The Philosophy of Personalism

A Study in the Metaphysics of Religion

By

ALBERT C. KNUDSON, Theol. D., LL.D.

Dean of Boston University School of Theology, and
Professor of Systematic Theology

THE ABINGDON PRESS

NEW YORK   **CINCINNATI**

KRAUS REPRINT CO.
New York
1969

Reprinted with the permission of the original publisher
KRAUS REPRINT CO.
A U.S. Division of Kraus-Thomson Organization Limited

Printed in U.S.A.

To

BISHOP FRANCIS JOHN McCONNELL

A DISTINGUISHED REPRESENTATIVE OF THE PERSONALISTIC PHILOSOPHY

AND

A WISE AND COURAGEOUS LEADER OF THE PROGRESSIVE FORCES

IN THE RELIGIOUS THOUGHT AND LIFE

OF AMERICA

CONTENTS

CHAPTER IV

CHAPTER V

PREFACE

THIS book is an exposition of personalism in the light of its historical development and in the light of contemporary philosophy.

The type of personalism here expounded and supported is that which received from Borden P. Bowne its clearest, most systematic, and most thoroughgoing expression. Special but not disproportionate attention is consequently devoted to him. One purpose of the book, though a quite incidental one, is to determine more precisely than has heretofore been done his place in the history of philosophy. Professor Bowne was a man of such striking personality, such extraordinary ability, and such far-reaching influence that a biography of him ought to have been written long ago. Fortunately, one is now in the course of preparation. It is being written by Bishop F. J. McConnell, who is pre-eminently fitted for the task. Here, however, it is the system of thought in its historical setting—not the man—with which we are concerned.

Considerable attention is devoted to the historical aspects of the subject, but the main purpose of the book is critical and constructive. It seeks to present in outline and to commend to the reader a type of philosophy that meets the needs of both the theoretical and the practical reason. Nothing at present is more needed in the field of religious thought than a revival of metaphysical theology. Much of current theology as well as philosophy has run into the shallows. Particularly regrettable is the

fact that not a little of the advanced theological thinking
of the day seems to be linking itself up with a crude
realism, dualism, pragmatism, or positivism. This represents a marked decline both in intellectual depth and
power as compared with the liberalism of a generation
or two ago. The result is a deplorable confusion of
thought on the part of many teachers of religion when
it comes to the fundamentals of the religious world-view.
Both in theology and philosophy there is great need of
coming to closer grip with the problems of metaphysics.
Clearer thought in this field will do much to save philosophy from shallowness and futility, and it will also help
to remove many of the common objections to the higher
beliefs and hopes of mankind. No system, in my judgment, is so well adapted to serve this double purpose
as that which constitutes the subject of this book. A
mastery of the philosophy of personalism will be of particular value to the student who is seeking to thread his
way through the labyrinth of speculation and to find a
firm basis for faith.

My special thanks are due Mrs. Borden P. Bowne for
the privilege of using several important letters, and also
Dr. Edgar S. Brightman and Professor Earl Marlatt for
their kindness in reading the manuscript and giving me
the benefit of their friendly criticism.

ALBERT C. KNUDSON.

"It is hard to classify me with accuracy. I am a theistic idealist, a Personalist, a transcendental empiricist, an idealistic realist, and a realistic idealist; but all these phrases need to be interpreted. They cannot well be made out from the dictionary. Neither can I well be called a disciple of any one. I largely agree with Lotze, but I transcend him. I hold half of Kant's system, but sharply dissent from the rest. There is a strong smack of Berkeley's philosophy, with a complete rejection of his theory of knowledge. I am a *Personalist*, the first of the clan in any thoroughgoing sense." Borden P. Bowne, in a letter dated May 31, 1909, and printed in *The Personalist*, 1921, p. 10.

"It is the unequivocal insistence upon the attribute of personality in all that is real which marks Bowne off from most of his idealistic colleagues. . . . To him the union of man and God is not one of identity or absorption, but, rather, one of mutual harmony or coincidence of purpose, which consists with and indeed presupposes the distinctness of selfhoods. Personality is the ultimate principle; it cannot be explained by anything else, but everything else can be explained by it. Thus 'personalism' becomes the distinctive name for Bowne's contribution to metaphysics, and as a summary account of the curve of metaphysical speculation since Kant, there is no more powerful and convincing chapter in American metaphysical writing than that of Bowne on 'the failure of impersonalism.'" William Ernest Hocking in the *Methodist Review*, 1922, p. 374.

CHAPTER I

THE DEFINITION OF PERSONALISM

PERSONALISM, like pragmatism, is a new name for some old ways of thinking. But it is not merely a new name. The new name, as in the case of pragmatism, represents a new emphasis and a new approach to some of the fundamental problems of philosophy and theology. What this new approach and new emphasis are will appear in a general way in the course of the present chapter and more in detail in the rest of the book. Here I need only say that the philosophical movement known as "personalism" is considerably broader and more complex than many seem to realize, and that, in order to be properly understood, it should be studied as a whole.

For the origin of the word "personalism" as a philosophical term we must go back over a hundred years. It seems to have first appeared toward the close of the eighteenth century, and then served as a general term descriptive of theism by way of distinction from pantheism. Schleiermacher so used it, in its German form (*Personalismus*), in his famous *Discourses* published in 1799;[1] and Goethe spoke of the distinguished theist, F. H. Jacobi, as a "personalist."[2] This general and more or less self-evident meaning attached to the term "personalism" during the nineteenth century, but it was used very rarely, even by scholars, and more rarely in Eng-

---

[1] Pages 256 and 257 of the German text.
[2] For this fact I am indebted to my colleague, Professor G. C. Cell.

land than in Germany. The German word *"Personalismus,"* for instance, was not rendered by its English equivalent in the translation of Schleiermacher's *Discourses,* published in 1893. The English translator, John Oman, did not apparently regard "personalism" as a word warranted by English usage. Indeed, as Professor Brightman[3] has pointed out, it does not even yet appear as a philosophical term in any of the standard English dictionaries except *The Oxford English Dictionary* (edited by J. A. H. Murray).

We are not, however, here concerned with the general philosophical use of the term, but with its use as the designation of a definite philosophical system; and this is of quite recent origin, falling within the present century.

In 1903 the veteran French philosopher, Charles Renouvier (1815-1903), published a book entitled *Le Personnalisme.* His philosophy had previously been known as "neo-criticism." But "personalism," he now says, "is the true name that fits the doctrine hitherto designated by the title neo-criticism."[4]

In 1906 there appeared in Germany the first volume of a work called *"Person und Sache"* (Person and Thing), written by a young philosopher by the name of William Stern, who in the subtitle describes his system as "Critical Personalism." The second volume was published in 1918, and the third and concluding volume in 1924.

In 1908 the name "Personalism" appeared for the first time, so far as I know, on the title-page of an Eng-

---

[3] *The Personalist,* 1922, p. 256.
[4] *Le Personnalisme,* p. iv.

lish book. The author was Borden Parker Bowne.[5] In
it he gave a compact but fresh restatement of the philosophic system which for thirty years past he had expounded in various books and journals and in his
classroom lectures in Boston University.

Thus within the brief period of five years we find
three representative and independent thinkers in France,
Germany, and America adopting the term "personalism"
as the proper designation of their respective systems of
thought.

Two years before the publication of Renouvier's work
on personalism there appeared a book by G. H. Howison, of the University of California, entitled *The Limits*
of Evolution (1901), in which the term "personal
idealism" was used to designate the metaphysical system there expounded; and the year following (1902)
this term was adopted as the title of a collection of

[5] Borden P. Bowne was born at Leonardville (now Atlantic High-
lands), Monmouth County, New Jersey, on January 14, 1847. Having graduated from New York University in 1871, he studied from 1873
to 1875 at the universities of Göttingen, Paris, and Halle, coming
under the influence especially of Lotze and Ulrici. In 1876, he became
professor of philosophy in Boston University, and in spite of attractive
offers from other universities such as Johns Hopkins, Yale, and Chi-
cago, remained in this position until his death on April 1, 1910, having
added in 1888 to his professorial work the office and duties of dean
of the Graduate School. In 1904 he was acquitted of charges of heresy
that had been brought against him, and in 1905-06 he took a trip
around the world, lecturing at various universities ·in the Orient.
Aside from *Personalism* and numerous articles in journals of one kind
and another he wrote the following books: *The Philosophy of Herbert
Spencer*, 1874; *Studies in Theism*, 1879; *Metaphysics*, 1882; *Introduction to Psychological Theory*, 1886; *Philosophy of Theism*, 1887; *Principles of Ethics*, 1892; *Theory of Thought and Knowledge*, 1897; *Metaphysics* (Revised Edition), 1898; *Theism*, 1902; *The Immanence of
God*, 1905; *Studies in Christianity* (comprising three booklets, previously published, on "The Christian Revelation," "The Christian
Life," and "The Atonement," and some additional essays), 1909;
The Essence of Religion (posthumous), 1910; *Kant and Spencer* (posthumous), 1912.

essays, published by eight members of the University of Oxford. Of these essays the most important from the philosophical point of view was that on "Personality, Human and Divine," by H. Rashdall. The term "personal idealism," as used by Howison and Rashdall, is synonymous with "personalism"; but the latter is the shorter and more distinctive term, and hence has in recent years been coming into more common use. It cannot yet be said to be a popular term. Many who might be classed as personalistic in their philosophy or at least as near-personalists, still avoid the term so far as they themselves are concerned.[6] But it is nevertheless steadily gaining in favor, and bids fair before long to have a well-established place in philosophical usage.

As yet, however, "personalism" has not received a fixed definition. The very word, it is true, implies that a philosophy so named must make the idea of personality central and basal, and must interpret reality in personal terms. But this still leaves unanswered many important questions. What, for instance, is a person? Does personality imply self-consciousness? Does it imply freedom? Are persons immortal? Is pre-existence to be ascribed to them? Were they created, or are they to be regarded as eternal? Are there sub-human persons? How low in the scale of being does personality go? And again how high? Are there super-individual persons? Are there superhuman personal beings? Is there a supreme, absolute Person? Or is ultimate reality a society of finite persons? Is God himself, if he exists, finite?

---

[6] See the interesting and informing articles by Professor Brightman on "The Unpopularity of Personalism" and "Why is Personalism Unpopular?" in the *Methodist Review* for 1921, pp. 9–28 and 524–535.

Is creative activity to be ascribed to him? Or is he to be regarded as simply the goal, the final cause, of the world? What, moreover, is the relation of nature to persons? Is nature wholly phenomenal? Or does it have existence for itself? Is it in its inmost being personal? These are all questions on which there are differences of opinion among personalists; and some of them are manifestly questions of fundamental importance. It is evident, then, that personalism does not at present stand. for a uniform body of doctrine. There are widely divergent types of personalism. It thus becomes our task to determine, if possible, the true or normal type.

Personalism and God

One would naturally suppose that personalism would be theistic. The very word, as we have seen, was, to begin with, a synonym for theism. And in addition to that, the central idea of personalism, the unique significance of personality, owes its origin to Christian influence. This was the great contribution made by Christianity to European philosophy. The idea was, of course, not altogether lacking in Greek philosophy. But Christianity concentrated attention upon the distinctively personal element in God and in the human soul as had not been done before. A personal God and personal immortality—these were the two foci in the ellipse of Christian thought. I would know God and the soul, said Augustine, these and nothing more.[7] It was this profound religious interest that led to the prominence of the personalistic tendency in Western thought. One would expect, then, that a philosophy, bearing the name of per-

[7] *Soliloquia*, I, 7.

sonalism or that might properly be called such, would be theistic; and, on the whole, the history of thought does not disappoint this expectation. The personalistic philosophies have, for the most part, been true to their theistic and Christian origin. But there are exceptions to the rule. We have both an *atheistic* personalism and a *pantheistic* personalism.

Atheistic personalism is represented by J. M. E. McTaggart[8] (1866-1925). He did not, I believe, call himself a personalist; but he might readily have qualified as such on the ground that he held that ultimate reality consists of a society of persons. It was his contention that Hegel should be so interpreted. The common view is that Hegel laid primary stress upon the unity of the world or upon the Absolute, and that he regarded concrete individuals or the many, as simply passing phases of the underlying reality. But this view, according to McTaggart, fails to do justice to the strong place occupied by the element of differentiation and multiplicity in the Hegelian system. Hegel held that multiplicity is essential to unity. One implies the other. The Absolute could no more exist without the world than the world without the Absolute. The whole meaning and significance of the Absolute lies in its being differentiated into the plurality of the world, and the whole meaning and significance of the parts of this plural world lie in their being combined into the unity of the Absolute. But if this be so, the individual need not necessarily be ultimately swallowed up in the whole; it is possible that he may be as eternal as the Absolute itself.

Hegel defined ultimate reality as spirit, and spirit, he

---

[8] *Studies in Hegelian Cosmology,* 1901; *Some Dogmas of Religion,* 1906.

held, can exist only in the form of persons. This at least
is McTaggart's view. The material world is phenomenal;
it has no existence apart from spirit. And the only differentiations of spirit that have sufficient vitality to
maintain a distinct existence of their own are persons.
Persons, therefore, alone are real. But they form a harmonious system, and this system is the Absolute. The
Absolute is not a personal being, it has no independent
existence, it exists simply as a system of selves. As such
a system it is superindividual; it is a spiritual unity. But
it is not personal, any more than a college, a goose-club,
or a gang of thieves. Nevertheless, as a system it is the
fundamental fact of the universe, and hence needs no
explanation any more than does the God of theism. There
is, therefore, according to McTaggart, no God. Ultimate reality is "a harmonious spiritual system," a system
made up of selves. "Nothing exists but persons connected in a unity." Beyond them and independent of
them there are no real beings of any kind. Hence it may
be concluded, since they alone are real, that they are both
immortal and eternal. Their very nature makes them
such, for they are constituent factors in an absolute system which in and of itself and apart from them has no
meaning or existence.

Such a view of the world is manifestly personalistic
in spite of its atheism. But it could hardly be regarded
as a characteristic or typical form of personalism. It
stands apart from the main current of personalistic
thought, and impresses one as a more or less artificial
and arbitrary variation from the accepted type. Though
interesting as an interpretation of Hegel and stimulating
as a criticism of theism, it is too far removed from those

motives that have hitherto been controlling both in theoretical and practical philosophy to be convincing. It is
in its main contention a philosophical novelty. As such
it is deserving of study, but it is not deeply enough rooted
either in speculation or life to give promise of permanence.

Two criticisms in particular may be brought against
it. First, a system as such, whether it be called the Absolute or not, is not self-explanatory. It is not a conception
which the human mind can accept as ultimate. Beyond
the harmonious system of selves there must be some
unitary principle that binds the selves together, and this
principle must be something other than the selves and
something more than a mere concept. To interpret unity
as a "system of differentiations" does not satisfy the
mind's demand for unity. To meet this demand there
must be a unitary being deeper than the system, and on
McTaggart's own principles such a being must be a
person. His theory of a "harmonious spiritual system"
thus requires for its completion a personal God.[9]

In the second place, persons, on McTaggart's theory,
have no real freedom. They are said to be self-determined. But complete self-determination, we are told,
is compatible with determination from outside; and the
power of contrary choice is explicitly and emphatically
rejected. That this view does not run wholly counter
to the theistic tradition is no doubt true. But it contradicts the main current of personalistic thought. Freedom is usually singled out as one of the most important
characteristics of personality. Insofar, consequently, as

---

[9] For an elaboration of this criticism see H. Rashdall's *Philosophy
and Religion*, pp. 96–101, 123–126.

McTaggart rejects freedom and a personal God, we may regard his personalism as a departure from the true type.

Pantheistic personalism is represented by William Stern (1871-), professor in the recently established University of Hamburg, to whom reference has already been made.[10] Stern describes his system as "critical personalism," thus differentiating it from what he calls "naïve personalism." The latter is theistic and dualistic. It opposes God to the world and the soul to the body. Critical personalism, on the other hand, is monistic both in its conception of the universe and of individual beings. Body and soul are not substances in the proper sense of the term. They are not two independent and separable forms of existence. They have a common ground and unity in a personal being that is "psycho-physically neutral," and that may be described as both "metaphysical" and "metapsychical." It is personal beings such as these that alone are substances. But their substantiality does not necessarily involve consciousness; it is neither material nor psychical. This holds true of God as well as of finite beings. God. is not to be conceived as a self-conscious spirit, standing apart from the world. He is the All-Person, who embraces in his own being the totality of the universe. All other personal beings are parts of him. Together they form a hierarchy of being, God being in one sense the apex of the pyramid and in another sense its all-encompassing ground and inner bond of unity. As distinguished from all other beings he is the absolute Person, since he includes all others in himself

---

[10] Compare Dr. Willy Moog, *Die Deutsche Philosophie des 20. Jahrhunderts*, 1922, pp. 150–157, and Dr. Reinhard Liebe's article on "Der kritische Personalismus und seine Bedeutung für die Theologie" in *Zeitschrift für Theologie und Kirche*, 1926, pp. 108–129.

and does not himself form a part of a higher person. But he does not exist independently of the world. "The world from above, regarded as actual unity, is the All-Person or God."[11]   This is manifestly thoroughgoing pantheism.

But the personal pantheism or pantheistic personalism of Stern has its distinctive features, due to a unique blending of Spinoza with Aristotle and Leibnitz. From Leibnitz Stern takes over the principle of individuality. The individual is real, a monad. It has its existence in itself, and is not simply a mode of the underlying reality. We cannot, therefore, say with Spinoza that there is only one substance. There are an infinite number of substances. Every individual being is a substance. But these substances are not self-existent in the sense that they are eternal. They are parts of a larger whole, and as such arise and pass away. They "have neither individual pre-existence nor postexistence."[12] There is also no freedom nor contingency connected with their origin. Their coming into being is not determined by general laws and so cannot be logically deduced, but it is none the less causally necessitated. And so also is their entire being. They act from inner impulses, but these impulses are determined by each one's nature and by the relation of each to the whole, so that there is no real freedom. Yet they are each said to have "an independent substantial existence."[13] They differentiate themselves from others and so are individual persons as well as parts of a larger whole.

---

[11] *Person und Sache*, I, p. 169.
[12] *Ibid.*, I, p. 185.
[13] *Ibid.*, I, p. 25.

This fusion of Spinoza and Leibnitz is supplemented by a motive drawn from Aristotle. The great Stagirite rejected Plato's theory of Ideas, insisting that all existence must be concrete and individual, but he distinguished in every individual being between "form" and "matter." These two factors he regarded as essential to every existing thing, and the relative proportion in which the two were combined determined the place occupied by each thing in the scale of being. All reality thus formed a hierarchy. At the lower limit was formless matter, and at the higher matterless form. This conception, which in modern times had been to a large extent superseded by the Cartesian distinction between mind and matter, is revived by Stern. He does not adopt the Aristotelian terminology. Instead of "form" and "matter" he uses the terms "person" and "thing" (*Sache*). But these terms are given meanings that bear a close resemblance to the Aristotelian terms. "A person," he says, "is that kind of being or existence which in spite of the plurality of its parts constitutes a real, unique, and intrinsically valuable unity, and as such, in spite of the plurality of the functions of its parts, achieves a unitary, purposive self-activity. A thing (*Sache*) is the contradictory opposite of person. It is that kind of being or existence which, consisting of many parts, constitutes no real, unique, and intrinsically valuable unity, and which, functioning in the many functions of its parts, achieves no unitary, purposive self-activity."[14] Thus understood, person and thing do not denote two distinct kinds of concrete objects. They rather denote the same object from different points of view. "What from

[14] *Ibid.*, I, p. 16.

above, seen as a whole, is person, is from below, viewed
as a sum of parts, thing."[15] "Person" is the active principle of unity, of self-preservation and self-development;
it is the "entelechy" or "form" of Aristotle. "Thing,"
on the other hand, is the passive principle of plurality,
of inert parts; it is "matter," and as such lacks individual
existence.

Every concrete object, insofar as it is a unified whole,
is a person. But a person is made up of parts, and these
parts, insofar as they are wholes, are also persons, and
these "persons" again have their "personal" parts. There
is thus a hierarchy of persons. Every finite person is
not only made up of parts but is itself part of a higher
person and in this sense a "thing." "Thing" is thus a
relative and to a certain extent negative term. It expresses the bare fact of plurality and potentiality, implied
in all existence. Person is the positive term. Every
actually existing being is a person, whether it be an atom,
a molecule, a cell, a family, a nation, mankind, or the
Absolute. Each has a unitary and purposive self-activity.
Bare thinghood, the mechanical principle, is everywhere
secondary, instrumental. It has no independent existence. In this sense Stern's *Weltanschauung* is idealistic
and personalistic. It gives universal primacy to teleology. Indeed, the absolute Person might be said to be
the teleological principle of the universe. But as such he
has no existence apart from the world; he is one with
it. All finite persons are parts of him.

This pantheistic or "hierarchic" personalism differs
not a little in form and tone from the atheistic personalism of McTaggart. But in their essential content the

[15] *Person und Sache*, II, p. 9.

two systems are not far apart. Stern's "All-Person" stands no closer to the God of theism than does McTaggart's "harmonious system of selves." If the latter is impersonal, so is the former. Both systems are also deterministic. Stern is less of an Hegelian than McTaggart, and so is more individualistic in his conception of causality, but he is not on that account less thoroughgoing in his necessitarianism. Indeed, in spite of his individualism Stern accords less significance to individual persons than does McTaggart. The latter affirms the immortality and eternity of finite spirits, but Stern explicitly denies both.[16] It may also be noted that McTaggart is more idealistic than Stern, and that he adheres more closely to the historic use of the word person. For him persons are conscious beings, and the world as a world of persons is an ideal world, a world of minds. He recognizes no extramental reality. Stern, on the other hand, tells us that "person" is a "psycho physically neutral term." It does not necessarily imply consciousness. Hence a personal world is not ideal in the mentalistic sense, it is "metapsychical" as well as "metaphysical." Here we have a lapse into Spinozistic realism with all its unintelligibilities.

But even more objectionable than this from the personalistic standpoint is Stern's novel and misleading use of the term "person." To extend the meaning of the word so as to include under it atoms, molecules, cells, and such universals as family, nation, and humanity, is to empty it of most of its positive content and to reduce it to an essentially impersonal level. Personality, thus understood, has very little value, whether applied to God

---

[16] *Ibid.*, I, p. 185.

or man. What Stern seems to have done is to rebaptize pantheism with an inappropriate name. The term "personalism," as we have seen, owed its origin to its implied antithesis to pantheism. To interpret it, then, in a pantheistic sense, as does Stern, is to do violence to historic usage. Theism is the only true form of personalism, and from this point of view the pantheism of Stern can hardly be said to have any appreciable advantage over the atheism of McTaggart.

We reject, therefore, both the atheistic personalism of McTaggart and the pantheistic personalism of Stern as nontypical, if not aberrant, forms, whatever value they may have as correctives of a mechanistic or crudely realistic type of philosophy. True, normative personalism must be theistic. But theistic personalism has not been cast in a single mold. It has been developed in a number of different ways. Before we take up what may be regarded as its classical and typical form, it will be instructive to consider three other developments of it that seem to be in one way or another defective.

Of these, the first is *personalism in the form of absolute idealism.* This might be called absolutistic personalism, and in some respects this would be a convenient designation. It would form a natural contrast to the "relativistic" type of personalism which we will next consider. But the term "absolutistic" is not altogether free from ambiguity. It might be applied to traditional speculative theism as well as to absolute idealism. The characteristic thing in absolute idealism is its stress on the wholeness of reality, on its organic unity, on what it calls the "concrete universal" or "notion," and its refusal to admit anything "other" to or separate from the Absolute. The Absolute, moreover, is "spirit," a rational unity, and as such embraces all the diversities of finite existence. It is this idea of a spiritual whole, a unitary and all-comprehensive experience, that is the key to Hegelian absolutism.

But how the unitary principle in absolute idealism is to be conceived is a point on which its expositors differ widely. Hegel now and then attributed personality to the Absolute, but how personality in these instances should be understood is a question. His immediate disciples divided into a left and a right wing, and at present his philosophy is interpreted from at least three distinct standpoints: the theistic, the Spinozistic, and the monadistic. McTaggart, as we have seen, adopted the last standpoint and reduced the Absolute to a mere "system of differentiations." But a system as such, a community, has no proper or distinct individuality, no center of experience. Hence "the Absolute is not God, and, in consequence, there is no God." Atheism, for McTaggart, is thus the logical outcome of Hegelian idealism. But this is not the conclusion commonly reached by representatives of this school. Most of them think of the Absolute as more than a "system," as an "individual," as a concrete whole of experience. But whether this all-embracing "whole" or "individual" is to be thought of as "personal" or not is a point on which they differ. Two of their most distinguished representatives, F. H. Bradley[17] (1846-1924), and Bernard Bosanquet[18] (1848-1923),

[17] *Appearance and Reality*, 1893; *Essays on Truth and Reality*, 1914
[18] *The Principle of Individuality and Value*, 1912; *The Value and Destiny of the Individual*, 1913.

approach Hegel from the Spinozistic point of view, and deny personality to the Absolute, taking a hostile attitude toward the personalistic type of thought in general. Bradley says that most of those who lay stress on the personality of God are "intellectually dishonest," and Bosanquet is hardly any less unfriendly to those whom he calls the "votaries of personality." Both of them speak of the Absolute as "superpersonal," but in so doing they virtually lapse into an agnosticism akin to that of Herbert Spencer, for no definite meaning can be attached to the phrase.

Many absolute idealists, consequently, frankly ascribe personality to the Absolute. Edward Caird[19] (1835-1908) and Josiah Royce[20] (1855-1916) took this position. Sir Henry Jones[21] (1852-1922) emphatically indorsed it. A. E. Taylor[22] (1869-) has in more recent years overcome his earlier impersonalism and adopted it. W. E. Hocking,[23] while he says he does "not love the word 'personality,'" thinks of the Absolute very distinctly under this form. And Professor Mary W. Calkins[24] has not only taken over from her teacher,

---

[19] *Evolution of Religion*, 1892; *Evolution of Theology in the Greek Philosophers*, 1904.
[20] *The Conception of God*, 1897; *The World and the Individual*, 1901. In a letter written to Doctor Brightman, July 16, 1913, Royce said: "I wish that somebody would tell me what my precise relation to Bowne is. I suppose that our agreements were rather on the increase toward the end of his work. I always prized him much; but each of us had many irons in the fire. I ought to have come closer to him before he left us."
[21] *A Faith that Enquires*, 1922.
[22] See his excellent article on "Theism" in *Encyclopedia of Religion and Ethics*. A brief autobiographical account of the factors that contributed to his change of view will be found in *Contemporary British Philosophy* (Second Series), pp. 270–272, edited by J. H. Muirhead.
[23] *The Meaning of God in Human Experience*, 1912.
[24] *The Persistent Problems of Philosophy*, 1907, 1925.

Josiah Royce, the idea of the Absolute as a person, but has made the term "personalism," qualified as "absolutistic," the designation of her own philosophy. Indeed, so prominently has she espoused the "personalistic" cause that she may properly be regarded as the most conspicuous representative of personalism in the form of absolute idealism.

That this form of the personalistic philosophy has been extremely influential and that it has on the whole stood in a sympathetic relation to historical theism and to Christianity, is well known to every student of philosophy and theology. But that the accord has not been complete is equally well known. The thoroughgoing theist feels that the idea of personality does not come to full recognition in absolute idealism, that there are certain characteristic features of Hegelian absolutism which necessarily obscure to some extent the personality both of God and man.

Religion and morality require a certain degree of separation between man and God, a certain amount of independence on man's part. Without it worship, responsibility, and contrition would have no rational basis. Religion, it is true, seeks union with God, but it is a union of will, of fellowship, a union that presupposes rather than excludes metaphysical otherness. It is, therefore, a prime concern of every sound philosophy of religion to guard the distinct individuality, the freedom and independence of the finite soul. And this end seems best attained by a strict doctrine of the divine personality. Personality is not necessarily exclusive, but it implies a certain degree of privacy, and this privacy has about it something sacred. In every person there is a holy of holies, which it would be sacrilegious to invade. And so the personal God,

> "whose pleasure brought
> Man into being, stands away
> As it were a handbreadth off, to give
> Room for the newly made to live,
> And look at him from a place apart,
> And use his gifts of brain and heart,
> Given, indeed, but to keep forever."[25]

To uphold such a view, however, is manifestly not the ruling motive of absolute idealism. It is primarily concerned not with the personality of the Absolute but with its all-embracing unity. Not the separateness of the finite individual, but his inclusion within the Absolute is the point stressed. Hence there is a tendency in absolute idealism to break down the exclusiveness of personality, to erase the boundary lines between personal beings, and to make the finite person simply a part of the Absolute. The consequence is a weakening of both the metaphysical distinctness and the unique worth of personality. Personality is made secondary rather than primary, and so the resulting system becomes a personalistic *absolutism* rather than an absolutistic *personalism*.

The degree of otherness, which theism ascribes to personality, stands opposed both to the "absoluteness" and the "idealism" of the Hegelian philosophy. The Hegelian conception of the Absolute is fundamentally that of a logical unity, but in the exposition of its meaning the spatial metaphor plays an important part, and the idea of a quantitative whole figures prominently. "The universe," we are told, "is incapable of increase."

---

[25] Robert Browning, *Christmas-Eve and Easter-Day*.

"There is nothing outside the Absolute." The Absolute, even though a self, includes all other selves and is in a sense identical with them. The finite self has nothing that it can call entirely its own. What is Cæsar's is also God's. All finite beings are parts of the Infinite and issue forth from its being by a kind of logical necessity. There is, therefore, no creation in the proper sense of the term. Creation implies metaphysical otherness, more or less of separateness of being; and for this the Hegelian Absolute hardly makes room. He or it is not a creator in the realistic sense. Efficient causation, as commonly understood, is not to be attributed to him; it is a mere "appearance." The finite self is an "expression" of the Absolute, and as such a considerable degree of privacy, freedom, and responsibility is claimed for it. "Nothing," we are told, "is so shut up within itself, and barred and bolted against invasion from without, as the self-conscious individual." Yet he is a part of the Absolute, and all his experiences are incorporated and transfigured in the one universal experience so that they enter completely into the eternal harmony without any discordant or resisting element in them. True otherness is thus denied the finite individual. What drives the absolutist to this conclusion is the specter of pluralism. He must at all costs have ultimate unity, and the only unity that seems to him closely enough cemented to meet the needs of the case is an all-embracing logical unity. Hence he turns a cold shoulder to creationism and that "relational individualism," as Bosanquet terms it, which forms the true basis of classical theism.

It is, however, not only the absolutistic element in Hegelianism that runs counter to the individualism of a thoroughgoing personalism; the idealistic element is also at variance with it. The otherness which personalism attributes to the individual consciousness implies a distinction between knowing and being. The reality of the individual is something other and more than a divine thought. He has an existence for himself, and this existence is not to be identified with the presence and activity of the absolute in him. He is in a sense and to a certain degree external to the Deity. His own thoughts, furthermore, are not identical with the objects which they apprehend, and no hypothetical participation of Reality in his own thinking processes makes them such. To him the world is "other," and so also is God. His ideas apprehend them, may be valid for them, but are not to be identified with them. The thoroughgoing personalist is thus a dualist in his epistemology. But not so the absolute idealist. He is an epistemological monist. For him the identity of knowing and being is a basic principle. The Absolute is himself Thought or Experience, and beyond Thought or Experience there is no reality. All reality is the product of thought, it is "constructed" reality. There is nothing "given" from without, no "thing-in-itself." This holds both of inanimate nature and of the finite centers of consciousness. The latter have no real otherness to God, they are but partial aspects of his one all-inclusive experience, an experience which is itself ultimate and identical with reality. The last trace of realism is thus banished from philosophy, and we have left what is literally an *absolute* idealism, an idealism which knows no other to thought, no ontologically distinct object, whether it be spiritual or material in nature.

That absolute idealism, as thus expounded, is necessarily hostile to personalism, cannot be fairly maintained, in view of the notable attempts that have been made to bring the two movements into harmony with each other. Indeed, it has been and is claimed by many that the only valid basis for a spiritual and theistic view of the world is to be found in the Hegelian type of philosophy,[26] But while we must recognize that there is a legitimate form of personalism linked up with the name of Hegel, and while we gladly welcome the powerful support that has come from that quarter to a religious world-view, it is, I think, clear from what has been said that personalistic absolutism does not express what may be called the true genius of personalism.   Normative personalism ascribes to the Deity a creative function and to finite spirits an individual and "real" character, which absolute idealism finds it difficult to assimilate.   Absolutism by its very nature leans toward pantheism.[27]

In rather sharp contrast to personalism in the form of absolute idealism stands the *relativistic personalism* of Charles Renouvier, to whom reference has already been made.   Renouvier's long and amazingly productive career as a writer on philosophical themes may be divided into three periods.   The first extended from 1842 to 1854, and may be called his "eclectic" period.   In it he advocated no definite system of philosophy, though he agreed with Hegel in maintaining that contradiction is a law of existence and hence that one may affirm both the infinite and the finite, both freedom and determinism,

---

[26] See Giovanni Gentile, *The Theory of Mind as Pure Act*, pp. 267ff.
[27] For a most excellent exposition of Hegelianism, as commonly understood, see *The Philosophy of Hegel* (1924) by W. H. Stace. See also *Idealism as a Philosophical Doctrine*, by R. E. A. Hoernle.

both unity and plurality. The second period began with the publication of the first volume of the *Essais de Critique Générale* in 1854, and may be regarded as continuing till 1885. This was his "critical" or "phenomenalistic" period, the period of his "neo-criticism." During it he reacted sharply against Hegelianism and all forms of philosophical absolutism, insisting on the law of relativity, on the principle of contradiction, and on the freedom of man. The third or "metaphysical" period was introduced by the publication of the *Esquisse d'une classification systématique des doctrines philosophiques* in 1885-86. Here Renouvier changes his interest. He begins to dwell, as he had not previously done, on such questions as the mystery of divinity, the beginning of the world, and the nature and origin of evil. This change of interest is reflected in the new name given his system. He now calls it "personalism" instead of "neo-criticism." To what extent this latest phase of his thought involved a departure from the principles laid down in the second period, is a question on which his followers are not agreed. Some see in it "another philosophy," something quite distinct from the earlier neo-criticism.[28] Others regard it as the logical conclusion of his life work, the crown of his entire system.[29] The latter was Renouvier's own view, and may be accepted as correct. In any case it is the connection of his personalism with his neo-critical relativism that gives to it its distinctive character.

The relativism of Renouvier had a double source. It grew out of both practical and theoretical considerations.

---

[28] So George Séailles, *La Philosophie de Charles Renouvier*, pp. 362ff.
[29] So André Arnal, *La Philosophie Religieuse de Charles Renouvier*, pp. 26ff.

The practical motives that led to it were chiefly his ethical interest in freedom, his religious interest in immortality, and his political interest in democracy. Freedom he regarded as a necessary presupposition of the moral life; without it duty, responsibility, and guilt would have no meaning; man would be simply an automaton. But real freedom seemed to him threatened, indeed, negated, by every absolutist philosophy. Such a philosophy gives us a "block-universe," and leads inevitably to determinism and pantheism. In the interest of moral freedom, consequently, Renouvier advocated a "relativistic" view of the world, one that denies to it the character of a closed system and leaves to the individual a measure of independent reality. The same concern for the individual appears also in Renouvier's defense of the doctrine of immortality. This doctrine gives to human life and particularly to the moral life a new dignity and sanctity. But it has no place logically in an absolutistic system. There the individual is engulfed in the Infinite, and no basis for human hope is left. It is, according to Renouvier, only as we hold to the finiteness of God and the relative independence of man that we can have a valid basis for the belief in immortality. In such a system the individual asserts himself as a "real" factor, and hence may well be immortal. He might even say as over against the Deity what Hamlet said as over against the Ghost:

"And for my soul, what can it do to that,
Being a thing immortal as itself?"

The "relativistic" philosophy does not require this view of man's destiny, but it at least makes it possible.

Yet another practical reason for Renouvier's opposition to philosophic absolutism is to be found in his democratic sympathies.   He was a child of the French Revolution, and as such saw in the absolute God of traditional theology the bulwark of political despotism. The "King of Heaven" he declared to be the "last support of kings on earth."   Hence he regarded it as the duty of the modern man to "dethrone the Absolute" in religion as well as in politics, and to transform the "Kingdom of God" from a monarchy into a republic or a kind of cosmic democracy, in which other persons besides God have their eternal place and rights.   This line of thought figured rather prominently with Renouvier, and so he has with some justice been spoken of as "the anarchistic theologian of the Republic of God."[30]

The foregoing practical considerations no doubt exercised considerable influence on Renouvier's philosophy, but the theoretical grounds of his relativism were, of course, those on which he himself laid chief stress. These grounds may be reduced to two: first, his thoroughgoing phenomenalism, and second, the principle of contradiction and the law of number.

The philosophy of Renouvier has been described both as a synthesis of Kant and Comte and as a synthesis of Kant and Hume.   He himself emphasized his connection with Kant.   "I avow frankly," he said, "that I continue Kant."[31]   It was this connection that led him to call his system neo-criticism.   He sought to do "for the critical strain in Kant what the German ontologists had done for the absolutist strain."   As they developed the Kantian philosophy into absolute idealism, so he, under the influ-

---

[30] George Séailles, *La Philosophie de Charles Renouvier*, p. 400.
[31] *Logique*, i, p. xv.

ence of Comte and Hume, developed it into a thorough-going phenomenalism. This, according to Shadworth H. Hodgson,[32] is his unique claim to distinction. He was "the first to produce a system of philosophical pheno-menism, based on the critical principles of Kant."

Kant himself was to a large extent a phenomenalist, and his phenomenalism carried with it the principle of rel-ativity. Knowledge, he held, is limited to the world of appearance or phenomena. What things-in-themselves are, that lie back of phenomena and cause them, we do not and cannot know. The categories of thought, with which the mind is endowed, and by virtue of which it builds up its world of experience, mask reality. The true nature of being is thus necessarily hidden from us; the very conditions of thought cast an impenetrable veil over it. It is only phenomena that we can know. In this respect, according to Kant, our knowledge is wholly relative.

Relativism in this agnostic sense, however, Renouvier rejected. For him there were no things-in-themselves, no substance or substances lying back of phenomena and vainly seeking to peer through them. The belief in such entities he characterized as "fetishism in philosophy." Phenomena themselves he regarded as constituting real-ity. But they are no simple elementary units. They each imply a perceptual process (*phenomène représentatif*). They are thus relative to consciousness. And they are also relative in the sense that they all stand in relation to each other. Nothing, Renouvier held, exists without relations, both "inner" and "outer." Everything is rela-

---

[32] See his articles on "M. Renouvier's Philosophy" in *Mind* for 1881, pp. 31–61, 173–211.

tive. Relation is a universal category. But it is not a category simply in the Kantian sense. It is a law of reality as well as of thought. For, from Renouvier's standpoint, there is no parallax between the phenomenal and the real. Reality is constituted by phenomena, and so is as relative in its structure as the phenomena themselves. There is no such thing as an absolute or unrelated being. The relativism, to which Renouvier's phenomenalism leads, is thus metaphysical rather than epistemological. It denotes finitism rather than agnosticism.

This becomes still more evident when we turn to the second ground on which Renouvier's relativism rests, the principle of contradiction and that of number. These two principles express essentially the same idea. Indeed, the principle or law of number may be regarded as simply the mathematical counterpart of the logical principle of contradiction. What they both affirm is, not the relativity of knowledge, but the relativity and finitude of being. Both are directed against the view, that there are fundamental antinomies in human thought and that these are somehow transcended and reconciled in an unknowable Absolute. This view Renouvier had himself at first accepted, but early in his career he revolted sharply against it, and thereafter made it one of his chief aims in life to overthrow it. The principle of contradiction, he insisted, is a fundamental law both of thought and of reality. Existence does not admit of the union of opposites. It cannot be both infinite and finite, both free and necessitated, both one and many. It must in each case be either one or the other. The principle of contradiction requires it, and it also requires that reality

be conceived as finite and many, not as infinite and one.
For all real existence is constituted by the categories—
relation, number, position, succession, quality, becoming,
causality, finality, personality—and these categories by
their very nature define and limit reality. A reality
without limits, an infinite reality, is therefore a contradiction in itself. Logic has no place for it. All reality
is "relative" to the categories, and so must be finite.

In further support of this conclusion Renouvier ap-
peals with particular confidence to the law of number.
All mathematicians, he says, since the time of Galileo
have regarded the idea of a "realized infinite" as absurd;
and if so, he asks, why should it be any less absurd for
philosophy? Every number, he points out, implies the
possibility of increase. It can be added to or raised to
a higher power. There can, therefore, be no such thing
as an infinite number, for that which is infinite admits
of no increase. "To speak, then, of an infinite number is
to speak of that which is rationally inconceivable, logically contradictory, metaphysically impossible."[33] An
infinite magnitude cannot, consequently, be ascribed to
the world. The law of number rules it out. It also puts
a veto on the idea of an "infinite regress" and on the idea
of infinite divisibility. All of these infinites are self-
contradictory. One might as well speak of a square
circle as of an infinite reality of any kind to which number may be implied.

From these considerations and those of a practical
nature previously adduced, it follows that both God and
the world must be thought of as finite. The world, according to Renouvier, had its beginning in time. Before

[33] André Arnal, *La Philosophie de Religieuse Charles Renouvier*, p. 40.

it there was no time, neither shall there be after it.   It
also has its limits in space.   There is no space outside it.
How this can be, cannot be represented to the imagination; we cannot comprehend it.   But it is required by the
principle of contradiction and must, therefore, be accepted
as true.   This, however, does not mean that the whole
world is within the reach of scientific knowledge.   Experience points to a realm beyond itself, a realm not infinite but of "indefinite" limits, a realm that transcends
human knowledge but one that is nevertheless included
within the finite world and stands in relation to that part
of it which is known.   This Beyond is the realm of belief, of possibles.   It has real existence; but of it we have
no knowledge in the strict sense of the term, except that
it is subject to the categories and is finite.

Having had a beginning, it might naturally be supposed that the world was created by some being or beings.
But this conclusion Renouvier for a long time resisted.
Causality, he argued, is a principle applicable only within
the limits of experience.   Beyond that it has no validity.
The beginning of the world must, therefore, be accepted
as an ultimate and inexplicable fact, a "limit-notion."
How or why it came into being we cannot say.   But this
need not disturb us.   For the idea of an absolute beginning is no more of a mystery than is the fact of existence
itself.   We can no more explain one than the other.   To
assume a First Cause or Creator of the world is no real
explanation.   Indeed, this hypothesis Renouvier in his
neo-critical period characterized as a "puerile fiction, un-
worthy of a philosopher's attention."[34]

But gradually his negative and hostile attitude to the

[34] *Psychologie*, iii, p. 252.

doctrine of creation gave way, as he became more metaphysical and personalistic in his thinking, until finally
in the *Esquisse* (1885-86) he himself adopted it as an
implication of his own finitism. From that time on it
became an increasingly prominent feature of his teaching. His earlier hypothesis of a causeless beginning he
now declares to be "insufficient, incomplete, alien though
not contradictory to the understanding,"[35] and in its stead
urged the necessity of referring the world to the free act
of a personal Creator.

The idea of an uncaused cause or causes was a fundamental one with Renouvier. He applied it not only to
the beginning of the world but to free acts. Freedom,
as he conceived it, is itself an uncaused cause, "not a bolt
out of the open blue," as one critic says, "but a bolt out of
nothing."[36] And as such it implies a finitistic view of the
world. This was a characteristic and original element in
his philosophy. Freedom, on the one hand, and finitism,
on the other, had been taught before his day, but that
there is a "necessary solidarity" between them seems to
have been new with him.[37]

As a result of thus emphasizing freedom and finitism
Renouvier was at first led to consider polytheism rather
more probable than monotheism; but after adopting the
idea of creation he naturally came to think of the Creator
as the sole Deity. This conclusion was also favored by
the unity of both the physical and moral order. Previously he had virtually identified the "deity" with the
moral and cosmic order, and had thought of him as per-

---

[35] *Année philosophique*, 1897, p. 33.
[36] Friedrich K. Feigel, *Der Französische Neokriticismus und seine
Religionsphilosophischen Folgerungen*, p. 73.
[37] See Paul Archambault, *Renouvier*, p. 58.

haps consisting of a "society" of gods. But now he thinks of the Deity as the unitary and self-conscious source and ground of the world. "The universal law," he says, "is the universal personality."[38]

The adoption of this view, however, did not lessen Renouvier's antipathy to the Absolute. He remained as hostile as ever, not only to the pantheistic Absolute but to the absolute God of speculative theism. The latter, indeed, was the special object of his invective and scorn. In him he could see nothing but a bundle of contradictions. Here, he said, is a being who is represented as unchangeable and yet as still thinking, willing, acting, as the All-Being and yet as distinct from the world, as the cause of all things and yet not the cause of evil, as the creator of free beings and yet as omniscient, foreknowing every act. These and other difficulties, or, as he would say, contradictions in the traditional idea of God, Renouvier was never weary of pointing out.

For him the idea of the absolute excluded that of personality. Personality implies determination, and this is negated by the very word "absolute." An eternal, infinite, unchangeable, omnipotent, omniscient, omnipresent being cannot in the very nature of the case be a person. These absolute attributes are, as a matter of fact, mere negations, "chimeras," "not exalted mysteries but sanctified absurdities."[39] There is no such thing as an unconditioned being. One might as well deduce the reality of nonbeing from the existence of being as the reality of the unconditioned from that of the conditioned. All existence must be concrete and finite. The phenomenal-

<hr/>

[38] *Monadologie*, p. 153.
[39] *Histoire et évolution des problémes métaphysiques*, 1901, pp. 289f.

ism of Renouvier, his relativism, his principle of contradiction, his law of number, his doctrine of freedom, his
conception of the categories—all these fundamental ideas
of his system seemed to him to require this conclusion;
and with it went necessarily the conclusion that God must
either be finite or cease to be an object of faith.

Finitude, however, applies only to the "quantitative"
side of God's being, to his power and knowledge. These
are necessarily limited by the freedom of man and by the
"logical" conditions of existence. But his moral nature
is subject to no such limitations. God may be morally
perfect, and hence "qualitatively" infinite. For moral
perfection — perfect righteousness, goodness, truth,
beauty—is a positive notion; it denotes something complete, realized, and so is not exposed to the same criticisms as the quantitative infinite with its negative and
self-contradictory implications.

God, then, according to Renouvier, is an ethically perfect Being, but finite. The latter conclusion, it should be
noted, was not arrived at as the result of an effort to
solve the problem of evil. It grew out of theoretical
rather than practical considerations. Renouvier was not
trying to relieve God of responsibility for the present
world-order; he was simply seeking to conceive his nature
in such a way as would be in harmony with his own
finitistic world-view. If all reality is finite, God, if real,
must, of course, also be finite. And if he is finite, he
cannot be eternal. But if he is not eternal, it would
seem that he must have had a beginning; and if he had a
beginning, it would seem that he must also have been
brought into being by some cause outside of himself.
These conclusions were not to Renouvier's liking, and he

sought in various ways to avoid them. He argued that they carry us beyond the limits of human knowledge, that they involve contradictions, that God cannot be thought of apart from the world, and hence that questions concerning his precosmic existence cannot be legitimately raised. So while denying the eternity of God, he was not ready to ascribe to him an absolute beginning. The result was that some of his followers, such as Dauriac, frankly took the position that God began to be, while others, such as A. Arnal and H. Bois, sought to interpret their master's teaching in such a way as to make it consistent with the eternity of God. From the standpoint of neo-criticism not a little can be said in favor of both of these views. But whichever of them Renouvier himself may have favored, he looked upon God as at present a temporal being, subject to the category of time. He held also the same view of his relation to space. He even went so far as to ascribe to God a kind of bodily organism. How this "integral, universal organism" is to be conceived, he admitted, surpasses our understanding; but some such view, nevertheless, is naturally suggested, if not required, by his theory of the relation of the categories to reality.

This finitistic conception of God seems to us unduly anthropomorphic. Associated with it in Renouvier's works there are also other conceptions of the past and future history of the world and man that seem to us extravagant and even fantastic. But in spite of these unconventional and dubious features the system as a whole is one of the most impressive phenomena in the religious philosophy of the nineteenth century. It is the most thoroughgoing attempt that has ever been made to build up a philosophical theology on a phenomenalistic and pluralistic basis. As such it has had a marked influence on theological thought in France, and indirectly, through its influence on William James, it has been an important factor in giving direction to the philosophical thinking of the Anglo-Saxon world during the past twenty-five years. James himself says that, if it had not been for the decisive impression made upon him by Renouvier's masterly advocacy of pluralism, it is doubtful if he would ever have freed himself from what he calls "the monistic superstition" under which he had grown up. He also acknowledges an even greater degree of obligation in connection with his doctrine of "The Will to Believe." At this point more fully perhaps than anywhere else he confesses himself a disciple of Renouvier; and this point, he says, is central.[40] It is, then, to Renouvier that American pragmatism must trace its immediate source. At first there were comparatively few, even in France, who recognized his significance, as did James. For various reasons, such as his difficult style, his lack of university connections and his secluded life, he was slow in gaining recognition for himself. But it is now quite generally agreed that he was one of the greatest and most influential thinkers of the past century. His finitistic or relativistic personalism stands out as the classical expression of that tendency in modern thought which may be described as a radical reaction against a monistic world-view. For fifty years he carried on a persistent warfare against all philosophical theories that seemed to him infected with "the metaphysical virus" of unity, and in the theological field he regarded it as his

[40] *The Letters of William James*, i, p. 186; ii, p. 44.

chief task to purge the idea of God of every taint of absolutism.

In this crusade against the Absolute, Renouvier emphasized several ideas that are of cardinal importance in a sound personalistic philosophy. He stressed the fact of freedom, and that in the libertarian sense; indeed, this was basal in his system. He developed an essentially monadistic view of the self, maintaining its independence and distinctness from other selves. He also made prominent in his later years the idea of creation, thus bringing out more clearly the thought of the divine causality and that of the objectivity and otherness of the world. These are all characteristic elements in Christian theism, and as correctives of a one-sided monism are in need of emphasis. In developing and enforcing them in a profound and original manner Renouvier made important contributions to the philosophy of personalism. But by rejecting the idea of the absolute and by insisting on a relativistic and finitistic view of reality, he gave to personalism a one-sided and defective expression. Personalism is as much interested in unity as it is in plurality, and, if it is developed in a thoroughgoing and consistent way, cannot dispense with the conception of an absolute Person.

Renouvier's polemic against the infinite and the absolute rests on inadequate grounds. For one thing he fails to distinguish between the pantheistic and theistic interpretations of these terms. The absolute for him means the unrelated, and the infinite the all. But this, as Bowne would say, is etymologizing, not philosophizing. Whatever meaning these terms might naturally have in view of their derivation, they denote in theistic philosophy simply the independent ground of things. The absolute and infinite being is one that does not depend for his existence on any other being, but has the ground of his own existence in himself, and is also the source and ground of all other existing beings. Such a being may limit himself by the creation of other free beings, but this self-limitation is not inconsistent with his absoluteness, rather is it an expression of it. If God could not thus limit himself, it might justly be urged that he was to that extent a limited Being. Of this fact, however, Renouvier seems to take no cognizance. For him, as above stated, the absolute means the unrelated, and hence, since all existence implies relation, there can be no absolute. For him also the infinite means the quantitative all, and this, when translated into concrete reality, turns out to be a mathematical absurdity. There can, therefore, be no infinite. The law of number puts a veto upon it; the very idea of a "realized infinite" involves a contradiction. But this argument implies an analytic as distinguished from an organic conception of reality[41] and has no force as against a genuinely spiritual and non-quantitative view of the Supreme Being. To insist, as does Renouvier, on making the law of number a fundamental principle of metaphysics must be set down as a piece of arbitrary dogmatism.

Having defined the absolute as the unrelated, Renouvier naturally finds a contradiction between it and the idea of personality, and that in a double way. Personality involves a distinction between the ego and the non-ego, and this means that a personal God can exist only

---

[41] For a fine statement of the contrast between the analytic and the organic or synoptic method in logic see E. S. Brightman's *Immortality in Post-Kantian Idealism*, pp. 17–25.

as he stands in relation to some being other than himself. But this relationship is negated by the idea of the
absolute and also by that of the infinite. An absolute
or infinite person is, therefore, a *contradictio in adjecto*.
The response to this argument, as has been repeatedly
pointed out by theistic critics, is that it mistakes a psychological form for an ontological distinction. The self
must have its object, but it may make its own states its
object; no metaphysical other is needed. There is, consequently, nothing in the idea of personality which excludes that of absoluteness. Rather are we warranted in
saying with Lotze that personality in its completeness is
possible only to the Absolute; and to this the converse
may be added that it is only in the form of personality
that the idea of the absolute can be consistently thought
through.

Again, Renouvier holds that the divine Person as
Creator is relative to the world and cannot be thought
of apart from it. What he is in his own nature, unrelated to the world, is a question that has no meaning.
It involves a contradiction. The creative activity of God
thus excludes his absoluteness. But if God has no existence apart from the world, one wonders what is meant
by creation. If God is creator of the world, surely he
must stand in a more or less independent relation to it.
Otherwise we would have pure pantheism—a viewpoint
particularly abhorrent to Renouvier. Evidently, this is a
place where his earlier relativism was transcended by his
later metaphysics without his fully realizing it. A Crea-
tor-God must, at least in some respects, be "absolute."

A special difficulty is created for Renouvier by the fact
that his phenomenalism prevents his making a clear dis-

tinction between phenomenal reality and metaphysical reality. For him the phenomenal is real and the only real; and if so, the categories of time and space are as valid for ultimate reality—if such an expression be allowed in this connection—as are any of the other categories. It is this that hampers the development of his personalism. While acknowledging that personality is the supreme category he fails to see that the categories as a whole have no independent existence and no self-evident application, but that they must find their interpretation in and through the living experience of the self. When this is seen, it becomes evident that a distinction must be made between the phenomenal and the metaphysical categories, or between the space-time world and the power-world. It also becomes clear that the power-world must be construed in personal terms; and this means that the categories must be subordinated to God, not he to them. It was Renouvier's failure to see this, that in a large measure accounts for the undeveloped state of his metaphysics.[42] His pluralistic relativism acted as a drag on his personalism, and prevented it from coming to its full fruition in the doctrine of an absolute Person.

We have thus far seen that both *absolutistic personalism* of the Hegelian type and the *relativistic* or *finitistic* personalism of Renouvier represent divergences from the typical form of theistic personalism. Another such divergence remains to be considered. This is represented by George H. Howison, to whom we have previously referred as an exponent of "personal idealism." Howi-

[42] For the many inconsistencies in his idea of God see F. K. Feigel, *Der Französische Neokriticismus und seine Religionsphilosophischen Folgerungen*, pp. 109-119.

son, like Renouvier, is a pluralist and an ardent upholder
of freedom as opposed to determinism.   But he is not
a relativist or finitist, at least not in the same sense as
Renouvier.   He looks upon God as an eternal and nonspatial Being, and emphatically denies that he is finite.[43]
Nevertheless, there is one important respect in which
he limits the being of God even more than Renouvier;
and it is this that also constitutes his chief point of divergence from classical theism.

While Renouvier in his later years affirmed the doctrine of creation, Howison rejected it.   God, he held, is
to be regarded, not as the First Cause of the world, but
as its Final Cause.   He did not create other persons;
they are all co-eternal with himself.   He is simply the
end, the goal, the ideal toward which they strive; and
in this sense, and this sense only, is he their bond of union
and the ground of their being.   Efficient causation is
not to be ascribed to him.   He exercises influence over
other beings only by virtue of a kind of spiritual attrac-
tion.   The influence is ethical in nature.   This is the
fundamental and distinctive note in Howison's "personal
idealism," and hence his system may not improperly be
called a *purely ethical* or *teleological personalism*.

In support of the idea of a noncreative God, Howison
adduces three main considerations.   The first is based
on the Kantian doctrine of the creative activity of
thought.   According to this doctrine it is the understanding that makes nature, not nature the understanding.
The individual mind is, therefore, not dependent on the
perceived world and its cosmic order; it is their creative
source.   Time and space are not independent existences,

---

[43] *The Limits of Evolution*, second edition, pp. 421f.

they are merely mental forms, and have their causal ground in the self-active spirit. Knowledge is *a priori*, and because it is such each individual mind is a creative agent. It belongs to the noumenal world, is self-existent, free, eternal, infinite. These different terms, as used by Howison, have all essentially the same meaning. Applied to the individual they assert his metaphysical reality, his underived existence, his independent causal efficiency, his likeness to God, so far as the purely ontological side of his being is concerned. Absolute ethical perfection belongs to God only, but other minds by virtue of their creative activity are as truly existent as he. They themselves produce the world of nature, and are in turn produced by nothing. They are eternally real. This conclusion, according to Howison, is involved in the fact of *a priori* knowledge in the individual.[44]

A second reason for denying that God stands in a creative relation to other minds is found in the social character of personality. The existence of one person involves the existence of others. For self-consciousness in the very act by which it distinguishes the self from others affirms their reality. Our self-certitude carries with it the certainty that we belong to a society of selves. Apart from such a society and the recognition of reciprocal rights and duties personality could not exist. The particularity of each individual implies as its background a social universality, and would be meaningless without it. And this means not only that other persons besides oneself exist, but that God could not exist without other persons nor other persons without God. For the individual in defining himself not only posits other persons

---

[44] *Ibid.*, chaps. i, iii, vi, and pp. 414ff.

like himself but also posits a supreme Person, an absolutely perfect Being, who stands in a relation of affection
to all other persons and who in his ideal nature constitutes the standard by which each person is measured.
This ideal Being is implicit in every self-consciousness
and is a constituent element in its definition. Hence if
the individual is real, God must be real. The existence
of self-thinking spirits implies the existence of God. In
this way Howison thinks it possible to revive the ontological argument, which in its original form sought to
deduce the existence of God from the idea we have of
him. But what we are here concerned with is the converse of this, namely, that the existence of God requires
the existence of other persons. Apart from them God
would not be God. Souls are as necessary to him as he
is to souls. Self-consciousness and true personality are
possible to him only if there are other free spirits to
whom he stands in the relation of *primus inter pares*
and who with him constitute an eternal and indissoluble
circle. The very conditions of personal existence exclude, therefore, the doctrine of creation in the traditional
sense of the term.[45]

A third argument urged against creationism is that it
is self-contradictory when applied to free beings. On
this point Howison is particularly emphatic.[46] No being,
he contends, that owes its origin to efficient causation, can
possibly be free. Such a being may appear to be self-
active, but it is only apparently so. Having been created
it is a mere effect, and all its activities are necessarily
predetermined. It might conceivably think itself free,

---

[45] *The Limits of Evolution*, especially pp. xxxiiff., 310f., 352f.
[46] *Ibid.*, pp. 332ff.

but this would have to be set down as a delusion. No really self-active intelligence can be called into being by a productive act, even though it be that of a divine agent. For a created intelligence would by the very fact of its creaturehood be an expression of the will and purpose of the Creator and not of its own independent selfhood. We must, therefore, according to Howison, choose between freedom and creation.

Essentially the same position was taken by Wilhelm Vatke in a work published a little less than a century ago.[47] Bernard Bosanquet has also indorsed it in his *Gifford Lectures* for 1912.[48] The latter scholar argues that to will a will is to will it in its every detail. For willing as an effect can have no existence apart from its cause. Consequently, if man is created, he cannot be free.

A somewhat different turn is given to this argument by H. Wildon Carr,[49] but his conclusion is virtually the same. Having defined a monad as in its nature "essential creativity" and as a living being that necessarily carries its past in its present activity, he argues that the creation of a monad or a human nature is manifestly impossible. For to create means to bring into existence what does not pre-exist, while a monad is a being whose very essence consists in its past existence. A monad without a past, a brand-new monad, a created monad, would, therefore, be a contradiction in itself. The present might conceivably be created, but a being, whose present existence is the outcome of the past, manifestly

---

[47] *Die Menschliche Freiheit in ihrem Verhältniss zur Sünde und zur Göttlichen Gnade, 1841, p. 401.*
[48] Pages 136f.
[49] *A Theory of Monads, 1922, pp. 55f.*

cannot be, for the past is clearly beyond the power of creation. Hence the idea of God as the efficient cause or creator of the world must be given up. According to Carr, it directly negates what he regards as essential to a monad, namely, its creativity and temporal inclusiveness, and, according to Howison, it destroys what is of the very essence of the self, namely, its freedom.

In addition to this argument and the two preceding ones Howison sees a considerable practical value in the rejection of creationism. If souls have not been created but are "co-eternal" with God, we may be assured of their immortality, and that without a belief in their pre-existence. The latter doctrine Howison refers to as a superstition, born of fancy. Furthermore, if nondivine minds are the creative sources of the phenomenal order and the events in it, it is evident that God is not responsible for the evil in the world, either natural or moral. As the ideal toward which all minds are struggling he is the source only of the good, and thus the age-old problem of evil is solved.

But whatever practical and theoretical advantages may be claimed for this unique form of personalism, its anti-creationism is not a doctrine that gives promise of any wide acceptance. For one thing, the positive arguments on which it is based are inconclusive. The alleged antinomy between creation and freedom has about it a certain formal stringency, but, like Renouvier's mathematical argument against the idea of the infinite, it impresses one as artificial and fails to carry conviction. How free spirits are made, of course transcends us. But that they cannot be called into being by an omnipotent Creator is an assertion devoid of logical warrant. Only on the basis of a mechanical conception of causality can it be claimed that every effect must be predetermined by its cause. Of a free Creator it certainly may be affirmed that he can create in his own image, even though the process is hidden from us. To tell how reality is made is not the function of philosophy, as Lotze so often reminds us. We may, then, dismiss Howison's contention, that the idea of creation is self-contradictory, as unwarranted. Nor does Carr's variation of the argument improve it. A monad might conceivably have a virtual or apparent past without an actual one. The lines in the structure of a being might point to a past that never existed. This, indeed, would necessarily be the case with every created being, whether free or determined. But this involves no logical or ontological difficulty. The difficulty in connection with creation is simply one of the imagination. We do not see how free and self-active beings can be created. But in the idea itself there is no contradiction.

Equally unconvincing are the arguments against creationism, based on the fact of *a priori* knowledge and the social character of personality. That *a priori* knowledge implies the creative activity of thought, and that this in turn implies a certain degree of independence and metaphysical reality on the part of the human mind, may be freely conceded. But that it implies the co-eternity of the human mind with God, is quite another matter. How the human mind can build up for itself a valid knowledge of the external world is, indeed, a mystery; but the mystery is not relieved by exempting the mind from causal dependence upon God. How a dependent being can attain to independent thought activity, we do not know; but both the dependence and the independence seem to be clearly given in our experience. At any rate, there is nothing in the creative activity of thought that necessarily excludes our being created beings. And the same is also true of the social nature of personality. That there is difficulty, from the monistic standpoint, in conceiving the moral absoluteness of God, has long been recognized. What object, it is asked, could the divine love have had before the creation of finite spirits? To this question, it is true, an ultimate personal pluralism provides an answer. But its answer is not the only one possible. One might think of eternal personal distinctions within the Deity which would give to him a social nature, or one might think of him as eternally creating free spirits. In any case, the metaphysical self-existence of nondivine minds is not essential to the personality of God.

It may also be questioned whether the practical advantages of noncreationism are not more than offset by its losses. If God is not responsible for any of the evil in the world, what becomes of the belief in Providence? God is virtually exorcised from nature and restricted to a merely ethical influence. And as for the immortality of the soul, is it certain that this belief has a firmer basis when grounded in the metaphysical separateness of the soul than when grounded in the divine purpose? The reverse would seem to be the case. Pluralism weakens rather than strengthens religious faith.

But the chief objection to a purely teleological personalism is to be found in its treatment of the principle of efficient causation. This principle it refuses to apply to the relation of minds to each other, whether human or divine. No mind is produced by another. Each is self-existent, and each is moved only by ideal or first causes.

In this respect Howison's system exceeds even that of Hegel in the absoluteness of its *ideal*-ism. It recognizes no coercive power whatsoever, in the relation of minds—the only realities—to each other. All minds or personal beings are governed solely by ideal forces, by conceptions of ends. And the one supreme end, the one absolute Final Cause, is God. That is his essential nature. He is the Omega, not the Alpha. One cannot but admire the thoroughness and boldness with which this teleological idealism is carried out; but those very characteristics are also its weakness. Not only does the system, taken as a whole, fly in the face of the great theistic and idealistic traditions, but it leaves reality suspended in the air, a kind of "cathedral in the clouds," a city without foundations. Final cause by itself is an abstraction. For its concrete realization it must be supplemented by efficient cause. The alphabet of thought is not content with an Omega; it requires an Alpha also, a first as well as a last. We cannot simply assume an ultimate society of minds as something self-evident. Beings such as non-divine minds are supposed to be call for explanation. The question as to their origin is one that insistently arises; no interdict can suppress it. And when once it is raised, it leads inevitably to a theory of emanation or to one of creation. The latter is the theory required by a consistent personalism. Only an arbitrary limitation of the causal principle can escape it. Logically efficient cause points as irresistibly to an absolute power as final cause does to an absolute goodness.

Having passed in review the atheistic, pantheistic, absolutistic, relativistic, and purely teleological forms of

personalism and adjudged them all in one way or another inadequate, we are now prepared to take up what
may be called *typical theistic personalism*. This form of
personalism had its chief sources in Leibnitz (1646-
1716), Berkeley (1685-1753), Kant (1724-1804), and
Lotze (1815-1881). Roughly speaking, it owes its spiritual individualism and activism to Leibnitz, its immaterialism to Berkeley, its epistemology and ethical conception of personality to Kant, and its first general and
distinctive formulation to Lotze. It was Lotze who took
the personalistic elements contributed by his predecessors
and wove them into a new type of theism. This he did
in such a masterful way, with such wealth of learning,
with such profundity of insight, and with such impressiveness of style[50] that he still stands out as the chief
protagonist of the movement. It is largely to his influence that the revival of theism during the past thirty or
forty years is due, a revival so marked that it is acknowledged to be the most striking movement in contemporary
philosophy of religion.[51]   To appreciate its significance
one need but recall the names of A. C. Fraser[52] (1819-
1914), James Ward[53] (1843-1925), A. J. Balfour[54]
(1848-), A. S. Pringle-Pattison[55] (1856-), J. Cook Wil-

[50] The following statement by Richard Falckenberg in his book on
Hermann Lotze, p. 13, is worthy of note: "Lotze is recognized as one
of the first stylists of Germany. His speech is music. Aside from
Paul Heyse and Friedrich Nietzsche I know no German who possesses
an equally fine feeling for the rhythm of prose."
[51] See R. F. Alfred Hoernlé, *Matter, Life, Mind, and God*, p. 190.
[52] *Philosophy of Theism*. Gifford Lectures for 1894-95 and 1895-96.
[53] *Naturalism and Agnosticism*, 1899; *The Realm of Ends*, 1912.
[54] *The Foundations of Belief*, 1894; *Theism and Humanism*, 1915;
Theism and Thought, 1923.
[55] *Hegelianism and Personality*, 1887; *The Idea of God*, 1917; *The
Idea of Immortality*, 1922. The first of these books has been characterized as "epoch-making." It is said to have done perhaps more
than any other book to shake the foundations of a rigid Absolutism

son[56] (1849-1915), H. Rashdall[57] (1858-1924), W. R. Sorley[58] (1855-), and C. C. J. Webb[59] (1865-), in England, Rudolf Eucken[60] (1846-1926) in Germany, and G. T. Ladd[61] (1842-1921) and Borden P. Bowne (1847-1910) in America. These men do not all have the same philosophical pedigree, and perhaps not one of them would with strict accuracy be called a Lotzean. Each has his own marked individuality, and they all differ to some extent, both from each other and from Lotze. But they all reflect in a measure his influence, and, in general, though with different degrees of completeness, represent the standpoint which I have characterized as typical theistic personalism.

This form of personalism differs from those already

---

and to quicken the growth of personalism (E. N. Merrington, *The Problem of Personality*, p. 131). The close intellectual kinship between Pringle-Pattison and Bowne is indicated by the following excerpt from a letter written August 17, 1908, by the Scotch personalist to Bowne relative to the latter's *Personalism;* "It is long since I read a volume with whose argument I more fully sympathized. I admire very much the clearness and simplicity with which you have stated the main contentions and the felicitous illustrations by which you sometimes help them out. In fact, I do not think I have anywhere seen the case for 'Personalism,' as you fitly call it, so broadly and victoriously stated. Your happy use of Comte's scheme, your 'transcendental.empiricism,' which refuses to try to explain the explanation, your demonstration of the objective reference in knowledge and the necessity of a mind at both ends, and the whole of your admirable discussion of causation are some of the points to which I refer. . . . Your proof that mechanical causality does not provide for change at all is, I think, most useful, and among minor matters I may be allowed to say that your illustration of the dream space and time (p. 130) is both happy and useful."

[56] *Statement and Inference*, 2 vols., 1926. Professor Wilson was regarded for many years as "by far the most influential philosophical teacher at Oxford." In a letter, written in April, 1914, he said that he always urged the study of Bowne "as the most important (to my mind) of the modern American philosophers."

[57] *Philosophy and Religion*, 1910.

[58] *Moral Values and the Idea of God*, 1919.

[59] *God and Personality*, 1918; *Divine Personality and Human Life*, 1920.

[60] *Main Currents of Modern Thought; Life's Basis and Life's Ideal;* etc.

[61] *Philosophy of Knowledge*, 1897; *Theory of Reality*, 1899.

discussed in that it bears a greater affinity to traditional theism. As over against a finitistic and also an exclusively teleological personalism it affirms the metaphysical absoluteness of God. It does not, however, use the term in the same sense as the Spinozistic and Hegelian absolutists do. For them the Absolute is either the undetermined ground of the universe or the all-inclusive whole; it is the all-pervading cause or the all-embracing experience. In either case it absorbs into itself all being and all power, and, logically at least, leaves to finite beings no independence. For traditional and personalistic theism, on the other hand, the Absolute has lost its blank negativity and its all-devouring unity; it is not the "unrelated" nor the "all." It is simply the one independent causal ground of the world. As such it excludes all other ultimate beings, whether they be personal, as Howison holds, or impersonal, as Plato and Aristotle assumed. All beings depend upon the Absolute and from it derive their existence. In this sense God is omnipotent. But his omnipotence does not necessarily deny to all other beings a measure of independence. He may provide for such independence by limiting himself. In a way he is already limited by his own nature, but in addition to this he may limit himself by calling into existence beings to whom a relative independence is granted. Such self-limitation involves no encroachment upon the divine absoluteness; rather is it an expression of it.[62]

Typical personalism is also in accord with traditional theism on the question of creation. Both ascribe to God efficient causation, and thus rule out Howison's idea of

---

[62] For an unusually fresh and suggestive treatment of this subject see F. J. McConnell's book, entitled, *Is God Limited?*

a noncreative Deity.   Both make creation a free act of
the divine will, and thus exclude all emanation theories,
whether Neo-Platonic, Spinozistic, or Hegelian—theories that make the world a part of God or a necessary
consequence of the divine nature.   These theories practically identify the world with God.   The doctrine of creation, on the other hand, distinguishes clearly between
the Creator and his works.   It conceives of the world as
having a certain objectivity or otherness as over against
its Maker.

This again leads to a third point of agreement between
normative personalism and classical theism.   Both are
dualistic rather than monistic in their epistomology.
They distinguish clearly between thought and reality.
Reality is something other and deeper than thought.
Thought is valid for reality but is not to be identified with
it.   At least this is true of human thought; and even
from the divine standpoint a finite being is not a mere
idea; it is grounded in a divine act and hence is more than
the thought which it expresses or by which it is apprehended.

There is thus a considerable degree of kinship between
personalism in its typical form and traditional theism.
But there are also distinct points of difference.   One is
to be found in the idealistic view of nature to which
personalism is inclined.   Theism has in the past been predominantly realistic.   It has regarded the material world
as created by God and as having thereafter a *quasi*-
independent existence.   Exactly what its independence
consisted in has never been made clear.   But some sort
of metaphysically real existence has been attributed to it.
This, however, personalism rejects.   It sees in the mate-

rial world simply a phenomenal order maintained by a divine or at least spiritual causality. In and of itself nature has no independent reality. It is ceaselessly produced by a power or powers outside itself. For a true conception of reality we must, therefore, pass beyond the material world.

This brings us to a second point of difference between personalism and historic theism. Personalism finds the ontologically real only in personality. "Inexplicable, as man's personal agency is—nay, the one perpetual miracle —it is nevertheless our surest datum and our only clue to the mystery of existence."[63] It is in our own inner experience that the idea of causality has its concrete source, and it is only through it that it can receive a valid interpretation. Causal reality must be interpreted in personal terms. In a vague way this was acknowledged by realistic theists when it came to the question as to the nature of the Divine Being. But they did not make it determinative in their theory of causality and reality in general. They distinguished between the First Cause and secondary causes in a way that produced confusion of thought and that deprived their own metaphysics of unity and consistency.

Yet another difference may be noted between personalism and classical theism. The latter movement has been more rationalistic than the former; in this respect it stands closer to the Hegelian philosophy. The traditional and Hegelian theists have been as a rule intellectualistic in their tendency. They have inclined to the view that the existence of God can be theoretically demonstrated, that the theistic argument can be made logically conclu-

---

[63] A. S. Pringle-Pattison, *Man's Place in the Cosmos*, 1897, p. vi.

sive. This argument they have formulated in different ways; but on its intrinsic cogency and its ability to convince the unbiased intellect they have been agreed. Both schools at this point have manifested a high degree of confidence in the self-sufficiency of reason. Personalism, on the other hand, is voluntaristic rather than rationalistic. It lays more stress on the will than the intellect and inclines to the view that life is deeper than logic. To formal argumentation it allows a place, its abstract validity it does not question, but mere reason, it holds, cannot bridge the gulf between thought and reality. At this point faith alone will suffice. So in the last analysis all knowledge rests on faith. Faith is the ultimate ground of every philosophical system. Demonstration is, then, impossible when it comes to the belief in God. But we can, nevertheless, go a long way toward establishing it by showing that it is the line along which thought moves with the least resistance, and that in it human nature finds its completest satisfaction.

Thus far we have considered the different forms of personalism in so far as they have to do with the idea of God. This has necessarily led us to take some account of the soul and the world. But for a more complete understanding of the personalistic philosophy we need to consider more fully its relation to these subjects.

PERSONALISM AND THE SOUL

The reality of the soul or self or "I" is the fundamental presupposition of personalism; it is even a more characteristic doctrine than the existence of a personal God. One might, as we have seen, be a personalist and yet an atheist. But one could hardly be a personalist and at the same time a disbeliever in the reality of finite persons. The belief in the real existence of individual minds or persons or souls or selves underlies all the different forms of personalism, and differentiates this type of philosophy from a thoroughgoing empiricism, on the one hand, and a thoroughgoing absolutism, on the other. As over against the Humian dissolution of the self into a mere bundle of perceptions and the pantheistic reduction of the self to a mere phase of the divine activity, all personalists hold that the self has a unique and distinctive character of its own. This much, at least, of Leibnitzian monadology is an essential and constituent element in a personalistic philosophy. Without real selves there is no personalism.

But along with this common conviction there is a wide difference of opinion among personalists as to the nature of the self, its freedom, and its destiny. So far as the nature of the self or soul is concerned, there are two main types of theories, the *substantialistic* and *activistic*. The purely empirical or positivistic theories are here not taken into account, since they deny the reality of the self. Assuming its reality, as the personalist does, we must think of it either as substance or as power of action. These two conceptions, however, do not exclude each other. From the beginning of speculation the ideas of substance and cause have stood in close relation to each other. The permanence of things has been referred to an abiding substance, and their changes to the same substance viewed as cause. But in ancient and mediæval thought the tendency was to make the idea of substance more fundamental than that of cause, and thus there arose the idea of a passive substance, an inert core of being, a substratum, that did nothing but exist, and that was more or less independent of the attributes and activities associated with it.

Against this conception of substance there has in modern times been a reaction. The tendency now is to regard activity as essential to being, and to deny reality to all forms of existence that lack the power of action. Substantiality, in a word, is being reinterpreted in terms of causality. This is true both in physics and metaphysics. Activism is taking the place of substantialism. The soul, consequently, is coming to be thought of as agent, not substance—an agent also that has no existence apart from its activities. It is the latter feature that is especially characteristic of the modern as distinguished from the ancient view. Plato regarded the soul as active. He even defined it as "the motion which of itself can move itself."[64] But that its very being consists in its activities was not his view or that of the ancient and mediæval thinkers in general. A thoroughgoing activism is a characteristic modern doctrine, owing its rise in no small measure to the influence of Leibnitz.

The substantialistic theories of the soul have taken three main forms. They have represented the soul as a material substance, as an immaterial substance, and as a thinking substance. The first of these was the early common-sense view; the second we owe to Plato, and the third to Descartes.

Men at first regarded the soul or spirit as akin to breath or air, a kind of refined matter. This is the view assumed throughout the Bible,[65] and it was also held by the early

---

[64] *Laws*, 896.
[65] See my *Religious Teaching of the Old Testament*, pp. 49, 223.

Greek speculators. Democritus regarded the soul as made up of fire-atoms, and similar materialistic views prevailed among the later Epicureans and Stoics. Such views, it is evident, furnished no satisfactory basis for the belief that the soul has a unique nature and is to have a unique destiny.

Hence Plato introduced the idea of an immaterial substance, a substance that is invisible and that has in itself the power of motion. The soul, he held, is such a substance; it is the invisible and incorporeal principle both of life and thought. This conception was adopted by Aristotle with some modifications and by the later idealistic thinkers, especially the Neo-Platonic, from whom it passed over into Christian theology and became an accepted doctrine of the church. But how such an immaterial principle as the soul was related to the body was far from clear. According to Plato the relation of the soul to the body was that of "a pilot in a boat"; but according to Aristotle the relation was far more intimate, indeed so intimate that the individual soul could hardly be thought of as having a separate existence. The question was one that evoked endless discussion. In the early church the tendency was toward the Platonic view, but in the thirteenth century the Aristotelian view, more or less modified, became dominant, partly because it seemed to furnish a better basis for the doctrine of the resurrection of the body. In whichever of these ways, however, the relation of the immaterial soul to the body was conceived, the soul was regarded as the principle of life as well as of thought.[66] This was made more explicit in the

---

[66] For a modern expression of this view see William McDougall, *Body and Mind*, pp. 372ff.

Aristotelian than the Platonic teaching, but it was by no means excluded by the latter.

Descartes' conception of the soul as merely a thinking substance stood, therefore, in sharp contrast with the teaching of the past. For him there was no vital, no nutritive or locomotive soul. The body was rather an automaton. Its essence and that of material things in general consisted in extension. The essence of the soul, on the other hand, was to be found in thought or consciousness. A clear-cut dualism of body and soul was thus established. The vital activity, which had previously bound the two together, was now denied the soul. The latter stood apart from the body as a purely thinking or conscious substance; a substance, however, it still remained, though the question as to whether it could exist without thinking, was commonly answered by the Cartesians in the negative.

The *activistic* theories of the self have not been so clearly defined as the substantialistic, nor have they always been clearly differentiated from the latter. They have grown up as a result of the new dynamic and idealistic interpretations of reality that have appeared since the time of Descartes. In this development three stages may be distinguished.

The first is represented by Leibnitz and Berkeley. These men in different ways destroyed the traditional conception of material substance or substances. Leibnitz argued that materiality or extension is an effect of an underlying force, and that this force in the last analysis must be conceived as spiritual. Souls are thus the causes of material phenomena, and hence must be regarded as essentially active in nature. Berkeley showed that the primary as well as the secondary qualities of things are ideas in our minds, and that the essence of things consists in their being perceived (*esse est percipi*). Things or ideas are, therefore, passive, while the percipient soul is active. Its very essence consists in perceiving (*esse est percipere*). Without its perceptive activity there would be no ideas and no world of things. Both Berkeley and Leibnitz thus gave greater significance to the activity of the soul than had been done before. They did not reject the idea of a soul-substance, but they interpreted it largely in causal terms. They thought of the soul as an agent rather than as a merely existing entity. Instead of setting it over against material things as a coordinate substance they made it rather the creative source of materiality. In this way they carried activity into the very being of the soul. But the nature of the soul's activity they did not analyze with sufficient thoroughness.

To make good this defect was the task Kant set himself, and his work marks the second stage in the development of the activistic conception of the self. By an exhaustive and penetrating analysis of human reason he showed that the mind does not passively receive its knowledge from without. It is creative; it builds up its world for itself. It does so by virtue of certain immanent principles. These principles or categories of thought predetermine the framework of experience and make experience possible. Instead, then, of being made by nature, it is rather the mind that makes nature. The world of nature, as we know it, is the product of the understanding. It is phenomenal, and as such dependent for its being on the creative activity of thought. The thinking, active self is thus the presupposition of all knowledge.

But, according to Kant, it is only the "empirical self" that we know. The real, "substantial" self is both unknown and unknowable. This distinction and others made by Kant in his discussion of the problem of the self did not do much to clarify thought on the subject; they rather confused it.[67] Nevertheless, there was one important outcome of his treatment of the problem. He discredited more completely than any of his predecessors had done the old idea of a soul-substance, and directed attention to the soul as given in experience. It now became clearer than heretofore that the only soul we know is the conscious soul. It is in conscious experience that the true nature of the soul is revealed. The consciousness-idea thus supplanted the substance-idea in the conception of the self, the activity of the self coming at the same time to be thought of more distinctly in terms of consciousness.

But consciousness seems to be an effect rather than a true agent. Hence the reduction of the soul to a merely conscious form of existence appeared to many equivalent to a denial of its reality. This was naturally suggested by the Kantian distinction between the empirical and the ontological self. To avoid the dissolution of the self it became, therefore, necessary to transcend the Kantian standpoint. This was done by

----

[67] "No sooner," says Professor Eugene W. Lyman, "had Kant exorcised the ego as a knowable soul from his system, and swept and garnished the place which it had occupied, than five other egos returned to the place left empty. For Kant tells us of the empirical ego, bound by the chains of causation; and of the ego as the transcendental unity of apperception, which is neither cause nor effect, neither substance nor attribute, but only a logical point of reference; and of the ego as a thing-in-itself, unknowable; and of the ego as a transcendental ideal, the goal of knowledge; and of the moral ego, which posits its own freedom. This is a real bedevilment of the situation" (*Journal of Religion*, 1924, pp. 128f.).

74 74THE PHILOSOPHY OF PERSONALISM

Lotze, who combined the idea of reality with that of consciousness or, rather, interpreted reality in terms of self-consciousness. For him there was no consciousness without a subject, no thought without a thinker, no activity without an agent. The very consciousness of unity and of self-identity put upon the soul the stamp of reality. No further evidence of its truly substantial character was needed.[68] But this is a conception which the analytic intellect has difficulty in accepting as final. Men are prone to detach the mental agent from its activity, thus virtually falling back into the old idea of a soul-substance. Or they separate the activity from the agent, thus leaving us with a mere psychical process, in which no real subject manifests itself. Against both of these fallacies of abstraction we need to be on our guard. The true activistic theory of the self finds the reality of the soul in self-consciousness and self-direction, and says with Lotze that when it is in a state of complete unconsciousness and complete passivity "the soul is not."[69]

As between the substantialistic and activistic theories of the self it is evident that personalism inclines to the latter.[70] Indeed, activism is a characteristic doctrine of what I have called typical personalism. Personalism of this type also holds to the libertarian as against the deterministic view of man, though its exponents vary not a little in the degree of stress which they place on human freedom. Along with the belief in freedom goes also the belief in immortality. William Stern, as we have already

[68] *Microcosmus*, i, 248ff.; ii, 645f.
[69] *Metaphysics*, p. 534.
[70] For an account of contemporary theories of the self see George A. Wilson, *The Self and Its World*, pp. 281ff. This book is one of the most substantial and important additions that have recently been made to the literature of personalism.

noted, rejects the latter doctrine, but personalists generally accept it. Some, such as McTaggart, Henry Jones, and Howison, attempt to demonstrate it as a truth of reason, but most personalists find its ground in the divine will and leave our assurance of its truth to faith in God. The reality of the self, they hold, does not necessarily imply its immortality.

PERSONALISM AND THE WORLD

Having considered the relation of personalism to the ideas of God and the soul, it remains for us to deal briefly with its conception of the world. Using the term in its broadest sense we may here distinguish between a *realistic* and an *idealistic* personalism. Realism in both its "naïve" and its "scientific" form holds to the extramental existence of the material world, but insofar as it is personalistic, it looks upon the world as created by a personal being. Things are thus as truly real as persons. This realistic view formed a constituent part of traditional theism, and in that connection has had a long and distinguished history. But under the criticism, to which it has been subjected by modern idealism, it has gradually been giving way. To common sense it will probably always commend itself; but in speculative circles it finds itself in a state of unstable equilibrium, tending, on the one hand, toward naturalism and materialism, and, on the other, toward spiritualism and idealism. The fundamental difficulty with it is that it has no clear and consistent conception of what reality is. It oscillates helplessly between the personal and impersonal points of view. So far as its relation to personalism is concerned it may be regarded as in a state of arrested development.

Thoroughgoing personalism is idealistic. It finds in personality the key to reality. Only the personal is metaphysically real. The material world is phenomenal. But there are two different ways in which its phenomenality may be conceived: the panpsychistic and the occasionalistic. Both of these views have been and still are widely held.

Panpsychism goes back to Leibnitz. Lotze indorsed it in his earlier years, and more recently it has been adopted by Mary W. Calkins, C. A. Strong,[71] C. A. Richardson, H. W. Carr, Edgar Pierce,[72] and many others. James Ward in his later years favored it, though he admitted that there was no means of deciding between it and occasionalism and regarded it as unimportant which view was held.[73] According to panpsychism material things are simply the "outside appearance" of underlying psychical entities. All nature has at its center living, active beings. Matter is "effete mind" or "undeveloped mind." Natural laws are firmly established "habits." Inorganic things are extreme examples of "fixed" or "stationary species," being constituted by agents of "extremely inferior mentality," "uncommunicating selves." Selves or psychical agents thus constitute the whole of reality. In favor of this view it is urged (1) that it gives to nature a certain independence, an existence for itself as well as others, and (2) that it is truer than occasionalism to the unity and continuity of nature, to the manifest gradations of being within it. But on the other hand, it may be objected to panpsychism that it reduces selfhood to such low terms that one is at a loss, from the personalistic standpoint,

[71] *Why the Mind has a Body*, 1903.
[72] *The Philosophy of Character*, 1924.
[73] *The Realm of Ends*, or *Pluralism and Theism*, pp. 482ff.

to determine in what its reality consists. Then, too, it may be urged with considerable force that appearances are against the theory. The orderliness of the material world and its apparent rigidity point to one will as their ground rather than to innumerable psychical entities. The latter supposition, whatever may be said in its favor, impresses most minds not only as inherently improbable but as more or less fantastic. A "philosophical romance," a "midsummer-night's dream" are not uncommon characterizations of it.

Personalism in its typical form, consequently, leans toward occasionalism. This was the view of Berkeley, of Lotze in his later years, of Bowne, of Rashdall, and is probably the view of most personalists. According to it nature has no independent forces resident in itself. It is "nothing more than the orderly and continuous intervention of God," a ceaseless product of the divine energizing. Things are not themselves "real" causes. They simply furnish the "occasions" on which God "intervenes." It is he who does everything. In him the world has its sole causal ground. There are no hidden entities lying back of the physical atoms. The material world is phenomenal through and through. Its essence consists simply in being a medium of divine revelation and a means of communication between finite spirits, "a system of occasions," as Lotze puts it, "for producing representations in spiritual subjects."[74] Other being than this it does not have. This view no doubt has its difficulties, but it is more thoroughly personalistic than panpsychism, and also stands closer to.both the scientific and common-sense conceptions of nature.

---

[74] *Metaphysics*, p. 170.

THE CONCEPT OF PERSONALITY

Our study thus far has given us a general survey of the personalistic movement in philosophy. We have seen the different forms which the movement has taken, have criticized these forms insofar as they seemed to us defective, and have sought to point out the distinctive elements in typical or normative personalism. But there is still one important aspect of the subject, that calls for more attention than it has yet received. This is the concept from which the term "personalism" is derived, the concept of personality.

It is a common opinion, one that we have already expressed, that the idea of personality owes its prominence in Western philosophy to the influence of Christianity. The extent of this influence may have been exaggerated. It may be that the idea of personality had a larger place in Greek philosophy than has generally been supposed. Too much stress may have been laid upon the fact that there was no technical Greek word to express the idea. In the case of Plato, for instance, A. E. Taylor has warned us against the danger of allowing the absence of the word to blind us to the omnipresence of the idea.[75] On the other hand, it may be that the modern conception of personality is not so completely the product of Christian influences as has been claimed. W. R. Inge, after pointing out that the New Testament writers and the early church fathers had no word for personality and did not feel the need of such a word, goes so far as to say that the modern conception—as expressed by Pringle-Pattison—is flatly contrary to Christianity and that its

---

[75] *Platonism and Its Influence*, p. 74.

general adoption would mean the mutilation and distortion of the whole body of Christian Theology.[76]   But while we may agree with Dean Inge and Professor Taylor that the influence of Christianity upon the development of the idea of personality has been exaggerated by some writers, there is no adequate ground for calling in question the common opinion of scholars on this point.

Whatever contributions the Greek thinkers may have made to the problem of personality they did not concentrate attention upon it in such a way as to make it a subject of urgent and compelling interest.   That was clearly the work of the Christian spirit.   To the believer in Christ the personality both of God and man was a matter of unique and vital concern.   For him God was in his essential nature a personal Being, a Being with whom he could hold fellowship, and the individual man was a being of infinite worth, an end in himself.   These convictions constituted the very breath of his spiritual life; and under their influence speculative thought necessarily took a new direction.   We see this perhaps most clearly in the stress placed by Christian philosophers on the idea of creation.   Creation means that God stands in a free, ethical relation to the world, that man is not the product of the world but its goal, that God, in a word, is a "Person." That this term was not applied to God in the early and mediæval church may seem to us strange.   Personality *in* God, as C. C. J. Webb puts it,[77] was affirmed, but not the personality *of* God.   This, however, does not mean that the modern stress on personality, both divine and human, is out of accord with the spirit of historical

---

[76] *Personal Idealism and Mysticism*, p. 95.
[77] *God and Personality*, p. 65.

Christianity. It may well be that bondage to philosophical tradition and other contemporary influences prevented the early and mediæval Christian thinkers from giving to Christianity its true philosophical expression. Dean Inge and others are no doubt right in pointing out that the traditional doctrines of the Trinity, Incarnation, and Atonement do not easily fit into the framework of our current personal idealism. But this may point to the need of a reformulation of these doctrines rather than to any want of harmony between the personalistic philosophy and the essentials of the Christian faith. That the personality of God and the sacredness of human personality express the true genius of the Christian religion, whatever may be said of its theology, is hardly open to question; and that these beliefs have received their completest philosophical justification in modern personalistic metaphysics, would seem equally clear. Personalism is *par excellence* the Christian philosophy of our day.

The derivation of the word "person" is uncertain. Its meaning, so far as its early philosophical and theological use is concerned, had a double source. One aspect of it came from the Greek word *hypostasis,* which denoted concrete individuality, and the other from the Latin word *persona,* which served as a translation of *hypostasis* but which originally designated an actor's mask, then the actor himself and later a party to a legal dispute, thus carrying with it the idea of social relationship and voluntary activity.[78]   It was in connection with the Trinitarian and Christological controversies of the early church that the term "person" first acquired theological and philosophical significance. An entire church council was once held

---

[78] See C. C. J. Webb, *ibid.,* pp. 35ff.

(362 A. D.) to determine its meaning and to decide the question as to the legitimacy of its use. The decision was favorable, and thereafter the word *persona* and its Greek equivalent *prosopon* were accepted as synonymous with *hypostasis*. The two originally distinct ideas thus combined in the term *persona* appear in the famous definition that has come down to us from Boethius (about 475-524 A. D.). A person is the individual substance or subsistence of a rational nature (*persona est naturæ rationabilis individua substantia*). The "individual substance" corresponds to *hypostasis,* and the "rational nature" to the social or universal element in *persona.* This identification of *persona* with an individual rational nature marks a radical change in the meaning of the word as compared with that which prevailed five centuries earlier. In one of the fables of Phaedrus (I, 7), a Roman writer of the first century A. D., the fox says of *persona* (mask), "What a mighty figure! but brain it has none."[79]

Boethius' definition of *persona* became the standard definition of the mediæval period, and C. C. J. Webb thinks that, taken all in all, it is still the best we have.[80] It brings out both the individual and the universal elements in personality, and is sufficiently broad in its scope to make room for those aspects of personality that in later times have received special emphasis. Webb mentions three of these aspects: incommunicability, self-consciousness, and will. The last two of these he associates with the names of Descartes and Kant, respectively, and the first he might have connected with the name of Leibnitz. "Incommunicability" manifestly stands related to

[79] Compare A. Trendelenburg, *A Contribution to the History of the Word Person*, p. 5.
[80] *Ibid.*, p. 47.

the "individual substance" of the Boethian formula, and
"self-consciousness" and "will" may be regarded as speci-
fications under the term "rational nature."

Three primary factors are thus involved in the idea
of personality and must be included in any adequate definition of it. These are individuality, consciousness and
will. Bowne was accustomed to mention only two, self-
consciousness, or the power to know, and self-direction,
or self-control; but the idea of individuality is implied in
the word "self," and this aspect of personality he always
emphasized. Rashdall[81] in his analysis of personality
singles out five elements: consciousness, permanence, a
self-distinguishing identity, individuality, and, most important of all, activity. But these may easily be reduced
to the three above given, since permanence and a self-
distinguishing identity are manifestly implied in the idea
of individuality combined with that of consciousness.

J. W. Buckham finds four constituent elements in personality, namely, self-consciousness, unity, freedom, and
worth.[82] Of these the first three correspond with our
analysis, since unity and freedom are only other names
for individuality and volitional activity. But "worth"
introduces a new factor, one that we recognize at once as
an important aspect of personality. The very qualities
of rationality and freedom imply it. A rational and free
being, by virtue of the very fact that he is rational and
free, stands apart from the world of things; he is an
end in himself. This was the fundamental thought of
Kant in his conception of personality, and one of his
most significant contributions to philosophy. A person

---

[81] *Personal Idealism*, pp. 370–372.
[82] *Personality and the Christian Ideal*, pp. 12-21.

from this point of view is not a mere self. The words "self" and "person" are sometimes used synonymously, and properly so. But, strictly, "person" is a narrower term.[83] It applies only to selves that have attained a certain degree of intellectual and moral development; a slave is not a person, nor is a child. Personality implies freedom and moral responsibility. It thus transcends the purely psychological or metaphysical plane, and takes on a distinctly ethical character. Here it is that the idea of worth enters. Whether this idea should be introduced into the analysis of personality will, therefore, depend upon one's standpoint. If we adopt the more restricted standpoint represented by the Boethian formula, we might omit it. But from the more comprehensive point of view it would naturally be included, and our analysis would then correspond essentially with that of Professor Buckham. We would find in personality four, instead of three, fundamental elements: first, individuality, which includes unity and identity; second, self-consciousness in the sense of power to know as well as to feel; third, will or free activity; and, fourth, dignity or worth.[84]

From the metaphysical point of view the most important thing connected with personality is the fact that in it unity and identity are co-existent with plurality and change. The self has many ideas, does many things, and

---

[83] For a clear statement of the precise meaning of the term "person" and the various related concepts, see *The Problem of Personality*, by E. N. Merrington, pp. 160-169. This is an excellent little book, distinctly personalistic in its standpoint. Incidentally, it may, however, be noted that the author makes the mistake of saying that Bowne, like Howison, built his metaphysical system upon personality as an ethical concept.

[84] For a more detailed and concrete analysis of personality, see the clever and instructive paper by Professor Earl Marlatt, entitled *"What Is a Person?"* published by the Boston University School of Religious Education (1925).

is subject to constant change, yet it is conscious of itself as one and as identical with itself. How this is possible we do not know, but it is nevertheless a fact given in immediate experience, and a fact of the profoundest philosophical significance.

Since the early days of Greek speculation it has been recognized that the basal and most difficult problem in metaphysics is so to conceive of reality as to provide for both identity and change, both unity and plurality. That the inner life of the soul throws some light upon the problem has also been recognized by idealistic thinkers since the time of Plato and Aristotle. But not until the rise in modern times of a more thoroughgoing form of idealism were the conditions for the solution of the problem at hand. Hegel found the solution in the self-differentiating unity of thought. Here we have a unity that requires diversity as its necessary logical counterpart, an identity that could not exist without change. But, however imposing the Hegelian dialectic may be and however great may be the advance that the Hegelian logic made upon that of earlier times, the whole system impressed most minds as moving in the realm of abstractions. The solution it offered to the world-problem seemed to be logical rather than truly metaphysical.

Hence a more concrete and empirical method was adopted by Lotze. He found the mark of reality in conscious self-existence, and directed attention to the fact that in self-experience we have an actual instance of the co-existence of unity and identity with multiplicity and change.[85] In personality we thus have an empirical solution of the age-old problem of metaphysics; in it we

---

[85] *Metaphysics*, paragraph 97.

have a sample or specimen of what reality is. But in human personality this specimen exists in an imperfect form. True reality and complete personality are to be found only in the 'Absolute. The Absolute is a person, and it is his personality that constitutes his reality. The two are identical.

But while this profound insight underlies the philosophy of Lotze, he did not make it the organizing principle of his system. The fact is he was not a great system-builder.[86] There is, as Henry Jones says, hardly any thinker of his magnitude who leaves his students in so much doubt as to his regulative ideas.[87] Edward von Hartmann at the close of his book on Lotze points out no less than nine important topics on which he thinks that Lotze vacillates between contradictory or mutually inconsistent views.[88] This criticism is not altogether fair to Lotze, but it is nevertheless true that he was too cautious and hesitating a thinker to take his profoundest insights and weld them into a logically articulated whole. For him personality was the key to reality, but the thorough and systematic exposition of this fundamental principle he did not attempt.

That task fell to a friend and former student of his. It is to Borden P. Bowne[89] that we owe what may be called *systematic methodological personalism*. It was he who first took the personalistic conception of reality, grounded it in the Kantian epistemology, developed its implications in a comprehensive way, and made it the

---

[86] See E. E. Thomas, *Lotze's Theory of Reality*, p. xv.
[87] *A Critical Account of the Philosophy of Lotze*, p. 5.
[88] *Lotze's Philosophie*, pp. 181–182.
[89] Bowne dedicated the first edition of his *Metaphysics* (1882) to the memory of his "friend and former teacher, Hermann Lotze."

center and constitutive principle of a complete metaphysical system. This principle he formulated in the statement that the categories of thought do not explain intelligence but are explained by it. The formula runs as a refrain throughout his entire *Metaphysics,* and expresses the most characteristic idea in his system as a whole. He transcended Lotze in other respects that will be mentioned later, but it was particularly in his elaboration and systematic exposition of this idea that he advanced beyond him. It was this aspect of his philosophy also that led him to say of himself that he was "a personalist, the first of the clan in any thoroughgoing sense."[90]

As we now look back over this chapter we see that our study has given us a general survey of the different types of personalism. The least distinctive type is the pantheistic personalism of William Stern, which makes personalism about equivalent to a universal teleology. Another type is pluralistic or finitistic. It is represented in different ways by the atheistic personalism of McTaggart, the relativistic personalism of Renouvier, and the purely finalistic personalism of Howison. Opposed to this type of personalism is absolutistic personalism, or personalism in the form of absolute idealism. This is represented by a number of distinguished thinkers of the neo-Hegelian school. What I have called typical personalism is neither pluralistic nor absolutistic, or, rather, it is both. It recognizes a permanent truth in both pluralism and absolutism, and so seeks to keep the scales evenly bal-

---

[90] For an admirable brief appraisal of Bowne and his relation to personalism, see E. S. Brightman's paper on "Personalism and the Influence of Bowne," read before the Sixth International Congress of Philosophy held at Harvard University in September, 1926.

anced between them. But the most distinctive form of personalism is not reached until personalism becomes a philosophical method as well as a body of conclusions. It is this that Bowne has given us, a systematic methodological personalism, in which the whole of metaphysics is organized around one central and all-illuminating principle—that of the self-sufficiency of personality.

In the light of these facts we may define personalism as *that form of idealism which gives equal recognition to both the pluralistic and monistic aspects of experience and which finds in the conscious unity, identity, and free activity of personality the key to the nature of reality and the solution of the ultimate problems of philosophy.* The detailed exposition and justification of this philosophical standpoint will be the task of the succeeding chapters.

CHAPTER II

PERSONALISM AS A THEORY OF KNOWLEDGE

John Dewey tells us that the time has come for philosophy to turn its face away from "vain metaphysics" and "idle epistemology"; and Bowne has said that, if men could and would give up philosophy altogether, he sometimes thought he would be willing to have them do so, for a great deal of philosophizing is "false" and "pernicious." But however false and pernicious much of it is, there seems no way of getting rid of it. Philosophy is too deeply rooted in the human mind to be eradicated. It is a spontaneous growth. Men are born unto it as the sparks fly upward. And if philosophy is thus unavoidable, so also are metaphysics and epistemology, no matter how "vain" and "idle" they may seem to those who are obsessed with the modern idea of utility. What philosophy at bottom aims at is a satisfactory theory of reality; and a satisfactory theory of ultimate reality is impossible without a satisfactory theory of knowledge. One may, it is true, take one's theory of knowledge for granted, and also one's theory of reality. But this simply means that the crude ideas of uncritical thought are accepted as final. That is what is done on the common-sense plane, and many scientifically trained minds never advance beyond it. In any case virtually all people have some vague notions as to what reality is and how we come to know it. This is true even of the agnostic. The question that confronts us, therefore, is not as to whether we will have a metaphysics and epistemology or not, but what kind of metaphysics and epistemology we will have. Are we to be content with the unreasoned convictions of common sense, or are we to attempt to arrive at some sort of rational and consistent view of the world? Between these alternatives we must choose. The question, in a word, is one between obscurantism and enlightenment.

Logically epistemology precedes metaphysics; before we are prepared to formulate a theory of reality we need to know something about the conditions and limitations of human knowledge.[1] But historically metaphysics preceded epistemology, and for a manifest reason. The human mind is so constructed that it goes directly to its objects. It at first takes no account of itself. It does not raise the question as to whether the knowledge of the object is conditioned by the activity of the subject. Indeed, no clear distinction between subject and object is made. The reality of the objective world, as it is given to us, is taken for granted.

This was true not only of ancient and primitive peoples in general, with whom we have only the fragmentary beginnings of speculation, but also of the Greeks with whom philosophy in the narrower sense of the term originated. Their earliest thinkers were physicists or metaphysicians. More accurately perhaps they might be called cosmologists or nature-philosophers. They were engaged in searching for the first or fundamental principle of the material world. Thales (c. 640-547 B. C.) found it in "water," Anaximenes (died c. 525 B. C.)

---

[1] For a different view see "The Emancipation of Metaphysics from Epistemology," by W. T. Marvin, in *The New Realism*, pp. 45-95.

found it in "air," Heraclitus (c. 535-475 B. C.) in "fire," and Empedocles (c. 490-430 B. C.) in a combination of water, air, and fire with earth, thus giving us four primordial elements. Others transcended the common empirical forms of matter. Anaximander (611-547 B. C.), for instance, found the original and true reality in "the Infinite" (*to apeiron*), an uncreated and all-embracing substance or mixture of substances; Parmenides (born c. 540 or 515 B. C.) found it in an unchanging as well as eternal world-stuff or Being, Anaxagoras (c. 500-428 B. C.) in a countless number of "seeds" or elementary substances, and Democritus (c. 460-357 B. C.) in an infinite number of qualitatively indeterminate atoms. Other primary principles of a more spiritual character were also recognized as, for example, the *logos,* or reason, of Heraclitus and the *nous,* or "thought-stuff," of Anaxagoras. But this did not alter the essentially objective and cosmological or metaphysical character of these early speculations. For the pre-Socratic and pre-Sophistic thinkers knowledge did not constitute a problem.

There were, however, factors at work in that early period which tended to precipitate the epistemological problem.[2] First, the lack of agreement among the philosophers raised the question as to whether they were not engaged in a hopeless quest. Instead of moving toward a common conclusion they seemed rather to diverge further and further from each other. Lapse of time increased the differences between them. Yet they all had the same objective world to deal with, the same material facts. Evidently, then, the ground of difference lay not

---

[2] On this problem see E. S. Brightman's *Introduction to Philosophy,* pp. 67–98. This book is the best general introduction to philosophy with which I am acquainted.

in the objective world but in the mind or minds which sought to apprehend it. Hence the feeling arose that the mind ought itself be made the subject of study. It was this that gave historic significance to the Socratic principle, "Know thyself." Self-knowledge, it is true, might lead to skepticism so far as cosmology is concerned, but in practical life it would yield valuable results, and in any case it was the necessary presupposition of any trustworthy inquiry into the nature of reality. Thought, consequently, took a subjective turn. The logic of the situation required it. The divergent conclusions of the physical philosophers forced the mind back upon itself, and made necessary a study of the conditions and limits of knowledge in general.

Two other factors also contributed to the same result. One was the sharp distinction drawn by Heraclitus between rational and sensible knowledge, a distinction made still more radical by Parmenides and the Eleatic School. Here two faculties of the mind were opposed to each other, and the question inevitably arose as to whether these philosophers were warranted in giving the preference, as they did, to reason over sense. In any case it was evident that their metaphysical conclusions were dependent on their epistemological assumption, and hence the latter called for investigation. Again, a distinction was made by Democritus between the primary and secondary qualities of things. The latter owed their origin to the mind; only the former had objective existence. This distinction manifestly had an important bearing on the conception of the material world, and modern science has confirmed it; but it is by no means a self-evident distinction. The significant thing about it is that it recognized a large subjective element in knowledge, and thus suggested the view that all human knowledge might be relative. Such a view was at least theoretically possible, and to appraise it aright it was necessary for thought to turn its attention upon itself.

The transition from metaphysics to epistemology or from cosmology to anthropology was effected largely through the work of the Sophists. These men were actuated by practical motives as well as by the theoretical considerations just brought out, but of the practical motives we need here take no account. The most noted Sophists were Protagoras (about 480-410 b. c.) and Gorgias of Leontini (483-375 b. c.) As to their exact teaching there is some difference of opinion. It is commonly held that Gorgias in his reaction against the rationalistic dogmatism of Parmenides went to the opposite extreme of complete nihilism, denying not only knowledge and the possibility of communicating it but also being itself. But it is doubtful if he meant to do anything more than deny the reality of the abstract being or thing-in-itself of the Eleatic philosophy. It is also commonly supposed that Protagoras in saying that "man is the measure of all things, of those which are, that they are, and of those which are not, that they are not," was thinking of the individual, and so denied to human thought all universal or objective validity, making truth simply a matter of individual taste, and teaching an absolute relativism. But it is quite possible that he meant by "man" not the individual man, but mankind, and so interpreted his doctrine was merely that of phenomenalistic empiricism. What he and Georgias did, then, was to maintain the rights of sense experience as over against the claims of what would to-day be called a rationalistic absolutism.[3] In any case, it was these men and the Sophists in general who first made knowledge a problem and the central problem in philosophy.

Their attitude toward the question of knowledge, while perhaps not so extreme as tradition has represented it, was on the whole negative. They adopted the sensualistic account of the origin of knowledge and denied to man the capacity for truth in the commonly accepted sense of the term. This skeptical conclusion they applied not only to the realm of science but also to that of morals and religion. The result was that the whole spiritual life of man was threatened. The authority of conscience was undermined, religious faith was left without assurance, and the high quest after truth was reduced to an idle dream. Had this tendency in Greek thought been allowed to work out its logical consequences in practical life, it would have led to the complete dissolution both of social order and of personal character; the supreme values of human existence would have been dissipated. Against it, consequently, a great idealistic reaction set in under the leadership of Socrates (469-399), Plato (427-347), and Aristotle (384-322). These men championed the cause of knowledge and, along with knowledge, the cause of faith and virtue. By their pre-eminent genius they set on high the spiritual interests of men, gave to them an immortal expression, and made them determinative in their own world-view. It was the first great clash in the field of intellectual combat between personalism and impersonalism, and personalism won the day. But vic-

---

[3] For a defense of this view see Theodor Gomperz, *Greek Thinkers*, i, pp. 450ff., 482ff.

tory in this realm is never final. Skepticism, sensationalism, and other forms of impersonalism spring up like weeds in human thought. They are constantly nourished by the lower elements of our nature. If they vanish for a while, it is only to reappear in new disguise, and then the conflict with them is again renewed. The controversy may take on new forms from age to age, but its main lines were laid down once for all by the great idealistic thinkers of Greece, and it is to them that we must go back for the earliest formulation of the distinctive principles in the personalistic theory of knowledge.

As over against the Sophists, Socrates, Plato, and Aristotle contended for the trustworthiness of reason and for its superiority to sense or to mere opinion. Socrates limited his interest in the validity of knowledge largely to its bearing on the ethical life, but the other two gave to reason a universal validity. And since their time the higher faith of mankind has for the most part been linked up with philosophical rationalism as opposed both to skepticism and to sensationalism. Now and then philosophical skepticism has been defended by theologians on the ground that it furnishes a basis for the doctrine of religious authority; if human reason is incapable of arriving at the truth, there is need of supernatural guidance either from Scripture or from the church. But skepticism of this kind has never been thoroughgoing. It has always assumed that reason was capable of weighing the evidence in favor of religious authority and of appreciating its cogency. It has also usually held that a considerable measure of religious truth was capable of rational justification. Then, too, the collapse of the older idea of authority has to a large extent removed the need

of the kind of apologetics which was based on philosophical skepticism. Valid authority, it is now seen,
must itself be rational. It must not only find an extraneous support in reason but must be an outgrowth of it.
There must be in religion and in its institutions something that both expresses and responds to a rationally
defensible need of human nature. What we are concerned about to-day, therefore, is to establish not the
religious incapacity of the natural man, but, rather, the
naturalness of religion and the validity of that part of
our nature that finds in religion its satisfaction. Occasionally religion is represented as wholly independent of
knowledge, but this is a radical mistake. Religion has
its cognitive side, and its truth implies the essential trustworthiness of the human mind. Indeed, the whole
religious appeal rests on the assumption that our faculties
are reliable, especially those that belong to the higher
ranges of our being; and these, of course, include our
reason. Any other view would be as inconsistent with
the truth of religion as with the dignity of human personality.

Skepticism has usually been linked with sensationalism
or empiricism. It was so in the case of Protagoras, and
reflection makes it evident that a thoroughgoing sensationalism leads necessarily to skepticism. But the full
logical consequences of the theory are often not drawn,
and hence we find sensationalism at times allied with
theology. Bishop Berkeley might be called a theological
sensationalist, and there is a considerable empiricistic element in Thomism or Aristotelian scholasticism, which
is still the official philosophy of the Roman Catholic
Church. But while Berkeley and the Thomists found in

sense-experience the source of knowledge, they did not deny the activity of the mind; they positively affirmed it. A consistent and thoroughgoing sensationalism, however, conceives of the mind as wholly passive, and this conception in the last analysis leaves no basis either for knowledge or for the high character and destiny of the soul. Plato, consequently, rejected the sensualism of his day, and urged the necessity of an independent reasoning faculty, of an *a priori* element in knowledge. He was the first to take this position in a clear and decisive way. He argued that the mind has ideas which are not derived from sense experience, and that it is in this realm of supersensible ideas that the true and distinctive nature of the human soul is to be found. This doctrine underwent various modifications and developments in subsequent ages until it finally culminated in the Kantian theory of the categories and the creative activity of thought. One may not be altogether satisfied with the Kantian formulation of the doctrine or with any other exposition of it, but it can hardly be denied that it is in the aprioristic theory of knowledge that the personalistic and religious conception of the self receives its most adequate expression.

Personalism, then, stands for the trustworthiness of reason and for apriorism or the creative activity of thought. These two doctrines in one form or another have, with a few exceptions, been characteristic of its epistemology since the time of Plato. A third principle for which it stands is what, in Kantian terms, is known as the primacy of the practical reason. This principle was to a certain extent recognized by Plato when he accorded the supreme place to the idea of the Good. But

on the whole, Greek thought was inclined toward intellectualism. However much practical considerations may
have actually influenced speculation, the tendency was to
ascribe pre-eminence to the intellect. It was the impersonal reason that stood highest among human faculties.
Undue importance was attributed to the syllogism. The
significance of the will and emotions for knowledge was
not adequately recognized. Some provision for them was
made in later Greek epistemology by the introduction of
the idea of revelation and authority, and this tendency
became still more pronounced when Greek philosophy
passed into the hands of the Christian Church.[4] But to
fuse faith and philosophy was not an easy task. There
was a constant tendency for them to break apart. Philosophy retained the early stamp of intellectualism, and faith
was bound up with the idea of an extrarational authority. Not until the time of Kant did the practical reason
establish itself within the precincts of philosophy as a
recognized principle of knowledge.

Kant himself, it is true, denied to the convictions
based on the practical reason the character of knowledge.
He distinguished sharply between knowledge and faith,
between the theoretical and the practical reason; and from
the purely epistemological standpoint he no doubt attributed a greater degree of certitude to the former than the
latter. But in the field of metaphysics he reversed the
order. There he destroyed knowledge in order to make
room for faith. Whatever valid convictions in that
realm are possible, he insisted, are based on the practical
reason. To it he gave the primacy in any complete world-
view. Thus he laid the foundations for a theory of knowl-

---

[4] Compare Windelband's *History of Philosophy*, pp. 219–229.

edge which gives due recognition to the volitional and emotional sides of our nature as well as the intellectual. This viewpoint manifestly harmonizes with the interests of religion and also with that type of philosophy which sees in personality something deeper, broader, and more divine than the perceptual or logical faculty. Personalism, consequently, accepts the primacy of the practical reason. At this point it parts company with the other main forms of idealism, and aligns itself with pragmatism and other voluntaristic types of thought which represent a reaction against the predominant intellectualism of the past.

Another respect in which personalism diverges from at least Hegelian idealism is in its conception of the nature of knowledge. This we pointed out in the preceding chapter. The common view is that there is a clear distinction between an idea and its object. My thought of a thing, "thing" being understood in the sense of "object," is different from the thing itself. To know an object implies that the object has an existence independent of my knowing it. Otherwise it would not be real knowledge. If thought and thing are identical, there might conceivably be either a mental state or an object in a certain relation, but there would be no true cognition. Cognition implies a dualism of thought and thing. So it plainly seems; and, as a matter of fact, this is the view that was generally held down to comparatively recent times. But since the rise of idealism there has been a tendency to reduce things to thoughts, and then, by way of reaction to this, the attempt has been quite recently made by neo-realists to reduce thoughts to things or to relations between them. These two movements are some-

times known as "pan-subjectivism" and "pan-objecti-
vism," or as "the great subjectivism" and "the great
objectivism."[5] The latter manifestly stands in direct
antithesis to the personalistic philosophy, but the former
also comes into conflict with it by virtually identifying
man and the world with God. Personalism attributes to
the individual soul a certain independence and regards
the world not only as independent of man but as in a
sense objective to God himself. In any case it refuses
to identify thought and thing so far as the human mind
is concerned. On this point it holds to the traditional
view. Its epistemology is dualistic.

These, then, are the main articles in the epistemological
creed of personalism: (1) the dualism of thought and
thing, or idea and object, (2) the creative activity of
thought, (3) the trustworthiness of reason, and (4)
the primacy of the practical reason. None of these articles is peculiar to personalism. It shares them all with
other philosophies. But taken together they constitute
a unique and coherent body of doctrine. The first has
to do with the nature of knowledge, the second with the
nature of thought, the third with the skepticism growing
out of the way in which the nature of thought and knowledge is sometimes defined, and the fourth with the question as to whether there are extraperceptual and extralogical grounds of knowledge. Each of these principles
will need to be carefully studied if we are fully to understand the personalistic theory of knowledge. In the following discussion they will be taken up in the order just
given.

[5] Compare W. H. Sheldon, *Strife of Systems and Productive Duality*,
pp. 38–221.

THE DUALISM OF THOUGHT AND THING

Reference has already been made to the fact that it is only in comparatively recent times that the dualism of thought and thing has been seriously called in question. That thought and thing seem to be "numerically two" and not "one" is generally admitted. But it is urged that this is mere "appearance," which needs to be resolved into simpler elements or into an underlying unity. Perhaps the chief criticism passed on the dualistic theory is that it leads to skepticism. It separates the idea from its object in such a way that there is and can be no certainty that the two correspond to each other. It creates a gulf between them which makes knowledge impossible. Hence the epistemological monist maintains that somehow or other the two must be brought together. Thought and thing, if the trustworthiness of our faculties is to be guaranteed, must in some way be reduced to unity and identity.

The problem thus raised is a complex and difficult one. There are many diverse views as to the nature both of the idea and the object, and this diversity complicates the question of their relation to each other. Furthermore, in the discussion of the question much confusion has arisen from the failure to keep the human and absolute points of view distinct and also from the failure to distinguish clearly between the epistemological and metaphysical aspects of the subject.

In dealing with the problem it may be best, first of all, to define more precisely what is meant by epistemological dualism and monism and what is implied in them. Their general meaning is clear enough, but exactly what they imply in concrete application is not so self-evident, nor is it altogether clear what their metaphysical implications are. For instance, can epistemological monism be consistently combined with a realistic philosophy, which recognizes the substantial reality both of minds and things? Is it possible for an idea and its object to be identical with each other, when the idea is owned by a subject metaphysically distinct from the object? The answer will manifestly depend upon the sense in which the terms "monism" and "identity" are used. If by epistemogolical monism is meant a metaphysical or factual identity of idea and object, it is evident that this is impossible on the basis of a substantialistic realism. Such an identity has its place in solipsism, in absolute idealism, and in a positivistic system like neo-realism where thought and thing are loosed from their anchorage in substance, either material or immaterial, and fused into a kind of neutral unity. But where minds and things stand in mutual externality to each other, it would seem clear that there is no way by which idea and object can be brought into real unity or identity. On this basis the idea may correspond to the object or be valid for it, but it cannot be factually or metaphysically identical with it. It matters not whether our experience of the object be mediate or immediate, the dualism necessarily remains.

The term "epistemological monism" is, however, sometimes used in a more limited sense to denote, not the actual oneness of idea and object, but their essential equivalence, in the sense that they coincide in their content to such an extent that there is no fundamental parallax between them. The secondary qualities of things are, of course, subjective; they belong to the perceived and not to the real object. At this point there is a dualism. But the primary qualities are objective. They are immediately experienced, and thus enter into the mind, constituting a bond of union between thought and thing. Here, then, we have epistemological monism combined wth substantialistic realism; "critical monism" it has been called.[6] But whether this is a proper use of the term "monism" is open to question. In any case the epistemological basis on which the theory rests is not one that will bear the test of criticism. The idea that we have an experience of the primary qualities of things so immediate that extramental existence is thereby guaranteed, is a conception that belongs to the pre-Humian and pre-Berkeleian stage of thought. How such an "immediate" experience of things is possible cannot even be made intelligible. The mind has no way of rubbing its nose, as it were, up against material reality and apprehending it without some mediating activity on its own part. And if this mediating activity is acknowledged, the term "immediate" as applied to perception turns out to be simply a designation of the remarkable rapidity of the process. In and of itself it has no epistemological significance. A process is not necessarily true because it is unusually rapid. The realistic appeal to immediate experience is, then, a broken reed, and the epistemological monism based upon it is simply a piece of crude sense dogmatism. Indeed, to call such an epistemological theory monism is misleading. The term "monism" ought to be reserved for an epistemology in which either things are reduced to thoughts, or thoughts to things.

---

[6] This view is represented by D. C. Macintosh, *The Problem of Knowledge* and *The Reasonableness of Christianity*, pp. 161ff.

It is not the disparity between the experienced object and the real object that makes an epistemology dualistic, but their mutual otherness. There might be a point for point parallelism between an idea and its object, and yet their relation to each other might be as dualistic as if there were no resemblance between them whatsoever. It is the existence of a stimulus external to the mind that constitutes the differentiating feature of epistemological dualism. Both personal idealism and absolute idealism deny any extramental reality to the material world. Yet the epistemology of one system is dualistic, and that of the other monistic. The reason for the difference is this, that personalism regards the soul as distinct from God and looks upon the world as a vast system of stimuli which serves as a medium of communication between God and man and between spirits in general. This system is in a certain sense objective and external to God as well as to man. In any case it exists independently of us. We do not make it but find it. What its exact nature is we do not know, but its causal ground we at least recognize as external to ourselves, and hence we distinguish between our own ideas and the objects which they apprehend. Absolute idealism, on the other hand, looks upon the Absolute as One who embraces in the unity of his own being both man and the world. The things that make up the world are his thoughts, and it is he also who thinks in us so that our thoughts are his thoughts, and since his thoughts are things, so also are ours. There is nothing "given" in knowledge, there are no external stimuli that impart anything to thought, no thing—or things—in themselves. Everything is generated within thought itself so that nothing exists but thought. Thus the antithesis of thought and thing is overcome and we have a monistic epistemology.

Against this epistemology two or three weighty objections may be raised. First, it does not remove the dualism of thought and thing from human knowing. The thoughts of the Absolute may conceivably be identical with things. But this is not and cannot be true of human thoughts. Things do not pass out of existence when we cease to think of them, nor do they come into being when we become conscious of them. The world manifestly exists independently of us. What it is in its essential nature we may not know. It may be a divine thought or system of divine thoughts, but whatever it is, it is objective and external to us. The theory that things are divine thoughts may help us to understand how we can know them, but it does not make them a whit less independent of our consciousness of them. Whether they be lumpish things or divine thoughts, we in either case discover them, we do not create them. Their existence is something distinct from our ideas of them. There is no way of escaping this conclusion. The dualism of thought and thing is for us, as Bowne used to insist, "ineradicable."

In the next place, if human thought is identified with the divine thought, as is done in the Hegelian epistemology, it becomes very difficult, if not impossible, to explain the fact of error. On the dualistic basis the explanation is simple. Here it is easy to see that our ideas may fail to harmonize with objective reality because of the careless or willful misuse of our faculties or because of physical and mental defects of one kind or another. But on the monistic basis, where idea and object are identical, it is hard to see how there could be any parallax between thought and reality. If an idea, whether true or false, is one with its object, it would seem that error must have its counterpart in reality, as well as truth. But such a conception would cancel error itself. If errors are themselves objective, the ideas by which they are apprehended cannot be erroneous. Yet this strange and self-contradictory theory of the objectivity of error has been broached and even advocated by some neo-realists.[7] Absolute idealists try to meet the difficulty by defining error as partial truth due to our finiteness. But this also virtually cancels error. For these partial truths or errors are not merely subjective with us. They form part of the experience of the Absolute and so belong to reality. A special difficulty, furthermore, arises from the fact that, while the Absolute thus thinks our thoughts with all their infection of error and ignorance, he is yet supposed to live in unclouded light, enjoying perfect knowledge of the truth. How these two antithetical forms of experience can be combined into unity completely surpasses us. The attempt to think it through can only lead to intellectual befuddlement. If ignorance and illusion are to be accounted for, there must be a more distinct separation between the human and the divine than absolute idealism permits. The fact of error is the Achilles' heel of every monistic epistemology.

A third criticism to be passed on the epistemology of absolute idealism is that it fails to distinguish clearly between thought and reality and also fails to give adequate recognition to the "given" element in experience. However we may explain it, there is a significant difference

---

[7] Compare Bertrand Russell, *The Problems of Philosophy*, p. 196, and E. B. Holt in *The New Realism*, pp. 303–373.

between what William James has called "acquaintance with" and "knowledge about"[8] and Bertrand Russell calls "knowledge by acquaintance" and "knowledge by description."[9] Acquaintance with a thing carries with it a sense of immediacy and an assurance of objective reality that indirect and inferential knowledge lacks. The latter may be valid for reality, but it finds its ultimate verification only in experience. What reality is, the human mind does not predetermine. It is something revealed to us through sensations and perceptions. We do not make it, we find it. It is in a sense given to us. Through external stimuli we are brought into contact with it and become aware of it. Reality is thus something other than our thought of it. Indeed, it is something deeper and richer than all thought. Even the divine thought needs to be set in reality before it can be said to be metaphysically real. The world is not mere idea; it is idea translated into deed. How this translation takes place we do not know. It is here that we have the ultimate and unfathomable mystery of being. Reality, as Lotze somewhere says, is a precipitate whose genesis we can never grasp.

Now, this conception of reality is one that absolute idealism rejects as a false realism. Reality and thought it insists on bringing together. It denies that reality is in any sense external to thought or that it is even a "plus" to thought. It also denies that there is anything "given" to the human mind that is other than or beyond thought. Thought is all inclusive. It embraces everything, both without us and within us. Our minds do not apprehend

---

[8] *Psychology*, i, 221f.
[9] *The Problems of Philosophy*, chap. v; *Mysticism and Logic*, pp. 209–232.

a world distinct from thought, but reality thinks *in* us and in this way the world comes to exist *for* us. Thought and reality are thus one. Thought also is constitutive, not simply "formal"; it receives nothing from without, it creates its own world. But however valid this view may be as over against a crude, realistic empiricism, it leaves us in a confused state of mind as to the nature of thought, both human and divine, and its relation to reality. We may admit that thought is creative rather than receptive and that there is no such magical immediacy about sense-experience as some realists imagine, but this does not necessarily mean that there is no "other" to thought which thought apprehends. Nor does it mean that there is nothing in human experience that may properly be described as "given," no raw material of the sensibility which owes its origin to external stimuli. We are dependent beings, and this dependence expresses itself in the recognition of a power not ourselves, a power that conditions our entire mental life. This power is not only within us, it is also without us; and the within and the without constitute for us a dualism which no human thought can escape. Nor can the divine thought wholly escape it. Thought and reality are not one even for God. We may say that the world is God's thought, but by thought in this case we mean, or should mean, not thought in the subjective sense of the term, but thought objectified, and objectified (it should be added) by the divine will so as to be in a sense an "other" to God. If we do not so understand it, if we regard the divine thought as identical with cosmic thought and as constituting a logical process, sufficient in itself, without a guiding or realizing will, we lose ourselves in a wholly abstract conception of

reality and fall into a devastating pantheism or naturalism. This is the peril that confronts absolute idealism,
and we can escape it only by surrendering its monistic
epistemology.

The epistemological monism of neo-realism or pan-
objectivism is even more untenable than that of absolute
idealism. As absolute idealism seeks to explain things
in terms of thought and thus to identify the two, so neo-
realism seeks to explain thought in terms of things and
thus to break down the dualism between them. But
"things" it interprets in a broader and different sense
from what the older materialism did. It denies to things
a substantial character.[10] There is no such thing as substance or cause in the older sense of the terms. Instead
of physical substances we have sensible qualities in certain aggregates or relations to each other. These aggre-
gated or related qualities constitute physical things. But
these things are not the only realities. Concepts are real,
and so also are relations. Indeed, relations are said
to be even more fundamental than sensible qualities, so
that in the development and refinement of thought the
categories of substance, quality, and relation may be
regarded as representing three successive stages.[11] Substantialism was succeeded by psychologism, and now
psychologism by a kind of logism. In any case the new
realism seeks to etherealize substance away into logical
relations, concepts and qualities, making consciousness
simply a special form of relation between these existent
or "subsistent" entities. Consciousness has, therefore,

[10] Compare E. G. Spaulding, *The New Rationalism*, pp. 270ff.,
308ff., 439ff.
[11] Compare R. B. Perry, *Present Philosophical Tendencies*, pp. 308, 310.

no independent existence. Instead of creating its objects it is itself created by them. It is not a secretion or a kind of motion, as the older forms of materialism asserted, but it is none the less intrinsically or fundamentally related to and dependent upon things. It is a process or phase or function or relation of its objects. Many different methods are employed by neo-realists and behaviorists to describe consciousness in such a way as to cancel its supposed uniqueness and thus remove the dualism of thought and thing. Holt speaks of subjective or psychical phenomena as "the subtle workings of integrated objective mechanisms." Montague tells us that "the potentiality of the physical is the actuality of the psychical" and that "consciousness is the potential or implicative presence of a thing at a space or time in which that thing is not actually present." Dewey says that "awareness . . . means things entering, via the particular thing known as an organism, into a peculiar condition of differential—or additive—change."[12] According to Perry, ideas are merely things in a certain relation. Things enter into the mind and, when they do so, become ideas. Ideas are, therefore, not distinct from things, but simply a subclass of them. They are those things that are known.[13]

In these different statements some strange things are said about consciousness and conscious states, but on examination it is evident that they leave the gulf between the psychical and the physical as great as ever. Ideas may be only things in a certain relation, but that relation is so unique that the things involved in it are

[12] Quoted by W. H. Sheldon, *Strife of Systems and Productive Duality*, pp. 189, 195, 210.
[13] See *Present Philosophical Tendencies*, p. 126.

as different from ordinary things as ever pure ideas were. Subjective states may be merely the subtle workings of an objective mechanism, but these "subtle" workings are as different from the ordinary workings of an objective mechanism as the older mental phenomena ever were. Memory may be described as the potential presence of the absent, but this makes it no less wonderful than it was before. Consciousness may be a peculiar condition of differential—or additive—change induced upon things, but this "peculiar" condition is as different from the ordinary condition of things as their representation in the form of ideas ever was. What neo-realism has given us is simply a verbal cement between thought and things—a cement that dissolves the moment the rays of criticism fall upon it. Thoughts do not become things by being merely called such. And even if we were to think of things as the ultimate source of thoughts, our thoughts would still remain distinct from the things by which they are produced. So far as we are concerned, the dualism of thought and thing cannot be transcended. Nor is there any way of deducing thought from things. From the standpoint of things, mind remains and will forever remain a miracle. Every attempted deduction of the mental from the nonmental and every attempted identification of thoughts with extramental things turns out upon investigation to be a pure verbalism.

Epistemological monism we then reject, so far as it has to do with the knowledge of the world. But how about self-knowledge? Do we not here have an identity of idea and object? From the metaphysical standpoint the answer must be, Yes. There is here no such ontological otherness as we have in the case of the self and the world.

The self knows itself; object and subject are one. But from the psychological point of view we still have the distinction of subject and object. The self as known stands opposed to the self as knower. This antithesis, however, is simply the form that knowledge necessarily takes. But the very fact that knowledge necessarily takes this form excludes even here the absolute identification of idea and object. The idea by which the self apprehends itself is not identical with the self. Nor is it merely a mirror of the self. The idea of the self is itself a thought product. Even in self-knowledge we have no experience so immediate that the activity of thought is dispensed with. Down below the level of articulate thought we no doubt have a self-experience in which self and experience seem merged together, but as soon as thought becomes articulate the idea formed of the self differentiates itself from the self. This also needs to be added, that the thought-process does not completely exhaust the being of the self. The self is deeper than any one of its activities, and in the elemental stirrings of the sensibility we have the necessary raw material of knowledge, without which thought would have no content. So within the life of the soul thought has in a certain sense its other. Still in self-experience and self-knowledge we have as close an approach to epistemological monism as is humanly possible. Nothing is given to the human mind with such immediacy and irrefragable certainty as self-existence. We have here the one impregnable bulwark against skepticism, as Augustine and Descartes taught us.

The problem involved in the debate between epistemological monism and dualism is, as we have already said, a modern one. It owes its rise largely to the skepticism growing out of the metaphysical dualism of Descartes and the Kantian doctrine of the creative activity of thought. These doctrines established an apparently impassable gulf between thought and its material objects so that it became a question whether thought by its very nature could apprehend objective reality. To offset this skepticism the claim was set up, on the one hand, that there are no independent things, that things are in the last analysis thoughts, and, on the other hand, that there are no independent thoughts, that thoughts are simply a subclass of things. Such an identification either of things with thoughts or of thoughts with things breaks down the middle wall of partition between knowing and being, and so leaves no ground for skepticism in its modern form. Now, in antiquity there was also a widespread skepticism, but it did not grow out of a profound dualistic system such as that of Descartes or Kant. Plato and his followers, it is true, taught the immateriality of the soul, but this did not raise for them an insuperable barrier between the knowing soul and the material world. Nor was the relation of the soul to the body so conceived either in the Platonic or Aristotelian schools that a direct interaction between them seemed impossible. Hence there was no felt need of asserting the identity of idea and object. The ancient and mediæval thinkers as a whole were epistemological dualists. Not even Parmenides was an epistemological monist in the modern sense of the term.[14]

It was Descartes who first established so sharp an antithesis between thought and thing and between the

---

[14] See T. Gomperz, *Greek Thinkers*, i, p. 178f.

soul and the body that an extreme monistic movement eventually set in as a natural reaction against it. Upon him, consequently, the monist looks with special disfavor. "In treating living bodies, even the human body, physically regarded as mere machines," says R. F. A. Hoernlé, "Descartes set the fashion of reducing biology to physics; he bequeathed to psychology and philosophy the body-soul problem; he burdened the theory of knowledge with the dualism of intramental ideas and extramental things; he divorced and isolated each individual mind alike from other minds and from the common world; he destroyed for psychology all chance of a concrete analysis of human minds by dividing the living man not only between a soulless body and a bodyless soul, but by dividing the soul further between a metaphysical, non-empirical substance and an abstract self-consciousness whittled down to the bare data of immediate experience. As far as any single thinker can be called so, he is the father of all evil in modern philosophy."[15]

Whatever we may think of this indictment, it is still true that it was the dualistic movement set on foot by Descartes and culminating in Kant that gave rise to the monistic attempt to identify thought and things. With this attempt, insofar as it rejects a fundamental metaphysical dualism, personalism is in accord. But insofar as it merges human thought in that of the Absolute or makes it a function of independent objects, personalism raises its voice in protest against it. Such a monism would destroy the independence and distinctive worth of personality, and would, as we shall see later, make knowledge itself im-

---

[15] *Studies in Contemporary Metaphysics*, pp. 240f. Reprinted by permission of Harcourt, Brace and Company.

possible. If personality is to maintain its integrity, it must be kept "a handbreadth off," both from the Absolute and from things; and this means an epistemological dualism, no matter what one's theory of things or of the Absolute may be. Descartes, then, was fundamentally right. There is a necessary dualism of thought and thing in human knowing. How this dualism is to be explained, is a problem that we for the present postpone. Here it may simply be said that the only satisfactory explanation of it is to be found in a theistic monism. If an intelligent Being is the ultimate source both of the thing-series and the thought-series, it is possible to understand at once their dualism and their parallelism, both of which are involved in the fact of knowledge. Apart from such a theory the parallelism of thought and thing remains an insoluble riddle. How amazingly intricate and marvelous this parallelism is, will become clear as we consider the second fundamental principle in the personalistic epistemology.

The Creative Activity of Thought

In perception thought is unconscious of itself. It goes so directly and so immediately to its object that men at first assume without question that the world exists in the form in which it is perceived. No distinction is made between primary and secondary qualities. The latter seem as objective as the former, and both are regarded as impressing themselves upon the mind from without. The mind is unique insofar as it has the power of receiving these impressions, but it contributes nothing to the content of the world which it perceives. So far as knowledge is concerned, it is passive. It is acted upon by forces outside of itself. The object completely determines the knowing process. All that the subject does is to serve as a reflecting surface or to furnish the capacity for receiving what the object gives. It may perform this function imperfectly, but as knower it has no other function. So it seems to spontaneous thought.

But however self-evident all this may at first appear, doubt eventually sets in. Our sense-experience deceives us. Things, we learn, are not always what they seem. And so the distinction arises between the apparent and the real. Appearances sometimes mislead us, and in any case they do not reveal to us the entire nature of things. Things act differently or appear differently under different circumstances. The question, consequently, arises as to what the true nature of things is, and thus metaphysical speculation begins. At once a double standard manifests itself—that set up by sense and that set up by reason. Philosophers at the outset generally favored the latter as against the former. It was Heraclitus who first sharply opposed the two to each other. But reason failed to save men from the uncertainties of sense. It led to no unanimity of opinion, and to most people seemed to have a less secure foundation than sense-experience. Hence a state of skepticism ensued. It is this that gives historical significance to the sophistic movement. The Sophists were the first seriously to call in question the validity of knowledge. Not only did they reject the conclusions of the metaphysicians, but sense-experience as a whole they regarded as devoid of objective validity. At least this was the view of Protagoras. He looked upon sense-perception as due to the reciprocal action of the subject and object but as different from both and, therefore,

without any counterpart in reality.   On this theory manifestly no knowledge was possible.

The skepticism precipitated by the Sophists gave to
the subjective element in thought a new importance.   It
was the subjectivity of sense-perception, according to
Protagoras, that nullified its validity.   The subject was
thought of as the destroyer of knowledge rather than its
creator.   If, therefore, knowledge hereafter was to justify itself, men must take account of the subjective factor
in its production as they had not done before. The philosopher must heed the Socratic injunction and first of all
know himself.   He must show that perception or thought
in general is not necessarily a distorting medium.   And
here the old cleavage between sense and reason again
arose.   Which, it was asked, is the more trustworthy,
which brings us nearer to reality? This question has been
a bone of contention down to the present day.   Spontaneous thought naturally favors sense as against reason,
and this represents also a persistent or constantly recurring tendency in the history of epistemological speculation.

The ancient theory, which reduced the mental life to
sense-impressions and their combinations, is commonly
referred to as "sensualism."   The corresponding modern
theory is called "sensationalism."   It also bears the name
of "associationalism" and "empiricism."   The former
term directs attention to the fact that sensationalists of
the past century found the principle of movement and
synthesis in the mental life in the laws of association;
the latter term brings out the fact that sensationalism
regards experience as the sole source of knowledge. The
theory in the course of its history has undergone various

developments and has had different metaphysical affilia-
tions. It has been associated with materialism (Epicurus), with idealism (Berkeley), and with positivism or
skepticism (Hume). The last named is the one with
which it is logically associated, but a preliminary account
of its relation to the other two will help to an understanding of the theory.

Sensationalism in epistemology is as natural to reflective thought in its first stages as is materialism in metaphysics. Hence an early alliance between them was
formed. The pre-Socratic philosophers were most of
them materialists and sensualists. But neither their materialism nor their sensualism was sharply defined.

The first clear definition of materialism appeared in
atomism, represented by Democritus (460-357 B. C.). The
sensualistic theory, however, which he also held, was not
clearly differentiated from rationalism; indeed, it was
combined with it. He regarded perceptions as due to
images cast off by objects, but he also regarded the high
philosophic conceptions of the structure of these objects
as due to images of a finer quality emitted by them. He
thus conceived of rational ideas as conveyed to the mind
in the same way as sense-impressions. He also held that
they were as much more trustworthy than the latter, as
their images were of a finer quality. Though a psychological sensationalist, he placed reason above sense. It is
even said that he put out his eyes so that he might be
less disturbed in his philosophical speculations.

But this alliance of sensualism with rationalism was to
a large extent broken by the later and more consistent
Epicureans, who made reason secondary and derivative.
They accepted the image theory of Democritus, so far

as sense-perceptions are concerned, but to the general ideas of reason they allowed no independent origin. They looked upon the higher forms of thought as due to the persistence or combination of sense-impressions. The latter they regarded as the only source of knowledge. The mind, they held, was wholly passive, and in this fact they found a defense against skepticism. If perceptions are due to the direct action of the images or effluxes of objects upon the soul and are in no way distorted by any activity on the part of the soul itself, there would seem no reason to distrust them. So by returning to the pre-Sophistic stage of thought and by not only assuming but asserting the complete passivity of the human mind, the Epicureans imagined that they had bridged the gulf between object and idea and had established within sense-impressions themselves a reasonably secure basis for their own materialistic philosophy. That their materialism transcended to some extent what was given in sense they realized, and so in their system the door to skepticism was not completely closed; but on the whole they maintained the bond between sensationalism and a sense-metaphysics. The result was that Epicureanism became a synonym for metaphysical materialism as well as epistemological sensualism and ethical hedonism.

Both Democritus and the Epicureans failed to grasp the unique and distinctive character of perception as a psychical act. This was to some extent due to their materialistic conception of the soul. But even those ancient and mediæval philosophers who followed Plato and Aristotle and accepted the doctrine of an immaterial soul held for the most part rather crude theories of perception. They, as well as their contemporaries in general,

seemed unable to get over the idea that in knowledge
the object is the determining factor and the subject
merely a passive recipient. The mind was spoken of as a
tabula rasa, a blank tablet; Aristotle's figure of the seal
and the wax was used to illustrate the perceptual process;
and the image theory of Democritus had considerable
currency. There were, it is true, other and profounder
conceptions. The skeptics denied that our percepts are
copies of external objects; Plotinus rejected the theory of
imprints or seal-impressions on the soul, asserting that
in perception the mind is active, not passive,[16] and Augustine put self-certainty above the certainty of the object.
But these were exceptions to the main current of ancient
and mediæval thought. Thinkers in general in those
days subordinated the knowing process to the object in
such a way that the reality of the object was supposed
to be given in thought itself. The objective reference
of thought was thus interpreted from the standpoint of
the object rather than the subject. It was not the subject
who objectified his thought; his thought was rather the
reflection of the object and would have been nonexistent
without it. Hence the object was regarded as implicit
in perception, and under those circumstances a sensationalistic idealism or subjective sensationalism could
hardly arise. The sensationalistic and empiricistic types
of thought in ancient and mediæval times remained bound
to materialism or realism.

Not until the time of Descartes was thought sufficiently
loosed from its anchorage in the object to take on a really
distinctive and independent character. It was now
sharply opposed to material or extended things and made

---

[16] *Enneads,* iv, 6, 1, 2.

the essential and exclusive feature of mind. Heretofore
mind or soul had been regarded as the source of vitality
as well as of thought, and hence as standing in such an
intimate relation to the body that it could receive from
without impressions more or less ready made. But now
it was defined as a purely "thinking thing" and hence
conceived of as separated from extended things by a
metaphysical gulf. Material things could, therefore, no
longer be thought of as impressing themselves upon the
mind or as generating in any direct way mental images
of themselves. Mental images were now regarded as immediate creations of the mind, and consequently it was
possible to think of them as arising without any direct
physical stimulus. They might owe their stimulus directly to God or to some external cause totally different
from the objects apprehended. The material world,
therefore, in the realistic sense of the term, was not necessary to explain sensations and perceptions. These mental
states in and of themselves contained nothing that was
inconsistent with an idealistic world-view. Descartes
himself thought that perception would be deception without the ontological otherness of the material object, but
the possibility of such universal deception he admitted.
The only protection he could find against it was the
veracity of God. Malebranche (1638-1715), however,
had no real place in his system for an ontologically distinct material world. He retained it, but his reason for
so doing was not so much his belief in the veracity of
God as his belief in the authority of Scripture.[17] Not
"the natural revelations of the sensations," but "the

----

[17] *Dialogues on Metaphysics and on Religion*, translated by Morris
Ginsburg, pp. 38, 75, 172.

supernatural revelation of faith," constituted for him the chief ground for believing in the existence of corporeal things; and this appeal to authority or revelation was of course an arbitrary or non-philosophical element in his system. So far as his system itself was concerned, he might as well have dispensed with the material world, for he made God the direct cause of all our sensations. This conclusion, which he himself declined to draw, was drawn by a younger contemporary, George Berkeley (1685-1753), who belonged to the English empirical or sensationalistic school of psychology. Berkeley denied the ontological existence of matter and thus gave to sensationalism an idealistic or subjective character that it had not previously had. Its earlier materialistic or realistic implications were sloughed off and sensations were now left as an orderly system of phenomena without any impersonal ontological content or support.

Berkeley's sensationalism, however, was not thoroughgoing. He eliminated the metaphysical object but retained the metaphysical subject. The next stage in the development of sensationalism consisted in the elimination of the latter also. This was the work of David Hume (1711-1776), who thus introduced the positivistic type of sensationalism. Sensations without a subject were now regarded as constituting the original atoms of the mental life. Through their combinations and associations the structure of reason was supposed to be built up. The whole process was conceived mechanically. No place was left for an independent mental agency. In this respect Hume's sensationalism marked a return to Epicurean sensualism with its conception of the complete passivity of the human mind. This conception of the

122 THE PHILOSOPHY OF PERSONALISM

mind is one of the two fundamental characteristics of sensationalistic empiricism. The other is the view that experience in the form of sensations is the source of all knowledge. By Hume, and his English successors for a century after his time, sensations were conceived of atomistically. Physics furnished the model for psychology.

But during the past thirty or forty years the biological analogy has been supplanting the physical. The cohesive bond in experience has been emphasized even more than its discrete elements and is regarded as equally original. Consciousness is now represented, not as a collection of sensations, but as a stream, a living, developing whole. The term sensationalism may still be used to designate this type of psychology, but it is a new kind of sensationalism, a sensationalism animated, not by aggregation, but by integration. Such a sensationalism lacks the clear-cut character of the older atomistic type. It sustains about the same relation to it that hylozoism does to atomistic materialism. The latter is the only pure type of materialism, but the former sometimes bears the name. So also sensationalism in its purity is atomistic, but in its more recent biological or "integrated" form it stands in a sufficiently close relation to the classical type to be designated at least occasionally by the same name. Both forms of sensationalism agree in making experience the sole source of knowledge, though they disagree in their conception of the original structure of experience. They also agree in eliminating the self, though on this point current sensationalism is both more conservative and more radical than its older form. In William James' representation of the individual "thoughts" as thinkers we have an approach to the self psychology, while in

behaviorism the self and even consciousness vanishes into
a system of physiological reactions. But whatever differences in detail there may be between its different
forms, the logical tendency of sensationalism as a whole
has been to reduce the rational to the irrational, the
spiritual to the sensuous, the personal to the impersonal,
and so to undermine the higher faiths of mankind.

Against this type of psychology and epistemology,
religious philosophy, consequently, has for the most part
set its face. It has contended for the reality of the self,
for the independence of reason, and for the creative
activity of thought. Its argument, developed through
the centuries, has assumed two main forms or passed
through two main stages. The first was initiated by
Socrates, Plato and Aristotle; the second by Immanuel
Kant. Between the two there is no radical difference.
One to some extent involves the other. But the method
of argument is different in the two cases. Plato laid
stress on the difference between sense and reason and on
the superiority of reason to sense. This might, it is true,
also be said of Kant. But he subordinated sense to reason in a quite different way from Plato. He developed
the theory that sense-experience is not due merely to
the sensibility but is constituted by thought or reason.
The sense world, therefore, has no independent existence
of its own, but flowers into being and becomes real only
through the creative activity of the mind. These two
lines of thought, the Platonic and Kantian, are the methods employed by reason to curb the tyranny of sense.
Both are called rationalistic by way of contrast with empiricism.

Platonic rationalism was modified in a significant way

by Aristotle, so that we have in the pre-Kantian period
an Aristotelian as well as a Platonic form of rationalism.
We shall consider each of these briefly.

The skepticism of the Sophists was directed against
both sense and reason. Neither in the perceptions, the
opinions, nor the philosophies of men could they find a
stable element upon which knowledge could be built.
Everything to them seemed to be in flux. This skepticism Socrates met by directing attention to the fixity
of the idea as over against the fleeting phenomena of
life. Particular things and events might come and go
and apparently leave no mark behind, but the common
element in them, the general idea, nevertheless persisted.
In ideas or concepts, therefore, we have a fixed element,
a solid basis for knowledge. But how do we arrive at
these concepts? This point Socrates did not make altogether clear. At times he emphasized induction as the
first step. But his own method he called spiritual "mid-
wifery" and this suggests that concepts are innate and
simply need to be helped to birth within the soul. No
definite theory on the subject, however, was formulated
by him. It was Plato who first developed the theory of
an *a priori* element in knowledge and insisted strongly
on the necessity of an independent reasoning faculty.
This faculty, he held, was not concerned with the data
of sense, nor even with general notions abstracted from
them, but with an independent realm of ideas. These
ideas, according to the common interpretations of Plato,
constituted a kind of conceptual double of the sense
world, but they preceded the latter. They were the original and eternal patterns, after which the things of sense
were made. The latter were copies, images, or imitations

of the ideas, and as such could suggest them to the mind. But the mind did not derive them from sense, it directly apprehended them. The activity of the mind or reason thus stood apart from that of sense as something distinct and independent.

This independence of reason Plato expressed by describing or defining its activity as recollection. In semi-mythical terms he represented the soul as having in a previous state of existence had a direct vision of the eternal ideas.[18] Hence he could say that we at present, by virtue of our reason, recollect "those things which our soul once saw when in company with God." The higher ideas of the mind do not then owe their origin to sense-experience. They arise within the soul itself. But while the term "recollection" thus implies the independence of reason, and its superiority to sense, it at the same time implies a view of thought that falls short of the modern conception of its creative activity. The soul, according to Plato, does not create its ideas, it remembers them. Ideas are in a sense objective to thought, objective even to God himself. We originally perceived them, and now recall them. The Platonic theory of thought and knowledge thus followed the analogy of sensuous and particularly visual perception. It left thought superior to sense but, like sense, passive and receptive as over against reality.

Neoplatonism marked a double advance beyond Plato. First, it carried the Ideas, which in the *Timæus* are represented as existing outside the Deity, into the Divine Mind itself, thus making them ideas of God. Second, it transformed Plato's "recollection" or "reminiscence" into a doctrine of innate ideas potentially present. Both of

---

[18] *Phaedrus*, 248f.

these doctrines found a place in Christian philosophy. The second was for a time supplanted through Aristotelian influence, but it was revived by Descartes and figured prominently in modern philosophy down to the time of Kant. It implied a greater degree of activity on the part of the mind than did the Platonic theory of "reminiscence," but it left undefined the relation of human ideas to divine ideas. The tendency was to subordinate the former to the latter. Augustine, for instance, said that the finite being cannot be its own light, and Malebranche carried this to a point where he said that we see all things in God. Leibnitz, on the other hand, laid so much stress on the concrete individual that he virtually taught us that we see all things in ourselves. In both cases, however, rational activity was regarded as having its own laws and as superior to the affections of sense as a revelation of reality.

It was this point that Plato especially emphasized. The sense world was to him in large measure an unreal world. Those who live on the sense plane he likened to prisoners in a cave so chained that they could not turn their faces toward the light, but could only see their own shadows and the shadows of moving objects back of them thrown against the opposite wall.[19]   As unsubstantial as these shadows were the things of sense to him. But as shadows resemble to some extent the objects that cause them, so is it with the things of sense in their relation to the Ideas. They are images or symbols of them. They participate in them. They do not, it is true, contain them in such a way that the Ideas may be obtained by abstraction from them; but they suggest them, prompt the mind to recall

[19] *Republic,* book vii.

them. There is thus some connection between sense and reason, but what Plato emphasizes is not the connection but the contrast between them. The sense-world is a shadow-land. The real world is the world of Ideas, apprehended only by reason.

This sharp contrast between sense and reason and between the phenomenal world and the world of Ideas was rejected by Aristotle, and thus there arose a new form of rationalism. Indeed, the Aristotelian epistemology is sometimes classed as empiricistic. The fact is it occupies a place midway between empiricism and Platonic rationalism. As a disciple of Plato, Aristotle continued to hold that knowledge consists in general ideas and that these ideas express the true nature of reality; they are not merely subjective concepts. But they have no real being, he contended, apart from individual things. They become real only in the concrete forms of existence revealed to us through the senses. Without sense-experience we could, therefore, have no knowledge of reality. But this does not mean that sense-experience is the sole source of knowledge. It is not so much through experience as in consequence of experience that we arrive at knowledge. In experience itself the universal ideas or intelligible forms are implicitly or potentially present, but they become explicit, and thus a basis of knowledge, only through the activity of reason. Reason, according to Aristotle, has a twofold nature; it is both active and passive. Exactly what he meant by this distinction has been the subject of much discussion. It probably should be understood from the standpoint of the opposition between "matter" and "form" and between "potentiality" and "actuality," which formed a characteristic and fundamental feature of Aristotle's metaphysics. The passive reason was matter or potentiality. It was a kind of *tabula rasa,* an "uninscribed tablet." The active reason was form or actuality. It was the causal or constitutive principle in thought. Through its agency the raw material, furnished by the passive reason, was worked up into intelligible forms. But while having distinct functions the passive and active reasons are not to be thought of as two entities. They are, rather, aspects of one and the same reason, just as every object, according to Aristotle, was compounded of both matter and form.

On this point, however, Aristotle was not altogether clear. His language concerning the active reason often suggests that he meant by it a separate entity, a super-individual, universal and immortal principle, immanent in human souls but detachable from them and from the passive reason identified with them. But whatever may have been his conception of the metaphysical relation of the passive and active reasons to each other, epistemologically he thought of them as intimately bound up with one another. The active reason by itself would be contentless, and the passive reason by itself formless. Both are necessary to knowledge, and both are in a sense organic to each other. The active reason does not create its own forms and impose them upon a foreign and more or less recalcitrant material. The sensations, perceptions, and images, contributed by the passive reason, already have the universal principles of thought immanent in them. They are potentially conceptual. What the active reason does is simply to extricate the concepts from their sensuous entanglement and thus to raise potentiality to

actuality. It creates nothing itself. It merely reads off
what is implicit or immanent in sense-experience. It thus
stands in essentially the same relation to conceptual objects that the organs of sense do to sensible objects. It
is receptive rather than creative. Hence Aristotle speaks
of the identity of thought with its object. "Actual
knowledge," he says, "is identical with its object." "In
the case of immaterial objects the subject thinking and
the object thought are one and the same thing."[20] By
this he meant that the object as pure form is "wholly
cognized, wholly penetrated by the mind, wholly taken
up into it." In other words, there are immanent both
in the mind and in things the same universal forms, so
that there is no parallax between thought and reality.
Thought reflects the true essence of things.

This form of rationalism differs from the Platonic in
that it denies the transcendence of concepts and holds
that they are immanent in sense objects. They can be
apprehended, it is true, only by reason, but it is only in
sense-experience that reason can apprehend them. Hence
it might be said that all knowledge is derived from sense-
experience. But while this sounds quite empiricistic,
Aristotle and his mediæval followers did not attempt to
deduce the laws of reason from sensations, nor did they
hold that bare sensations are the only valid revelations
of reality. In these two fundamental respects they dis-
agreed with what may be called traditional empiricism.
They held that the intellect or reason is as original a
faculty as is the sensibility, and that it is not bare sensations, that are the source of knowledge but sensations
informed with reason. Reason is immanent in sensations

[20] *De Anima*, 431a, 430a.

and perceptions. If it were not so, it would not be possible by an abstracting and generalizing process to extract conceptual knowledge from them. At bottom, then, the Aristotelian epistemology was rationalistic. But it rejected the theory of innate ideas and conceived of reason as so firmly anchored in sense that the Platonic epistemology seemed to it alien in spirit. It is for this reason that the modern Aristotelians, the Thomists, find it apparently so difficult to understand or to deal sympathetically with Plato and Kant, the two philosophers who emphasize most strongly the total disparity of sense and reason. But what here needs especially to be noted is that both in the Platonic and the Aristotelian epistemology, a certain independence is ascribed to sensation, perception and memory-images. They are represented as preceding thought and having a kind of existence apart from it. They may be mere copies, shadows or potentialities, but insofar as an independent existence is accorded them, they are always on the point of setting up in their own right and claiming to be the sole source of all knowledge. Both Aristotelian and Platonic rationalism thus left the door open to sensationalism and empiricism. They did not realize that thought itself is not only active but creative, and that sensations and perceptions as well as concepts are the products of its creative activity.

Not until the epoch-making work of Immanuel Kant (1724-1804) was this truth clearly grasped and firmly established. Before his time all schools of thought agreed in regarding receptivity as the most important characteristic or function of the human mind. Knowledge was thought of as something given to us. In sense-experience it was supposed that we receive impressions from without and in the realm of reason it was held that we either read off what is implicit in sense-experience or bring to consciousness what is innate in the human mind. As to the nature of the external stimulus in sense-experience there was wide difference of opinion. Theories varied all the way from the effluxes of Democritus to the divine will in Berkeley's system. There was also no agreement as to whether perception implied the extramental existence of the object. Down to the time of Berkeley the common opinion was that it did. In this implication it might be deceptive. Some extreme skeptics asserted that it was, and others, such as Descartes and Malebranche, admitted theoretically that it might be. But whether the implication was valid or not, it was generally held that sense-perception carried with it a realistic view of the external world. Berkeley was the first to contest this view effectively. He showed that our perceptions do not necessarily imply the metaphysical existence of the objects perceived. Our sense-experience might be produced within us by the divine will; but produced it nevertheless was by some foreign power rather than by the mind itself. Even Leibnitz' windowless monads did not create their own objects; they, rather, reflected what was given implicitly in themselves. It was Kant who first made the individual mind a determining factor in the manufacture of experience.

So long as sense-experience was accepted as something epistemologically ultimate, as something co-ordinate with or independent of thought, reason and the higher spiritual interests of men were left with an insecure title. They had on their flank an unsubdued and ambitious foe. The things of sense, no matter what might be said of their shadowy, imitative and purely potential character, were always on the verge of setting up a claim to primacy in human life and thought. And there was no decisive way of gainsaying that claim, so long as the data of sense-experience were admitted to be ultimate, self-sufficient, and self-evident. The one effective and conclusive method of dealing with the sensationalistic claim is to show that sensations are themselves thought-products and that they have no definite or articulate character until they have been fashioned into being by the creative activity of thought. This it was that Kant did. He did not content himself, as did Aristotle, with reducing the sensibility to "potentiality," nor, as Plato did, with stigmatizing the phenomena of sense as mere shadows. He subjected sense-experience to a searching examination and showed that the sensibility as the passive recipient of external stimuli could yield nothing but fleeting and discontinuous impressions, "an elusive phantasmagoria without intelligible contents." Sensations in and of themselves, without the impress of thought, have no unity or identity. They are as evanescent as their physical stimuli, and, so far as content is concerned, have hardly enough definiteness to be described as "a big blooming buzzing confusion." Indeed, they are simply the raw material of thought, its abstract presupposition. As soon as they become definite enough to be called sensations of anything, they already have the work of thought stamped upon them. Sensations, as commonly understood, and still more perceptions and memory-images are, therefore, the products of thought activity. What the passive sensibility contributes has no articulate character. It is not even a shadow of reality, nor is it a potentiality. In and of itself it could develop into nothing rational. It is in itself utterly impotent. As over against reason it has no independence, it is like clay in the potter's hand. For it to set itself up as a rival would, therefore, be absurd. It is itself completely subject to thought, completely molded by it. Rational thought, consequently, need not hereafter fear the aggression of sense; it is securely enthroned. This was Kant's method of vindicating the claims of reason and the higher interests of men.

As is evident from the preceding paragraph, Kantian rationalism is more thoroughgoing than either the Platonic or Aristotelian. It takes away from sense the last shred of cognitive independence, and reduces it to a state of inarticulate passivity where it has not even a voice with which to protest against the dominance of reason. Whatever cognitive value it *seems* to have, it owes to thought with its *a priori* principles. But while Kantian *apriorism* is thus the most highly developed form of rationalism, it differs from both the Platonic and Aristotelian types in being purely "formal" in character. Aristotle, it is true, rejected Plato's conception of thought as "recollection," and the later Aristotelians rejected the doctrine of innate ideas. They thought of the truths of reason as evolved only from sense-experience and in connection with it. But they regarded these truths as having a definite content of their own and as expressing the essence of things. The same was also true of the Platonic "ideas," whether conceived as innate or as purely objective. Kant, on the other hand, looked upon the categories as the structural principles of experience without which experience would be impossible, but which in turn would be formal and empty apart from experience, as much so as the rules of grammar in abstraction from living speech. The categories find their meaning and application in the facts of experience and apart from these facts are altogether vacuous. It is the fleeting impressions of sense that furnish the content of experience, but this content would be formless and meaningless without the activity of thought. It is the categories that give unity and fixity of meaning to the chaotic flux of the sensibility. The operation is, of course, one that lies beneath the threshold of consciousness, but without it consciousness itself would be impossible.

In criticism of this Kantian epistemology it is sometimes urged that it derives its strength from the inadequacy of the older atomistic type of sensationalism. That discrete sensations, even though aided by the laws of association, cannot account for the mental life as a whole, is freely conceded. On that point Kant and his disciples are admitted to be right as against Hume and the associationalists. If experience consisted originally of atomic sense impressions, the relating activity of thought would be necessary to explain the coherent character of experience as we now have it. But the Humian assumption with reference to the original structure of sense-experience, we are told, is mistaken. Experience in its most elementary form is organic. It includes relations as well as sensations. Both belong to the stream of consciousness and each implies the other. We do not, therefore, need the relating activity of thought to account for the coherence of experience. Experience is coherent, to begin with, and its coherence is no more in need of explanation than its discrete elements. Both are ultimate facts of experience, and must be accepted as such. They are given to us, and beyond them the mind cannot go. Hence we may discard the complex machinery of the Kantian categories as superfluous. The newer integrated type of sensationalism has rendered it unnecessary.

But this criticism, plausible as it may at first seem, misses the point of the Kantian argument. The defect in the older sensationalism did not consist simply in its failure to account for the relations in which sensations stand to each other. It was natural that its Kantian opponents should fix attention upon this defect. Granted, they said, that the human mind is furnished at the outset with a series or collection of sense-impressions, it would still be impossible to account for the coherent aspects of experience. To explain them the creative activity of thought is needed. But in taking this position the Kantian epistemologists never for a moment conceded the sensationalistic assumption that sense-impressions actually constitute the original units of the mental life. It has always been their contention that sensations as distinct psychical units cannot be accounted for by the passive sensibility. They themselves are thought-products; and if so, it is evident that this is far more clearly the case with "the stream of consciousness" and the complex relations involved in it. If, therefore, the Kantian argument is valid against the older atomistic type of sensationalism, it is still more decisive against its current organic or "integrated" form. Current sensationalism is really a capitulation to Kantian criticism in much the same way as current positivism has arisen from the capitulation of the older materialism to idealistic criticism. The effort is made in both cases to save the naturalistic element in the traditional systems by conceding a certain truth to apriorism in the one case, and to idealism in the other. But the effort is doomed to failure. A sensationalism which recognizes as elementary the complex thought activity involved in the stream of consciousness, has already surrendered one of the two fundamental principles of empiricism, namely, the passivity of the human mind. So long as the latter principle is adhered to, there is no way of getting beyond fleeting and inarticulate sense-impressions. "This insight," as Bowne says, "is Kant's great contribution to philosophy, and it remains, in spite of all criticism, a permanent possession of reflective thought."[21]

What interests the personalist most, however, in connection with the doctrine of the creative activity of thought is not the doctrine itself, important as it is from the epistemological point of view, but its metaphysical implications. The first of these is the reality of the self. A certain kind of substantial reality has been attributed to the soul or self from ancient times, quite independently of the question as to its creative activity in the knowing process. Indeed, only in a very imperfect way was the creativity of thought recognized by any school of philosophy before the time of Kant. Reason was asserted by many to be independent of sense. But both reason and sense were regarded as, in large part at least, the passive recipients of a ready-made knowledge. The knowledge might be regarded as due directly to God, or as imparted through physical media, but in either case it was supposed to be received from without. It was "given" to the mind. Yet the mind was thought of as "real," as having

[21] *Personalism*, p. 56. Reprinted by permission of Houghton Mifflin Company, publishers.

a kind of substantial existence in spite of its passivity. But what such an existence would be or mean, is far from clear. Pure passivity would seem to deprive reality of all positive content. "If we admit," says Eucken, "that absolutely everything comes into the mind from outside, there is neither sense in nor authority for ascribing to the spirit a peculiar existence."[22] The spirit asserts its reality in and through its activity. And this activity must manifest itself in the realm of thought, if the independence of spirit is to have any meaning. For it is thinking that constitutes the essence of the soul, and it is only insofar as thought is active and creative that it becomes a constitutive factor in the world. The ultimate theoretical basis for the reality of the self is, therefore, to be found in the creative or constitutive character of its thought-activity.

It is only a further explication of the same idea when it is pointed out that thought as a creative process implies the unity and identity of the self. If the mind were wholly passive and perception a mere act of receptivity, we might conceivably get along without a self. Percepts would then have a kind of thing-like existence attributed to them. They would be looked upon as passing in bodily fashion from object to subject and as somehow floating in the stream of consciousness without the sustaining power of thought. But when this crude theory is outgrown and perception is seen to be a subjective process, involving a complex relating activity, the need of a unifying mental principle becomes evident. Knowledge, for instance, exists only in the form of the judgment, and the simplest judgment involves at least two elements, a

[22] *The Fundamental Concepts of Modern Philosophical Thought*, 1880, p. 90.

subject and a predicate. These, however, can be brought together only by some principle that embraces them both, and that principle we call the self. Our mental life is complex, and over against this complexity the soul must be one. It is also a ceaseless flow, and over against this temporal flow the soul must be permanent as well as one. There is no possible way of escaping this conclusion. The existence of the self is involved in every denial of it. Without the unity of the self a rational consciousness would be impossible; "perception," as Plotinus quaintly said, "demands a gathering place." And without the identity of the self the mental life would vanish into an incoherent flux. Thought as an active and creative process requires as one of its fundamental conditions a unitary and abiding self.

Another important metaphysical consequence of the doctrine of the creative activity of thought is that it makes possible an idealistic view of the world. It does not require such a view. There is nothing in the subjectivity of thought that is necessarily inconsistent with the theory that the external world is an exact double of the perceptual world. But the subjectivity of thought does deprive this theory of its traditional support. The strength of naturalistic realism has lain in the apparent immediacy of knowledge. But this immediacy, it is now seen, is illusory. Knowledge is something built up within the mind itself. The existence of an extramental double of our perceptual world is, therefore, an assumption. It is not given in perception itself. Indeed, the study of perception has made it clear since the time of Democritus that many of the qualities we ascribe to things have no extramental existence. "Only in opinion," said Democritus, "consists sweetness, bitterness, warmth, cold, color; in truth there is nothing but atoms and empty space."

But if the secondary qualities have no counterpart in reality, it is evident that our perceptions are no mere copies of the external world. The perceptual world contains something more and other than the real world. Yet there is apparently a marvelous adjustment of the two to each other. The physical stimuli are totally different from the resulting sensations and perceptions, yet there is an orderly relation between them, a kind of pre-established harmony. The stimuli in and of themselves leave with us the impression of incompleteness, and so also does the entire material world when robbed of its secondary qualities. It is a barren, poverty-stricken world; and this forces on us the conviction that, if it has any extramental existence at all, it is an embryonic or purely instrumental type of existence. It does not exist simply for and by itself. It exists in order to be known, and hence finds its completion and meaning in knowledge. Knowledge, in a word, is organic to nature. It is not "a barren rehearsal" of it. It adds something to it, it completes it. In this sense the understanding makes nature, and thus man, banished from the geographical center of the universe by the Copernican astronomy, is reinstated as the immanent goal and crown of nature. Without man, or at least intelligent beings, to apprehend it, nature would be a merely inchoate form of being, without articulate character. This is the Copernican revolution initiated in philosophy by the Kantian doctrine of the constitutive activity of thought. It restores to man his lost primacy and gives to the material world an altogether new significance. We now see "the earth and every common sight appareled in celestial light."

The Trustworthiness of Reason

It is, however, possible to draw a skeptical conclusion from the subjectivity of thought, and hence it becomes necessary to consider the question as to the trustworthiness of reason. If thought does not directly and immediately apprehend external reality, it may misapprehend it. This is at least a theoretical possibility. To avoid it thinkers have either appealed to intuition or have constructed a theory of epistemological monism. The latter in both its idealistic and realistic forms is, as we have already seen, quite untenable, and the former leaves us in the realm of magic. Thought and thing constitute a dualism which human thinking cannot escape, and which it cannot by any metaphysical power of its own transcend. The mind builds up its world for itself, and, consequently, if thought is valid for reality, there must be a parallelism between them. But that this is the case can never be demonstrated. The validity of knowledge is, and must remain, an assumption. There is, therefore, no way of absolutely closing the door to skepticism. Skepticism, however, exists in various forms and degrees, and the more important of these we need briefly to consider.

In antiquity an extreme form of agnosticism was deduced by some thinkers from the Heraclitic doctrine that all is flux. The argument was that nothing can be affirmed of that which everywhere and in every respect is changing. Aristotle, for instance, tells us of a certain Cratylus, "who finally thought that one ought not to say anything, but merely moved his finger; and who found fault with Heraclitus for saying that it is impossible to enter the same river twice; for he himself thought one could not do so even once."[23]   This radical type of skepticism had not a little vogue in ancient Greece. For a time it gained possession of the Academy, Plato's School, so that the term "Academician" became a synonym for an extreme skeptic. Most of the arguments by which it was supported are now obsolete, but it is interesting to note the way in which Augustine met it. "Without any delusive representation of images or phantasms," he said, "I am most certain that I am, and that I know and delight in this. In respect of these truths, I am not afraid of the Academicians, who say, 'What if you are deceived?' For if I am deceived, I am. For he who is not, cannot be deceived; and if I am deceived, by this same token I am. And since I am if I am deceived, how am I deceived in believing that I am? For it is certain that I am if I am deceived. Since therefore, I, the person deceived, should be, even if I were deceived, certainly I am not deceived in this knowledge that I am. And, consequently, neither am I deceived in knowing that I know. For, as I know that I am, so I know this also, that I know."[24]   This line of thought occurs again and again in Augustine, and may be regarded as the basal principle in his philosophy. But its full significance was not appreciated by his contemporaries nor by his mediæval followers. Not until the dawn of the modern era did men realize that it really marked a turning-point in the history of speculative thought.

It was Descartes who, in his famous *Cogito, ergo sum* revived the Augustinian conception of the primacy of

[23] *Metaphysics*, 1010a.
[24] *The City of God*, xi, 26.

self-consciousness and gave to it a permanent and conspicuous place in philosophic speculation by making it
the foundation of his own system. The immense significance of this conception lies in the fact that it transferred
the center of gravity of human certainty from the objective to the subjective realm. Aristotle and Aquinas would
have regarded as absurd the idea that the existence of the
soul is immediately and indubitably certain, while that of
matter is a later inference. For them certainty attached
quite as much to the material object as to the mental
subject. To give the primacy, consequently, to self-
knowledge, as did Descartes, marked a very important
change in speculative thought. It was this change that
constituted the germ out of which grew the great idealistic systems of the modern age.

This stress on self-certainty, however, important as it
was, did not solve the problem of skepticism. It did
bring out the contradiction involved in absolute agnosticism. Even doubt implies a doubter. This contention
is valid, regardless of the theory we may have of the self.
All thought involves some sort of conscious existence.
To deny this would be to deny thought itself. But the
important thing, after all, in connection with thought
is not the fact that "I think" and that "therefore, I am,"
but the question as to what I think and whether I think
correctly or not. This question is not one that can be settled by the bare fact of self-existence. There is no logical
bridge leading from self-certainty to the validity of
knowledge in general. The Augustinian and Cartesian
argument does exclude absolute nihilism, but it leaves the
door open to skepticism so far as the knowledge of the
external or objective world is concerned. And no logical

injunction requiring the closing of this door can be issued. It may, however, be pointed out that such skepticism is wholly gratuitous. On the factual side it leads to the absurdity of solipsism, and from the standpoint of conceptual thought it implies a distinction between rationality and truth. Our reason, it is urged, may require certain affirmations concerning the objective world, but there is no way of knowing that reality corresponds to them. Other intelligences might be differently constructed from what we are, and hence might have a very different view of the world. Rationality does not necessarily mean actuality. Such formal doubt as this is always possible, but it is also, as Bowne used to say, "always barren." It has no positive foundation whatsoever, rests on a bare theoretical possibility, and implies the abdication of reason itself.

The lesson to be learned from such skepticism as this is that there can be no standard of truth other than that furnished by reason itself. The mind must be its own judge. No external authority, whether it be that of theology or the hypothetical "truth" of skepticism, can possibly take its place. Truth and rationality must be equated. To drive a wedge between them, as formal skepticism does, is the height of unreason; it is an act of volition, of caprice. In the very nature of the case reason must be the ultimate test of truth. But this does not mean that reason itself is infallible in the sense that its objective validity cannot be doubted. Such doubt is possible. Its possibility is implied in the fact of error and in the necessary dualism of thought and thing. We must, it is true, as rational beings assume the validity of reason, but this assumption is itself a matter of faith.

To accept reason, quite as much as to reject it, is at bottom an act of volition. The element of trust cannot be eliminated from knowledge. Anselm was right when he said that he did not seek to understand so that he might believe but he believed in order that he might understand.[25] In the last analysis all knowledge rests on faith.

This fact makes formal doubt possible, but it by no means legitimizes it. Only reason can dethrone reason, and so in the very act of seeking to dethrone itself it reasserts its own sovereignty. In other words skepticism, if it is to be rational and not merely capricious, must assume the validity of the reason it seeks to overthrow. But while absolute agnosticism is thus self-contradictory, there are less extreme forms of it that have had considerable vogue. In modern times skepticism has been associated with sensationalism, on the one hand, and with the Kantian epistemology, on the other. Sensationalism has usually admitted the truths of objective fact but has denied the truths of reason. The latter it has ascribed, in Hume's well-known phrase, to "the mind's propensity to feign." There are, therefore, no objectively valid categories. The subjective principles of thought are precipitates either of individual or race experience, or they are the deposits of social pressure, the preconditions of social life. In any case they represent nothing intrinsically valid. They are the products of contingent facts, and hence to universalize them is unwarranted. They must, as J. S. Mill said, be "limited to a reasonable degree of extension to adjacent cases." On the moon, two plus two might, for all we know, make five.

The effective and decisive reply to this type of skepti-

---

[25] Proslogium, chap. i.

cism is to be found in the Kantian doctrine of the creative activity of thought. This doctrine, as we have seen, makes it clear once for all that the categories cannot be imported into the mind from without. They cannot be produced by experience or by any mysterious social pressure. They are themselves the conditions of experience. Without them articulate experience would be impossible. We must then assume that they are inherent in the mind itself. They belong to its original outfit.

But this theory admits of another and profounder type of agnosticism. The categories of thought may belong to the structure of the human mind and may be universally applicable to experience, but beyond experience it is possible that they may have no validity. They condition experience and hence are law-giving for the world of phenomena, but this very fact raises a question as to whether they do not erect a barrier between us and things-in-themselves, whether, in a word, they do not mask reality so that we can never know it as it is in itself. This conclusion Kant drew and persisted in holding. But it is self-contradictory. If the categories of thought— being, causality, identity—do not apply to things-in-themselves, these things are not only unknowable, they are also unaffirmable. The distinction between knowable phenomena and unknowable things-in-themselves is, therefore, untenable, and with it Kantian agnosticism falls to the ground. One might, it is true, surrender the unknowable things-in-themselves, and yet hold to a kind of phenomenalism, restricting not only knowledge but also reality to phenomena. But such a metaphysical phenomenalism would also be self-contradictory. Phenomena, in order to be phenomena, must be phenomena of some-

thing; and they must also stand in relation to a percipient. In and by themselves they are mere abstractions. If
viewed as real, they presuppose both object and subject,
and to some extent reveal both. A thoroughgoing phenomenalism, therefore, which rejects both thing and
thinker, is inconsistent with the very nature of phenomena. But the implications of the doctrine are seldom
thought through. Indeed, in its common form the doctrine is unclear, and hardly amounts to anything more
than a convenient excuse for neglecting the deeper and
more difficult problems of thought[26] and for occasionally
belaboring metaphysics and theology.

No valid basis for agnosticism can then be found in the
Kantian distinction between phenomena and noumena.
As sensationalistic agnosticism succumbs to the Kantian
criticism, so Kantian agnosticism succumbs to its own
inner contradiction. There is no rational ground for
drawing an impassable line between appearance and
reality and excluding the latter from the realm of knowledge. These two terms are correlative and find their
true meaning only in their relation to each other. A
reality that appears to no one, not even to itself, would,
indeed, be unknowable, but it would also be unaffirmable;
and an appearance that appears to no one and is the appearance of nothing would be an empty abstraction. All
knowledge must be to a certain extent a knowledge of the
real. To exclude the metaphysical from the range of
human knowledge is either sheer arbitrariness, or it rests
on ignorance of what metaphysics is. Metaphysics has to
do with the causal ground of phenomena, and without
such a ground phenomena from both the objective and

---

[26] Compare Will Durant, *The Story of Philosophy.*

subjective points of view would dissolve away into a meaningless flux. The metaphysical is implicit in all knowledge. And if one goes a step further than the phenomenalist and denies the possibility of our knowing anything, he cuts the ground from beneath his own position. For the very denial of knowledge implies a certain amount of knowledge. Otherwise the denial would be as untrustworthy as the affirmation. It is this fact that foils every attack upon the possibility of knowledge. The attacker cannot find a place outside the intelligible world on which to plant his batteries without renouncing the claims of rationality, and he cannot find a place for them within the intelligible world without assuming the knowability of the world in the very act of denying it.

We must, then, hold to the essential trustworthiness of reason. But this does not mean that reason apprehends reality with an immediacy which excludes the possibility of doubt. Doubt is possible; no logical interdict can be issued against it. We may point out its barrenness from both the practical and the theoretical points of view, and we may point out its inner inconsistency the moment it begins a positive attack upon its opponents. But its theoretical possibility we must admit, and this possibility is not without its significance. It excludes the monistic identification of thought and thing, and brings out the fact that an act of volition lies at the root of reason. Reason is at bottom founded on faith, faith in its own objective validity. This faith is immediate and instinctive, but it is not coerced. It is an act of ratification which the free spirit passes upon itself, and as such it is ultimate. It is not deduced from anything outside itself. No logical mechanism makes it necessary. It is, rather, an axiomatic act, an act, however, that is not confined to the intellect but embraces also the æsthetic, the moral, and the religious faculty, and affirms the autonomous validity of each. All our faculties, the theoretical as well as the practical, thus find their ultimate justification not in the demands of abstract logic but in an act, and that act is an *auto da fe*.

This initial faith, however, so far as it has to do with the intellect, is only a faith in its essential trustworthiness. It does not exclude nor does it attempt to explain away the fact of error. It frankly admits it as a most patent fact of our human life. Nothing could be more manifest than the wide prevalence of erroneous views. In almost every field of inquiry we find contradictory opinions, half of which at least must be false. But this raises a difficult question. How can the fact of error be harmonized with the trustworthiness of reason?

In answering this question we are introduced to one of the most characteristic features of the personalistic philosophy, as expounded by Bowne. It is his persistent contention that freedom alone can provide a solution of the problem.[27] The positive argument runs as follows: Our faculties are so constructed that they have a native capacity for truth; but in order that truth may actually be attained, they must be used with care. When they are not so used or are deliberately misused, error arises. Truth, in other words, is made possible by the essential trustworthiness of our faculties. If our faculties in their normal operation might lead us astray, it is evident that

---

[27] See his *Metaphysics* (1882), pp. 123f.; *Introduction to Psychological Theory*, pp. 227f.; *Metaphysics* (Revised Edition), pp. 406–408; *Theory of Thought and Knowledge*, pp. 239–244; *Personalism*, pp. 198–202; *Theism*, pp. 123–127.

all faith in reason would be at an end. But while the trustworthiness of our faculties makes truth possible, it does not guarantee its attainment. Our faculties do not operate automatically in the sense that they necessarily lead to truth; this would deny the fact of error. They need to be guided by a standard immanent within them, and this guidance is possible only on the assumption that the human spirit is free. Freedom is, therefore, necessary to the trustworthiness of reason; without it there would be no way of accounting for error.

The negative argument in support of this conclusion, as presented by Bowne, consists in showing that every system of thought which denies human freedom and makes error necessary overthrows reason itself. This contention is supported by several considerations. In the first place, it is pointed out that a necessitarian system destroys the distinction between the true and the false by making both of them mechanical effects. The mechanism by which they are produced may be either spiritual or material. In either case they are simply the resultants of nonrational forces. The views that we call "true" and those that we call "false" have the same source. The common idea that the former are rationally grounded while the latter are not, is, therefore, a mistaken one; and with the removal of this distinction all essential difference between them vanishes. That one view is called true and another false is a mere accident.

One might, to be sure, hold that, however produced, some ideas correspond with reality while others do not. But in this case we would need a standard by which to distinguish between the two groups of ideas, and no such standard could be found. We could not find it in the necessity of true ideas and the contingency of false ones, for, according to the theory, all ideas are alike necessary. Nor would the appeal to normality help out, for it would be equally difficult to determine which ideas are normal and which not. Quite as unsatisfactory, and even more so from the necessitarian point of view, would be a popular referendum on the subject. For, aside from the fact that there is no logical connection between the notion of truth and that of a majority, it is probable that a large majority would vote in favor of the belief in freedom as against the belief in necessity. If false ideas are, therefore, as necessary as true ones, there would seem to be no means of distinguishing between them. The very notion of a rational standard would be abrogated.

But, even if we should assume the existence of such a standard, it is evident that we would be unable to use it without freedom. To use a standard we must be able to compare our ideas with it, to direct the course of our thought, to withhold judgment, to retrace our steps, to review the facts again and again, to study their relations to each other, until finally the coherent whole sought by the intellect is made clear. And all this implies real freedom. No mere mimicry of its processes will suffice. Indeed, without true freedom all argument and all attempt at persuasion become absurd. For whether employed by necessitarian or libertarian they imply on the part of the person addressed self-control in thought and responsibility for its exercise. The necessitarian in arguing his case thus assumes the very freedom that he denies. From this self-contradictory position there is no escape on the necessitarian basis. It is, as Bowne says, "one of the traditional imbecilities" of the discussion of freedom that this fact has been generally overlooked. The question has been discussed with almost exclusive reference to moral action, when as a matter of fact the purest illustration of self-determination is to be found in the operations of pure thought. Without freedom rational thought would be impossible, reason would collapse. For on the necessitarian theory the distinction between truth and error or between rational and irrational beliefs would vanish; and if it were retained, there would be no rational standard by which it could be determined which beliefs are true and which false; and, finally, if such a standard did exist, only a free being could use it. This argument was developed again and again by Bowne and might be said to be structural in his system as a whole. With him it was a fundamental conviction that freedom is necessary to save reason from shipwreck.

"I know of no philosopher," says Professor George M. Duncan, of Yale University, "who so ably and so persistently insisted upon the impossibility of basing a theory of knowledge on any necessitarian system, materialistic or pantheistic, any system, that is, that robs the finite person of essential freedom. Bowne never tires of insisting* that proper rationality is possible only to free agents, persons, and that on the plane of freedom alone truth and error first acquire significance. There are passages in practically every one of his books that ought to be regarded as classical on this point."[28] To this statement I should be quite ready myself to subscribe. There is, however, another eminent thinker who took the same view as Bowne of the relation of knowledge to freedom, and who laid considerable stress upon it. Renouvier, in a

---

[28] *Methodist Review*, 1922, p. 385.

number of his books,[29] argues that the only satisfactory explanation of error is to be found in freedom and that necessitarianism leads logically to skepticism. For this insight he confesses himself indebted to his friend Jules Lequier (1814-1862), whom he speaks of as "an original and profound thinker." But while declaring with Lequier that freedom is "the positive condition of knowledge, the means of knowledge," he did not develop the idea so thoroughly, nor did he make it so basal, so central, and so decisive in his system as did Bowne. Still, it is a matter of interest to note that on the fundamental principle itself he was in full accord with his personalistic colleague in America.[30]

The argument outlined above, by which Bowne sustains his contention that the trustworthiness of reason implies human freedom, has not received the attention that it deserves. No necessitarian, so far as I know, has ever attempted a response to it. Whether this is due to its irrefutable character and the consequent feeling on the part of the opposition that it is good tactics to ignore it, or whether it is due to its abstract nature and hence limited influence, I shall not venture to say. To me the argument seems unanswerable. In any case it is an important item in the personalistic epistemology.

A second point to be noted in connection with the personalistic belief in the trustworthiness of reason is that

---

[29] *Essai de critique générale: Traité de psychologie*, ii, 96, 419ff.; *La nouvelle Monadologie*, 139ff.; *Les Dilemmes de la Métaphysique pure*, pp. 170ff.; *Histoire et solution des problémes métaphysiques*, p. 460.

[30] Augustine (*De vera religione*, 33, 61; *De Trinitate*, xi, 10, 17) and Descartes (*Meditation* IV) also attributed error to the freedom of the will, but neither of them developed the epistemological and metaphysical significance of this fact as did Bowne. See *Die Lehre vom Primat des Willens bei Augustinus, Duns Scotus und Descartes*, by Dr. Wilhelm Karl, 1886.

this belief implies a theistic monism.   There is, as we
have seen, a dualism of thought and thing; but if knowledge is to be possible, there must also be a parallelism
between them.   The question, consequently, arises as to
how this parallelism can be accounted for.   The only satisfactory solution of the problem is to be found in a
monism that transcends the dualism of thought and thing
without destroying it, a monism, in other words, that
traces the origin both of finite minds and the world of
things to a common underlying intelligence.   According
to this theory minds are created in the image of the basal
intelligence, and things are an expression of thought and
so homogeneous with it.   There is, consequently, no necessary disparity between our thought and the world of
things.   Things, being rooted in thought and an expression of it, are naturally open to our apprehension and
understanding.   Only in this way are we able to explain
the necessary dualism and parallelism of thought and
thing.   Theistic monism is the ultimate solution of the
problem of knowledge.   That knowledge is possible,
cannot, it is true, be demonstrated.   But faith in its possibility is implicit in all rational discourse, and on this faith
with its implied parallelism of thought and thing personalism rests its entire case.   In its epistemology it thus occupies a middle ground between agnostic dualism, on the
one hand, and a monistic identification of thought and
thing, on the other.

THE PRIMACY OF THE PRACTICAL REASON

Thus far we have dealt with the problem of knowledge
in general, and more particularly with theoretical knowledge, that is, knowledge insofar as it has to do with real-

ity in its existential rather than its qualitative aspect. We have considered the nature of knowledge, showing that it implies a dualism of the thought-series and the thing-series. We have made it clear that thought involves a complex mental activity and that the mind builds up its world for itself. We have also seen that knowledge implies a parallelism as well as a dualism of thought and thing, and that, while it is theoretically possible to doubt this parallelism and hence also the validity of knowledge, such doubt is a mere negative possibility. It has no rational basis. Knowledge justifies itself. But while reason is strong enough to stand on its own feet, it has its presuppositions. It implies both freedom and a theistic monism. Without the latter there would be no way of accounting for the dualism and parallelism of thought and thing, and without the former reason would shatter on the problem of error. Rationality as well as morality is an achievement, and as such it implies the possibility of error as morality does the possibility of sin. But if error and sin are necessary, there is manifestly an end to faith in reason and conscience. The fact of error can be harmonized with the trustworthiness of reason only on the assumption that it owes its origin to the freedom of the human mind.

All this, however, has had to do only with knowledge in general, and more especially with knowledge in its more manifest forms, that is, knowledge as mediated through the perceptual and logical faculties. Such knowledge, as we have seen, has its presuppositions that point toward a personalistic world-view. But no stress has as yet been laid on the idea of value, nor has the question been raised as to whether the emotional and volitional aspects of our nature have a cognitive function and what degree of significance attaches to them from this point of view. That this question is one of vital importance to the religious believer is evident. For to him ultimate reality is not only knowable and not only intelligent; it embodies in itself all those elements of worth associated with personality. All religion is based on faith in the goodness of the world-ground. A God without righteousness and without good will might be omnipotent and omniscient, but as such he could not be an object of religious faith. What faith is primarily concerned about is the moral character of God, his personality in the full ethical sense of the term. But has this faith any rational basis? It manifestly has only on the assumption that the affective and volitional aspects of our experience have a cognitive significance, that they contain within themselves a warrant for our making certain affirmations about ultimate reality. In other words, religious belief implies the objectivity of values, it assumes that knowledge is not restricted to sense-perceptions and logical deductions from them. On the contrary, the deepest truth about reality, it insists, is derived from our ethical and spiritual nature, from that practical and vital experience that lies back of all purely intellectual processes. Its standpoint, in a word, is voluntaristic. It holds that life is deeper than logic. This in substance is the truth expressed by the Kantian doctrine of the primacy of the practical reason, to which personalism attaches itself and which constitutes the fourth article in its epistemological creed.

It was Kant who first gave to the practical reason or the idea of value an independent and established place in philosophy. Before his time philosophy was predominantly intellectualistic; no system made the problem of value central or even expressly considered it. But this does not mean that the problem was entirely absent from earlier philosophizing. To some extent it has been implicit in all speculation. And it will contribute to a better understanding of the personalistic teaching on this point if we consider briefly the history of the idea of value in pre-Kantian thought.

Here we naturally begin with the Platonic and Aristotelian philosophies. In them the valuational factor played a considerable part. It appears first in Plato's Idea of the Good. Exactly what he meant by this Idea is a matter of dispute. Some identify it with God, while others deny the identification. It is also a question to what extent the term "Good" was conceived of as ethical and to what extent it expressed merely the idea of order, permanence and stability. In any case the idea of value attached to it, and the value expressed by it was thought of as objective, and not only as objective but as the truest and highest form of reality. "The good," says Plato, "may be said to be not only the author of knowledge in all things known, but of their being and essence, and yet the good is not essence, but far exceeds essence in dignity and power. . . . That which imparts truth to the object and knowledge to the subject is what I would have you term the idea of good and that you will regard as the cause of science and of truth as known by us. . . . Science and truth may be deemed like the good, but not the good; the good has a place of honor yet higher." What the sun is "in the visible world in relation to sight and the things of sight," that "the good is in the intellectual world in relation to mind and the things of mind."[31]   It is the source both of knowledge and of being. To it the phenomenal world stands not only in a participative or imitative but also a dependent relation. The Idea of the Good is the final cause of the world, and to it not only phenomena but all other ideas are subordinate. In this profound conception we have the germ of a complete philosophy of value, but it was not developed by Plato into a distinct epistemological principle, nor was it differentiated from other modes of thought in such a way as to make it is the characteristic and controlling factor in his own system. However fundamental it may have been in his thinking, it appears rather incidentally in the exposition he has left us of his philosophy as a whole.

Another valuational factor in Greek philosophy is to be found in the idea of an ascending scale of realities. Things appear in different degrees of perfection, the lower being subordinated to the higher. This idea is implied in Plato's conception of the good as the supreme reality, to which all other ideas and all phenomena stand in a subordinate or dependent relation. It is also implied in the distinction he made between form and matter, things being conceived of as sharing or participating, in different degrees, in the forms or ideas that constitute their real being or essence. This distinction, however, was not developed in a systematic way by Plato. It was Aristotle who took it up and made it the organizing principle of his entire system. He arranged all beings in a scale of development according to the degree in which form in each triumphed over matter, or actuality over potentiality, the highest form being wholly free from

[31] *Republic,* book vi, 508, 509.

matter or potentiality. This highest form corresponds to the good of Plato's system, and as the supreme object of desire is the cause of movement in the world of becoming. It is thus itself the Prime Mover. But while its moving power lay in its attractiveness it did not embody in itself the idea of worth so distinctly and so fully as did the Platonic idea of the good. It was itself "unmoved," "the thought of thought," and not the soul of goodness, going forth in creative and providential activity, as was the Platonic Deity. Still it was regarded as the *perfect* Being, self-conscious and in this sense personal, representing an ideal of value as well as mere perfection of existence.

A third element in the Platonic-Aristotelian philosophy that may be called valuational is the principle of teleology. This principle is implied in the Platonic idea of the good and the Aristotelian gradation of being, but it is not necessarily bound up with either, except insofar as they both involve a theistic world-view. Indeed, the teleological principle has been affirmed on a subconscious plane, but whether it can be consistently maintained on that level is open to serious question. In any case, however conceived, it involves a standard of value and excludes a purely mechanistic view of the world. It looks upon nature as dominated by an end, or an indefinite number of ends, to be attained.

The idea of value thus exercised considerable influence in ancient philosophy, but it was not treated as a separate problem, nor was its affective and volitional basis clearly recognized. It was for the most part conceived intellectualistically. This was more true of Aristotle than Plato, but ancient Greek thought in general was inclined toward

intellectualism. It found the ideal of life in passive contemplation rather than in practical activity. And even
after philosophy became the handmaid of Christian theology, this intellectualistic bent persisted. It manifested
itself both in practice and theory. In practice it found
expression in the monastic movement; men and women
withdrew from the normal activities of life, thinking
that the way of salvation lay in undisturbed meditation
and contemplation. In theory it revealed itself in the
early Christian contrast between reason and faith, a contrast that in the mediæval period under Aristotelian influence took the form of a distinction between "natural"
and "revealed" theology. The line of division between
these two types of theology was not a fixed one. It was
drawn in different places by different thinkers. But, in
general, it was assumed that natural theology was based
on the perceptual and logical faculties and that these faculties alone yielded knowledge in the proper sense of the
term. Revealed theology rested on authority, and though
its content might have the greatest religious value, this
value was no evidence of its truth. Truth must be either
factually or logically established, or confirmed by divine
authority. The latter method lay beyond the scope of
philosophy. Hence demonstration by appeal to the facts
of experience or to the self-evident principles of reason
was regarded as the only human means of arriving at
truth. Much that was of religious value could, it was believed, be established in this way. The existence of God,
for instance, and the immortality of the soul were supposed to be capable of proof. Intellectualism thus served
as a support of faith.

But it was an impure intellectualism that served this

purpose. Valuational elements were unconsciously intermingled with the logical, and as the stricter methods of
modern thought separated the two, the tendency was to
find less and less support for religion in the pure intellect.
Empiricism, for instance, was carried by Hume to a point
where it denied the validity of the categories of substance
and cause, rejected the soul as a datum of experience, and
undermined religious faith altogether. Natural science,
furthermore, was construed in a mechanistic sense and
rigidly excluded the teleological principle. Its epistemological ideal was that of a completely dehumanized world,
a world without purpose and without distinctions of
value. Such was the goal toward which modern intellectualism tended, and it was in opposition to this tendency
that the Kantian doctrine of the primacy of the practical
reason was developed. Kant accepted the traditional distinction between the intellectual and the practical and the
antithesis created by modern science between the mechanical and the teleological. Indeed, he accentuated both,
establishing a clear-cut dualism between knowledge and
faith. But he reversed the Aristotelian standpoint by
giving the primacy in metaphysical matters to the practical as over against the theoretical reason. The latter
alone, he admitted, gives us knowledge, and in the phenomenal realm it is supreme, but beyond that it has no
jurisdiction. In a total world-view it occupies, therefore,
a secondary place. Only the practical reason warrants
affirmations about ultimate reality, and these affirmations
are in the nature of practical postulates rather than intellectual insights. They belong to the realm of faith rather
than knowledge, but faith in this case is grounded in the
moral nature, and the moral nature stands in its own

right. It represents an independent realm of value, that in and of itself justifies a theistic world-view.

This Kantian doctrine is fundamentally sound, but in the form in which it was presented by Kant it has not altogether shaken itself free from intellectualistic prejudices. The line of distinction, for instance, between knowledge and faith is not so sharp as he draws it. Knowledge is not absolutely limited to the phenomenal world, nor is it even in that realm wholly free from an assumptive element. The theoretical reason itself implies faith, and also for its own satisfaction requires us to pass beyond the phenomenal. It cannot permanently dispense with the metaphysical categories, nor can it completely eliminate from its own world-view the element of value.

The latter point is illustrated by the fact that thought cannot complete itself without the category of purpose, and purpose manifestly involves the idea of a good to be attained. The lower mechanical categories—space, time, causality—leave us among isolated things and events. They give us no systematic totality. It is only as we rise to the plane of free causality, guided by purpose, that we are able to bring the scattered fragments of reality into a coherent whole. Mechanical causality may bring things into connection with each other, but the connection lacks completeness. Things are left open at both ends; there is no starting-point and no goal. It is only as the different lines of causality emerge from a common center and converge toward a common end that they form a unitary system; and this manifestly implies purpose. The systematic totality, sought by the theoretical reason, cannot, consequently, be realized on the theoretical plane. We must ascend to the practical reason

with its realm of ends and values before thought can complete itself in a unitary world-view. The disinterested intellect is not sufficient unto itself.

This insufficiency appears also at the beginning of the intellectual quest as well as at its end. Knowledge, before it can become a rounded system, must call in the category of purpose, a principle borrowed from the practical reason; and so also at its very inception, in its most elementary forms, it requires as its presupposition an act of faith, which likewise is rooted in the practical reason. Knowledge begins by assuming that the world is intelligible and that we are able to understand it. That this is actually so, we can never demonstrate. We simply accept it on faith, and faith is primarily an act of volition. It springs out of the vital needs and interests of the mind. These needs and interests are subjective; they are practical and ideal in nature, a kind of *modus vivendi* with the universe; and they are also fundamental. They are the ultimate source of our mental activities. We do not create them; they, rather, create us, they are constitutional within us. And as such they stand in their own right. Logic does not legitimate them. All it does is to guide them so that in their natural unfolding they do not go astray. So far as their own fundamental validity is concerned they need no legitimation from without. They are autonomous validities, and it is only as they are recognized as such that knowledge becomes possible. The mind, in the very nature of the case, cannot demonstrate its own presuppositions. It must accept them. It must assume that whatever its own inner nature with its various needs and interests requires for its satisfaction, is true, if there is no decisive evidence to the contrary. Beyond these

inner needs and interests it cannot go. The intellect represents such an inner or subjective interest quite as much as do the other forms of mental activity. It, as well as they, is anchored in life, and cannot break away from it. Life itself as an original and creative impulse is the source and ground of all knowledge.[32]

It is in this sense that the primacy of the practical reason is to be understood. This doctrine does not necessarily mean that theoretical knowledge is limited to the phenomenal realm; it rather means that all knowledge rests ultimately on faith. Faith in reason is the beginning of knowledge, and faith can be justified only by itself. We cannot demonstrate the validity of faith. We begin with it, and in this sense the primacy belongs to it or, in Kantian language, to the practical reason.

But this is something quite different from the pragmatistic or utilitarian interpretation of truth. Personalism does not find in utility the criterion of truth or a substitute for it. It does not subordinate the theoretical to the practical in such a way that the practical becomes the organizing center and the independent norm of the mental life. That is not necessarily true which "works." The intellect has laws and rights of its own. These laws and rights, it is true, imply the practical principle of faith, but the faith that founds reason is not a faith exterior to reason but one immanent in it. Knowledge does not, therefore, need to go outside of itself to find validation. The faith that validates it is implicit in it. Hence knowledge is an autonomous validity quite as much as morality, art and religion. No one of these is in

[32] For a fine elaboration of this view see the "Introduction" to Bowne's *Theism*, pp. 1–43.

its essential nature dependent upon the other, and no one has a right to domineer over the others. All are independent and co-ordinate forms of mental activity, and each can maintain its own integrity only by asserting its essential independence of the others. To subordinate the intellectual to the practical in the way that pragmatism does is to destroy truth itself by making it purely instrumental. On the other hand, to subordinate the practical interests of life to the purely intellectual, as rationalism has done, is to divest the former of much of their legitimate content and to deprive them of their pristine power. A balanced and sound viewpoint is attained only as we recognize the independent validity of each of the four fundamental interests of the human mind. One might, indeed, regard each of these interests as an expression of a deeper underlying reason, and hence speak, as does Troeltsch, of a religious *a priori,* a moral *a priori,* and an æsthetic *a priori* as well as a theoretical *a priori.*[33] This method of expression brings out the essentially independent and irreducible character of these different aspects of life, and implies that they all have a common and indestructible basis in reason. The term "reason," however, is in danger of suggesting the purely intellectual or logical, and hence we need to remind ourselves that it is here used in a broader sense. The common source and bond of union between the different *a prioris* is to be found in something deeper than the formal reason; it is to be found in that deepest of all rational unities, the personal spirit. Personality with its fundamental needs and interests is the fountain-head of

---

[33] See my article on "Religious Apriorism" in *Studies in Philosophy and Theology,* edited by E. C. Wilm, pp. 93–127.

all that passes under the name of reason, whether it be theoretical or practical.

In the light of this fact it is evident that personalism occupies a position midway between pragmatistic relativism, on the one hand, and abstract intellectualism, on the other. As against intellectualism it insists on the priority of faith to knowledge, but as against relativism in every form it insists with equal vigor on the independent rights of the intellect. It has been said that according to pragmatism man is like a vessel that carries a crew but no passengers. Every one on board has to work his way. And this may be true. The human intellect does work its way. It plays its part in life, but it is not the abject slave of any foreign taskmaster. It exists for itself as well as others. And what it is in itself is quite as significant as the service it may render to any other human interest. But important as this is, it is even more important, in view of the history of speculation, to recognize the fact that the intellect does not exist for itself alone, that it stands in relation to life as a whole, and that this broader relationship determines to no small degree its significance and also conditions the interpretation of its fundamental principles. It is the recognition of this fact that gives to personalism its voluntaristic cast and that leads Bowne to say so frequently that "life is deeper than logic."

The four epistemological principles we have considered in this chapter, as we have already said, are none of them peculiar to personalism. But taken together they constitute a distinctive body of doctrine. To one who reviews the present chapter it is evident that there are two fundamental problems in epistemology. One has to do with the validity of knowledge in general and the other with the objectivity of values. The first of these underlies the first three principles we have discussed, and the second underlies the fourth. In both cases personalism takes a mediating position. In the first instance it avoids the extremes represented by epistemological monism, on the one hand, and skepticism, on the other. It accepts the dualism of thought and thing, and that in the accentuated form represented by the doctrine of the creative activity of thought. Yet it holds to the trustworthiness of reason, founding this conviction on our instinctive faith, a faith, however, that is logically justified by theistic monism. It thus steers a middle course between agnostic dualism and an impossible identification of thought and thing.

The second problem involves a conflict between a one-sided intellectualism, on the one hand, and an equally one-sided voluntarism on the other. In this conflict personalism leans toward voluntarism; it holds to the primacy of the practical reason. But at the same time it distinctly rejects the more extreme form of this doctrine. A thoroughgoing voluntarism, it contends, leads to relativism, and relativism means the overthrow not only of truth but of the other ideal values also. The interests of truth, goodness, beauty, and God belong together. To cast discredit on one is to weaken faith in all. Hence personalism insists on the trustworthiness of both the theoretical and the practical reason. The latter is primary and more inclusive, but the former also stands in its own right. Both, when thought through, involve faith in the ideal, and faith in one form of the ideal is as valid as faith in any other form. Faith in the cognitive or intellectual ideal is easier and more common than faith in the moral, æsthetic and religious ideal, but the latter faith is logically as valid as the former. The conflict between intellectualism and voluntarism thus turns out to be a conflict between two types of faith or value; and the solution of the conflict lies in a recognition of the validity of both. This is the position taken by personalism. It seeks to maintain an even balance between the two conflicting tendencies by pointing out that both have their basis in a common faith; a faith that springs up spontaneously in the human mind and that finds its ultimate justification in life itself.

CHAPTER III

PERSONALISM AS A THEORY OF REALITY

SOME philosophies are predominantly epistemological and others predominantly metaphysical. Personalism belongs to the latter class. It has its own well-defined theory of knowledge. This theory we expounded in the preceding chapter. It contains a number of significant principles, principles of far-reaching import. But it is, after all, only preliminary in character, an introduction to the personalistic theory of reality. Lotze used to pass rather severe strictures upon those philosophers who sought to avoid the field of metaphysics. He spoke of their "pretentious occupation with theories of cognition," likening it to the constant whetting of the knife which, he said, "is tedious, if it is not proposed to cut anything with it." He also compared it to "the tuning of instruments before a concert," except that it is not "so necessary or useful."[1] The true objective of every systematic philosophy is a theory of reality. Not the knowing process but the object of knowledge is what philosophy as well as common sense is ultimately interested in. Without a metaphysic philosophy remains a mere torso.

But it is nevertheless true that since the time of the Greek Sophists thinkers have not been able simply to take knowledge for granted. The trustworthiness both of sense and reason was then seriously challenged, and since that time the challenge has been renewed again and

---

[1] *Metaphysics*, p. 12.

again so that it stands as a perpetual threat to the philosophic quest, as a flaming sword seeking to bar the way to the tree of knowledge. This foe must, therefore, somehow or other be disposed of before we are prepared to construct a theory of reality. Then, too, a careful study of the conditions and limits of knowledge is necessary before we are prepared to launch upon the metaphysical enterprise. This study and its conclusions we have outlined in the preceding chapter. Of these conclusions there are three that have a direct and important bearing upon metaphysics.

In the first place, we have seen that there is no valid reason for limiting knowledge to the phenomenal realm and thus denying the possibility of a rational theory of reality. A purely formal doubt as to whether human rationality equates with truth is, as we have seen, possible, but such doubt can in the nature of the case have no rational standing. To doubt or reject reason is itself an irrational act. Rationality is for us necessarily the test of truth, and the only reasonable question that can be asked with reference to reality is as to how we must think of it. A reality that is antithetical to thought, a reality that we do not and cannot think, is for us nonexistent. But can we form a rationally consistent theory of reality? This has been denied on the ground that knowledge is limited to states of consciousness or to phenomena. Things-in-themselves, we are told, we cannot know. They are necessarily hidden from us, for the very categories of substance and cause are either due to the mind's propensity to feign or are immanent mental principles, limited in their application to phenomena. The former of these theories was Hume's, the latter Kant's. Both of them we have found to be untenable. The sensationalism of Hume, if logically carried out, would lead to the complete disintegration of knowledge, indeed, to pure nihilism. And the agnosticism of Kant is fundamentally self-contradictory. It denies that the categories are applicable to things-in-themselves, and yet it asserts that things-in-themselves exist, although the affirmation of their existence implies the application of the metaphysical categories to them.

But not only are the Humian and Kantian types of agnosticism logically self-destructive, they are based upon a mistaken notion of what metaphysical reality is. According to Hume, for instance, the soul, if real, ought to manifest itself in the flow of consciousness as a distinct and abiding entity; and since it does not thus manifest itself it is to be adjudged unreal. According to Kant, the real or transcendental self could not manifest itself in consciousness without becoming subject to the categories and thus ceasing to be "real" and becoming phenomenal or empirical. Hence Kant declared the real self to be unknowable. It was his belief, and also that of Hume, that the soul, *if* real or *as* real, must have a sort of thing-like existence. This existence might manifest itself in consciousness, as Hume held it must if real, or it might lie beyond consciousness, as Kant contended; but in either case it was conceived as an objective "substantial" form of existence, an existence constituted by an abiding core of reality. In this core of being were to be found the unity and identity of the self when viewed as real. Hume denied its reality, Kant affirmed it, but both had essentially the same notion of what reality is; and this notion was an erroneous one. They thought of reality as a self-

existent entity independent of consciousness and, therefore, constituting a standard by means of which the
reality of consciousness itself might be tested. This led,
in one case, to the denial of the self and, in the other, to
the denial of its knowability. The escape from these
negative conclusions and from metaphysical skepticism
in general is to be found in a reinterpretation of the idea
of reality. True metaphysical reality does not consist in
any mere substance, material or immaterial, passive or
active, which somehow persists through time, but in the
unifying and self-identifying activity of consciousness.
When this is realized, the Kantian distinction between the
empirical and transcendental self at once breaks down.
It is now seen that the only real or transcendental self
is the self that reveals itself in consciousness. Any other
self, hidden behind consciousness, is a pure fiction, the
product of "the bungling reflection of the philosopher."

The same is also true of reality as a whole. The idea
that there is an unknowable thing-in-itself, vainly seeking
to peer through the masking veil of phenomena, is a complete illusion. The only way that either God or man can
know anything is through its phenomena or modes of action. To separate a thing from its activities is to fall into
the fallacy of abstraction; and yet it is apparently the
popular belief that metaphysics is by its very nature concerned with this abstract and unreal thing-in-itself. What
has given such impetus to positivistic types of thought in
our day, is largely this strange misunderstanding. Most
of the polemic against metaphysics is based upon it. True
metaphysics has, of course, nothing to do with the futile
quest after pure or abstract being. The whole idea of a
thing-in-itself is the product of a misguided logic, and

the agnostic relativism, based upon it, is due, as Pringle-Pattison says, to "an elaborate and perfectly gratuitous mystification." What differentiates metaphysics from other lines of human inquiry is simply this, that it is, as William James said, "an unusually obstinate attempt to think clearly and consistently." Against such an attempt intellectual shallowness and mental indolence will naturally protest; and it is these human weaknesses that are the chief sources of the antimetaphysical propaganda of our day. But serious minds should not be misled by it. Get-rich-quick methods are even less trustworthy in the field of philosophy than in that of finance. Profound and painstaking reflection is the necessary price of all unusual achievement in the realm of knowledge; and this, when we are concerned with the question of an adequate world-view, leads inevitably to metaphysics. Every attempt that has thus far been made to bar the way to metaphysical inquiry has proven arbitrary and futile. This our personalistic epistemology has made clear. No mortal or immortal is justified in stationing himself on the border of metaphysics and saying to the inquiring mind, "Thus far shalt thou come but no further."

A second important conclusion to be drawn from our study of epistemology is that reality is "given" to us. We do not create it, we find it. This does not mean that the mind is the passive recipient of a ready-made knowledge; the contrary view we have maintained and expounded at length. But it does mean that the world is in a sense objective to us and that it is revealed to us in experience. We do not construct it out of whole cloth. Thought and thing are not identical. The thing-world is given to us, no matter how much it may be reshaped by the creative activity of thought. Our thought has no resources within itself which enable it to create reality or to determine what in detail it must be. For this we must wait upon experience. It is in experience, and experience only, that reality is revealed to us.

The theory of reality must, therefore, begin with experience; and its task must be not to construct or reconstruct it, but to interpret it. In this respect the function of metaphysics is but a continuation of that of science. For science, although it is primarily concerned with discovering, describing, relating and correlating facts, has also to some extent the task of interpreting them. The Copernican astronomy, for instance, is a scientific interpretation of the world as it appears to sense. The same is also true of the atomic theory, the theory of evolution, and all other theories that seek to explain the present sensible order by reference to past phenomena or to existing entities that might conceivably become phenomenal under certain conditions. Such explanations as these lead us to nothing ultimate. But they carry us beyond the region of sensible experience. We have never seen atoms nor the astronomical heavens, nor have we observed the long processes of cosmic and animal evolution. These existents and processes are all thought constructions; they are not given in experience, they are interpretations of it. They thus belong to the same rationalizing type of activity that we have in philosophy.

What differentiates scientific from philosophical or metaphysical theories is that the former do not take us beyond the phenomenal order. They infer from facts and events that we have experienced other facts and events that we have not experienced but that might conceivably have been experienced. These inferred facts and events serve as explanations of observed phenomena, but they do not themselves transcend the phenomenal realm. They are not productive agencies. They belong, if real, to the phenomenal order and are on the same level with experienced facts and events. They explain or interpret the latter only in the sense that they supplement their fragmentary character by establishing new sequences and coexistences and thus satisfy more fully the mind's demand for connectedness in things. But the causal ground of this connection lies as completely beyond scientific theory as it does beyond our sense-experience.

It is the function of metaphysics not simply to interpret facts by inferring additional facts of the same order but to interpret them in a more fundamental way by inquiring into their underlying cause and their informing purpose. Only as we know the agent or agency that lies back of phenomena do we really know what they are. Only then do we know whether they have a meaning or purpose beyond the bare fact of their existence in a certain order of sequence and coexistence. This, then, is the unique task of metaphysics, to decide how we must think of the causal ground of the phenomenal world. Causal agency itself lies beyond our immediate observation. We do not and cannot see cause. But reason requires us to affirm it. Without it the connectedness of things would vanish. Phenomena would be suspended in the air without ground and without any cohesive bond between them. This bond or ground, however, must not be conceived of as in any sense a double of the phenomenal order or as a pure thought-construct distinct from and unrelated to phenomena, or as the generator of our experience in such a sense that the world has no externality to our thought. There is a "given" element in our experience, and it is this that introduces us to reality. Without it our minds could not even make a beginning. The "given" element is the raw material out of which knowledge is built up. To it we must, therefore, go for our initial point of contact with the real world, and out of it we must construct our theory of reality. Metaphysics thus begins, as does science, with experience, and what it aims at is simply a more complete and systematic rational interpretation of experience.

A third conclusion, to which our epistemology led us and which has an important bearing on metaphysics, is that reality or our knowledge of it is not necessarily to be confined to the limits set by the perceptual and logical faculty. That it is so limited, is a traditional intellectualistic prejudice. This prejudice has its basis in the fact that sense-perception and logic seem more objective than the other forms of mental activity and thus manage to get themselves more generally recognized. But all knowledge, as we have seen, rests upon faith, and faith is "feeling appreciative of value." This is true of the faith that underlies theoretical knowledge as well as that which underlies our convictions of a practical nature. The latter may or may not be properly called knowledge. But there is no fundamental or absolute difference between them and what is commonly called knowledge from the perceptual or logical points of view. All convictions, whether founded on the theoretical or the practical reason, derive their ultimate validity from faith, faith in our intellectual, moral, æsthetic, or religious nature. And faith in one form is in principle just as valid as any of

the other forms of faith. We are not, therefore, warranted in restricting the objective validity of our convictions to those of a theoretical nature. We may, if we
wish, limit metaphysics to considerations based on the
perceptual and logical faculty and refer all questions that
have to do with the objectivity of value to the philosophy
of religion. But such a division of labor has no other
justification than that of convenience and custom. To
some extent we shall adopt it, devoting attention in this
chapter chiefly to theoretical considerations. But it should
be borne in mind that there is no sharp line of demarcation between metaphysics and the philosophy of religion.
One to a large degree involves the other. And if we here
deal mainly with a view of reality based on the theoretical reason, this by no means closes the door to that larger
and richer conception of reality which the practical reason and the religious nature demand.

Metaphysics is thus not to be construed as standing in
an antithetical relation either to theology or to science.
It is a supplement to the latter and an introduction to the
former. It carries the cognitive quest beyond the phenomenal limitations of science into the realm of productive causality and purpose. At the same time it con-
structs an outline view of reality into which moral and
religious faith will fit and upon which it may build. Faith
of this practical character, it is true, may flourish independently of any systematic inquiry into metaphysics.
It may even be conjoined with a large degree of metaphysical skepticism. But this is an unnatural alliance. Faith
in religion cannot be permanently divorced from faith in
the intellect. If the latter is untrustworthy beyond the
limits of phenomena, it is probable that the former is also.

One type of faith is bound up with the other. To restrict knowledge to the phenomenal realm is, as we have seen, unwarranted, and in most cases amounts to nothing more than a verbal intimidation. Much of current naturalistic positivism reminds one of the cuttlefish, which, when attacked, ejects an inky fluid that conceals it from its foe. It is this that makes of positivism a menace to the higher interests of men; it hides from them its true nature. As a matter of fact, current positivism is by no means metaphysically neutral. It is a polemic against a reasoned metaphysics and a tacit apology for the crude naturalistic metaphysics that springs up spontaneously on the sense plane. The truth is that the human mind is so constructed that it cannot dispense with a metaphysics of some kind. And it is also true that the sense-metaphysics of uncritical thought is the prolific breeder of naturalism, materialism, necessitarianism, and atheism, systems which, when carried to their logical conclusion, involve not only religion and morals but also reason itself in disaster. To make this clear and to develop a rational and self-consistent theory of reality is, therefore, a task of the greatest practical and theoretical significance.

In our study of the personalistic epistemology we singled out for discussion four fundamental principles which, when taken together, distinguish it from other theories of knowledge. The same method will be adopted in our study of the personalistic metaphysics. Only here there are six instead of four principles that may be singled out as fundamental to and characteristic of the personalistic position:

First, personalism holds that reality is concrete and individual. It thus leans toward pluralism and natural realism. It does so in the interest of the reality and independence of the finite person and also in the interest of a more distinct and clearly defined conception of the Infinite than has prevailed in many philosophies.

Second, it stresses the unity of the world and the world-ground. In this respect it leans toward monism and absolutism, thus satisfying the religious demand involved in the feeling of absolute dependence and also the intellectual demand for a universe as distinguished from a "multiverse."

Third, it maintains that reality in its essential nature is active. In other words, it interprets substance in terms of causality. It thus falls in line with modern physical theory and also with the modern tendency to conceive of the soul as a mental agent rather than as mere substance.

Fourth, it takes an important step beyond modern energetics and contends that energy or causality must ultimately be interpreted in terms of volition. Here personalism breaks with the realistic systems of the past and becomes idealistic.

Fifth, it holds that matter is phenomenal, and that in a more thoroughgoing sense than any realistic theory would admit. This follows necessarily from its interpretation of causality. Not only does personalism deny extramental existence to the extended matter of sense-experience but also to its dynamic ground. It conceives of the whole material world as the ceaseless product of the divine energizing. Indeed, in its thoroughgoing form it holds to the complete ideality of space and time.

Sixth and finally, it contends that personality is the key to ultimate reality. Abstract thought leads to fundamental antinomies such as those between identity and change, the One and the Many, freedom and necessity. A solution of these antinomies is possible only in personal experience. Here we have in very fact, however we may account for it, a union of personal identity with change, of conscious unity with multiplicity of experience, and of freedom or self-control with uniformity or necessity. If we, therefore, conceive of ultimate reality as personal, we have in that conception an answer, and the only adequate answer, to the fundamental questions of speculative thought.

In the remainder of this chapter it will be our task to expound the foregoing principles in the light of their historical development.

INDIVIDUALITY

Personalism begins its theory of reality with the affirmation that metaphysical existence can be predicated only of that which is individual and concrete. The universal and abstract are essential as ideas; without them thought would disintegrate. In making a statement about a thing we are required to use a universal; and all things, we assume, have qualities of one kind or another. But these qualities and universals have themselves no thing-like existence. There are individual trees but no tree in general. There are white objects but no independent self-existent whiteness. This seems self-evident to common sense but it has by no means been such to speculative thought. Many great and influential thinkers have given to the universal and the abstract a metaphysical

significance that common sense denies them.   The result
has been a long-drawn-out debate which has been one of
the most stubborn in the history of philosophy.   It appeared in its classic form in the conflict between realism,
on the one hand, and nominalism or conceptualism, on
the other.   But it has by no means been confined to that
historic struggle.   The debate has been implicit in all the
great systems of philosophy, and is not yet at an end.

It was Plato who first championed the cause of the universal in the field of metaphysics.   Socrates had insisted
on the possibility of knowledge and had pointed out that
knowledge consists in general ideas, but he had confined
his interest almost exclusively to the realm of ethics.
What he aimed to do was to save morals from the disin-
tegrating individualism and relativism of the Sophists,
and this he did by his stress on the fixity of the idea as
over against the flux of mere perception and opinion.
The conclusion he reached had a decisive significance for
science or knowledge in general, but the development of
this significance he did not himself undertake.   He was
content to establish an epistemological basis for ethics.
It was Plato who took the Socratic conception of knowledge and transformed or developed it into a metaphysic.
For him concepts or ideas were not only valid in the ethical realm, they were universally valid; and not only did
they have objective validity, they had ontological existence.   At least this was the view attributed to him by
Aristotle, and this has also been the common interpretation of his teaching.   According to it Plato held that
true reality is to be found in a super-sensuous realm of
ideas.   These ideas were conceived of as immaterial, but
immateriality he did not identify with spirituality.   In

his later writings, it is true, there seems to be a tendency
to identify the two,[2] but in his system as a whole ideas
are kept distinct from souls. They have an existence of
their own, indeed represent the highest form of existence,
and since they are *general* ideas, it is implied in their existence that a higher degree of reality belongs to the universal than the particular. Tree is more real than trees
and man than men.

This idealistic doctrine, so strange to common sense,
owed its origin in part at least to the objectivity of ancient epistemology. The mind was regarded as relatively
passive, not creative. It received its knowledge from
without. The object was *given* to it. Hence even a concept, if true, must have an objective source; there must
be something in reality corresponding to it. Otherwise
there would be no way of explaining its origin. For it
was assumed that consciousness did not have the power
to create its own content; it could only receive what was
given it. And so Plato, since he held that ideas are not
given in perception, ascribed to them an independent
existence and accounted for our knowledge of them by
the theory that in a previous state of being our souls
had a direct vision of them, a vision which, though forgotten with our advent into the present earthly life, is
gradually recalled to mind by the perception of similar
corporeal things. The objective reality of Ideas was thus
with Plato a corollary of the validity of conceptual knowledge, and it was such because of the assumed passivity
of the human mind in the knowing process. This at least
was one source of his theory of Ideas. But however the
theory originated it introduced into philosophy a logical

---

[2] See Gomperz, *Greek Thinkers*, iii, p. 173.

idealism that in subsequent ages has been the chief main-
stay of universalism in its struggle against individualism.

Aristotle rejected the extreme form of universalism or
realism represented by Plato and carried on a persistent
and vigorous polemic against it.   Its origin he attributed
to the influence of the Heraclitic doctrine that all things
flow.   If this doctrine be true—as the upholders of the
Ideal theory believed—knowledge becomes impossible
from their standpoint.   For thought, they held, to be
valid must have objects corresponding to its own universal and permanent ideas.   But such permanent entities are not to be found in the sense world.   Hence Platonists, going in this respect beyond Socrates, drew the
conclusion that the universals, without which thought is
impossible, have a separate and supersensible existence.

One criticism passed on this theory by Aristotle is
that it gives us simply a conceptual double of the perceptual world.   A man-in-himself or a horse-in-itself is
merely a pale reflection of the concrete reality which we
perceive, differing from it only in this respect that it is
eternal while the latter is perishable.   So Aristotle said
the Platonic Forms or Ideas were nothing more than
"eternal sensible things"; and such a view as this he regarded as superfluous and barren.   It multiplied entities
unnecessarily and explained nothing.   It was, he said, as
if a man should think himself unable to count a set of
things until he had doubled their number.   For the Ideas
are impotent; they produce no motion or change.   And
to say that they are exemplars and that other things participate in them is to use "empty words and poetical meta-
phors."[3]

---

[3] See Aristotle's *Metaphysics*, 1078b, 997b, 1079b.

More significant than these criticisms, however, is Aristotle's contention that the Idea or Form, which was regarded as the essence of a thing, cannot exist apart from the thing of which it is the essence. Essence and thing belong together and are meaningless in separation from each other. This criticism of the Platonic theory was directed, not against the reality of the ideas, but against their transcendence, and as such it marked the transition to Aristotle's own theory. He held that the ideas or forms are immanent in particular things and have no existence apart from them. Every existing thing or substance was for him individual.[4] In this sense he rejected the Platonic universalism. But, on the other hand, universals were for him real and objective; they were not simply our notions or conceptions. They existed as common entities in the individuals included under them and yet were apparently not to be identified with the individual substances themselves. The latter also were to be distinguished from their sensible qualities or accidents.

The individual thing, consequently, as Aristotle conceived it, was composite. It stood in a double relationship that prevented complete inner unity. On the one hand, it stood in the relation of substance to its own phenomenal manifestations, and, on the other, it stood in a subordinate relation to the species to which it belonged. The species or universal constituted the essence of the individual substance, and the individual substance in turn constituted the essence of the perceptible phenomena. We thus have three stages of reality in the Aristotelian conception of the individual: the species, individual sub-

---

[4] *Ibid.*, 1003a.

stance, and accidents or phenomenal manifestation. This analysis is not strictly adhered to by Aristotle. The tendency on his part is, rather, to merge the first and second, and in one noteworthy passage in the *Metaphysics* he even eliminates them both.[5] His main interest, however, leads him to emphasize the second factor, namely, that substance is individual. But, emphasize this as he will, he cannot rid himself of the Platonic conception of the superior reality of the species or the universal. So in spite of himself he remains a realist. The individual, as he thought of it, was not "individual to the innermost fiber of its being." It was divided against itself by the presence within it of the immanent Idea. The latter did not admit of being completely individualized, and hence what Aristotle has given us is, after all, a bastard individualism, an illegitimate fusion of species and accidents.

A step in the direction of a purer individualism is represented by Neo-Platonism, at least so far as the human soul is concerned. Plato and Aristotle had left the individual soul in an insecure position. They had subordinated it either to the world soul or the universal active reason in such a way that its real independence and permanence were threatened, if not actually denied. Plotinus, on the other hand, explicitly ascribed to the individual man a distinct eternal nature, "Form," or "Idea," and thus sought to rescue him from absolute dependence upon a more universal substance and from the danger of absorption by it. But his motive in formulating this conception was primarily religious, and it cannot be said that it was clearly and logically grounded. The representation of the real individual as an "idea" tended to obscure his

---

[5] See Gomperz, *Greek Thinkers*, iv, p. 81f.

uniqueness and individuality. For an "idea" by its very nature is universal. Plotinus, therefore, even in his conception of the individual soul, did not entirely succeed in extricating himself from the coils of realism. This was also true of the Christian Platonists and the later Christian Aristotelians. They affirmed the substantiality and immortality of the individual soul, but they did not define its individuality in such a way as to make it individual through and through, nor did they ground its individuality in their philosophic systems in such a way as to make it secure. Orthodox philosophy remained in the main realistic or universalistic in its bent down into modern times in spite of the Aristotelian stress upon the individual character of all true existence.

It was Leibnitz who first developed the principle of individuality in a thoroughgoing way, divested it of its universalistic ingredients, and made it basal in a great idealistic system. This system he called a monadology. It stands sharply opposed to Spinozism and to every system, whether naturalistic or idealistic, that subordinates the individual and concrete to the universal and abstract. It holds that there is not simply one substance but many, and that every true substance is a monad, a unique and unitary being, entirely distinct from every other substance. This type of individualism differs from the individualism of earlier thinkers in three main respects. First, it insists on the absolute separateness and uniqueness of the individual or monad as had not been done before. "The monads," said Leibnitz, "have no windows through which anything could come in or go out." They are completely isolated from each other; they act by virtue of forces resident in themselves. They are "incorporeal automatons." They also differ from one another; no two are alike. "Each monad," we are told, "must be different from every other." And this difference is not merely superficial. It is rooted in a unique "internal principle." There is, therefore, no *common* substance in the different monads. Each is individual to the very core of its being.

In the second place, individuality, according to Leibnitz, consisted not in an "Idea" or "Form" or a passively conceived "substance," as had previously been held, but in the power of action. This view tended still further to bring out the unity and uniqueness of the monad. For the terms "Idea" and "Form" suggest something universal in content, and the term "substance," when passively conceived, suggests something that might be common to different individuals. All these traditional terms, therefore, leave the individual incompletely unified and individualized. What distinguishes one individual from another is the way it acts rather than any peculiar substance that it contains. To find the essence of an individual in its power of action is, therefore, more completely to individualize it. Then, too, the term "power" does not lend itself to the imagination the way the term "substance" does. It suggests more naturally something invisible, something having a generating center to its being, something subjective, akin to what the finite spirit experiences in itself. It points, in a word, to a *unitary* agent, as the traditional conceptions of the individual did not.

A third point to be noted in connection with Leibnitz' view of individuality is that he found its one true exemplification in the soul or in soul-like beings. It is here that we have the key to his view as a whole. The sepa-

rateness of the individual and its automatic activity were
both ideas borrowed from self-experience. The only concrete illustration of force is that found in the willing,
striving, acting self. It is self-determination that furnishes us with our only type of real causality. The idea
of cause is carried over from self-experience into the objective world. Then, too, it is in self-experience that the
separateness or isolation of the individual finds its true
source and meaning. This is a characteristic feature of
our experience upon which poets have often dwelt. Our
"spirits live in awful singleness, each in its self-formed
sphere of light or gloom." "Yes," says Matthew Arnold,
        "in the sea of life inisled
    With echoing straits between us thrown,
    Dotting the shoreless watery wild,
    We mortal millions live alone."
Between us lies "the unplumbed, salt, estranging sea."
In plain didactic terms Pringle-Pattison has expressed
this thought in a passage that has been frequently quoted
and much criticized. "Each self," he says, "is a unique
existence, which is perfectly impervious . . . to other
selves—impervious in a fashion of which the impenetrability of matter is a faint analogue. The self, accordingly,
resists invasion; in its character of self it refuses to admit another self within itself, and thus be made, as it
were, a mere retainer of something else. . . . The self is
in truth the very apex of separation and differentiation.
. . . Though the self is in knowledge a principle of uni-
fication, it is in existence or metaphysically a principle of
isolation."[6] It is this conception of the self that we find
in Leibnitz and that gave to him the distinctive elements
in his idea of individuality. For him the only true ex-

[6] *Hegelianism and Personality*, 1887, pp. 216f.

188 THE PHILOSOPHY OF PERSONALISM

istence was individual, and since the soul was the key to
individuality it was for him also the key to reality. In
this respect he might be called the first personalist.

Personalism attaches itself to the Leibnitzian monadology, and by virtue of this relation stands opposed to
the two great realistic or universalistic systems of modern
times, Spinozism and Hegelianism. The "concrete" universalism of Hegel, it is true, differs in important regards
from the "abstract" universalism of Spinoza, but, as commonly understood, both are at one in denying true reality
to finite individuals or monads and in claiming it exclusively for an absolute and universal Spirit or Substance.
The error into which both fall is what Bowne calls "the
fallacy of the universal." Another fallacy, akin to this
and in principle the same, is "the fallacy of abstraction."
Bowne calls these "structural fallacies," and his elaboration of them is one of the most fruitful contributions
made to modern logic.[7] They are "structural" in the
sense that they spring up spontaneously in human
thought; men almost inevitably fall into them. They
are by no means confined to such system-builders as Spinoza, Hegel, and Spencer. They appear in the crudest
forms of thought. Nor are they peculiar to any one type
of philosophy. Materialists fall into them as readily as
idealists. So common, indeed, are they that one is warranted in saying with Bowne that the fallacy of the universal is the universal fallacy.

The essence of this fallacy consists in overlooking the
truth of metaphysical individualism and in mistaking

---

[7] In his doctor's thesis, entitled *Lotze und Bowne; Eine Vergleichung
ihrer philosophischen Arbeit*, pp. 6of., Gilbert H. Jones points out that
one of the most striking differences between Bowne and Lotze is to
be found in their treatment of logic, Bowne being fresher, more independent, and more original in his method.

class terms for things or the classifying processes of our
thought for the processes of reality.   It is, of course,
evident that when we classify things we do nothing to the
things themselves. They remain as separate and individual as ever. When we abstract from them their activities,
we do not, of course, create any new entities.   Force,
for instance, has no existence apart from things themselves. The reality is always acting things. There is no
independent and self-existent "action" or force.   The
same is also true of matter. There are individual material things, but matter as a general or abstract term has
no counterpart in reality. So likewise there is no such
thing as pure Being or Substance or Spirit or Thought.
These are all abstractions. Yet they have figured prominently in the history of speculation as the ultimate and
all-inclusive realities. Against this persistent tendency,
which goes back to the beginnings of speculative thought,
personalism raises its voice in sharp criticism. It
pronounces realism or universalism in its abstract ontological form a stupendous illusion. All reality, it insists,
is concrete and individual. This is the first article in its
metaphysical creed, and it is only the logical counterpart
of this when Bowne in his theory of thought makes the
fallacy of the universal the most pervasive and fundamental of all fallacies.

In insisting on metaphysical individualism personalism
is primarily concerned with the reality of the finite self.
It thus stands for pluralism as over against absolute
monism. In this connection it is a matter of interest to
note that Jean Wahl in his recent work on *"The Pluralist
Philosophies of England and America"*[8] credits Bowne,

---

[8] Page 319. See Bowne's *Metaphysics* (1882), pp. 130, 355.

whom he inaccurately characterizes as a commentator and disciple of Lotze, with having introduced the word "pluralism" into the English language. The pluralism, however, for which personalism stands, is distinctly limited in character. It presupposes an underlying unity, and that in a more direct and intimate sense than is implied in the Leibnitzian monadology. This leads us to the second fundamental principle of the personalistic metaphysics.

UNITY

By unity we here mean, not that unity which is implied in the idea of individuality, but the unity implied in the idea of a universe, the unity of the world-ground. The term "individuality" has also been used in the same restricted sense. Bosanquet, for instance, tells us that there can be only one individual, and that the Absolute.[9] But this use of the term seems to me confusing. Traditional usage is against it, and personalism in particular, as we have seen, employs the term in a different sense, a sense applicable, it is true, to the Infinite as well as the finite, but not applicable in an exclusive way to either. To bring out the unique relation of the Absolute to the world or the unique characteristic of ultimate reality it seems better to use the term "unity." The world is one as well as many. This affirmation is only second in importance to that which asserts the concreteness and individuality of the real.

The quest after an ultimate unity goes back to the very beginning of philosophy, and represents the dominant tendency in the history of metaphysical speculation as a whole. This tendency has often been carried to extremes.

---

[9] *The Principle of Individuality and Value*, p. 68.

It has threatened to destroy the principle of individuality altogether, and has subordinated the world of concrete reality to a realm of vague and empty abstractions, "the solemn shadow-land of unchangeable ideas." Numerous reactions to it have, consequently, been evoked. These in their more extreme expressions have taken the form of dualism, pluralism, and positivism. But however vigorous these reactions may have been, they have never succeeded in suppressing the *rational* demand for unity. Sense-experience is manifold and pluralistic; but reason is unitary and systematic. Indeed, monism, as even Kant recognized, is the deepest demand of reason. Both the principle of logical subordination and that of causality point to a unified whole, a unitary world-ground. Things are connected as well as distinct from each other. There is a community as well as an individuality of being; and it is the particular province of the reason to direct attention to the former and to seek to form a clear conception of it. The monistic tendency has, consequently, been dominant in the history of thought. The most influential thinkers, both of ancient and modern times, have agreed that "the ultimate pluralism of spontaneous thought must be exchanged for a basal monism."

How this basal monism is to be conceived, however, is a point on which there has been wide diversity of view. Three main types of theories may be distinguished: the materialistic, spiritualistic, and pantheistic, or Spinozistic. Of these the first was the earliest to come to clear expression. It appears in its most definite and distinctive form in the atomism of Leucippus and Democritus. Their atomic materialism may be regarded as bringing to a close the pre-Socratic philosophy. But materialism in this or any form is not and cannot be a true monism. It may be said to be qualitatively monistic in the sense that all reality is conceived of as material in nature. But this common quality does not unify existence. The atoms in spite of their qualitative resemblance remain distinct and individual. The atomic theory is thus an extreme form of pluralism. Indeed, atoms themselves cannot be regarded as true units. For unity denies composition and divisibility, and this means that nothing extended in space, no matter how small, can be a unit, since space is infinitely divisible. The thing might itself be actually indivisible, but this would not constitute it a true unity, since its indivisibility would be due simply to the great cohesiveness of its parts. Everything extended in space is necessarily a compound, an aggregate. True unity cannot, therefore, be ascribed even to a material atom, to say nothing of the material universe. Materialism in its atomic form and in any form that conceives of ultimate reality as spatial is the negation of true metaphysical monism.

The great spiritualistic reaction against materialism began with Socrates, Plato, and Aristotle. But these thinkers also failed to attain a true monism. They rejected the materialistic conception of matter as metaphysically real, and yet they did not succeed in completely shaking themselves free from it. For Plato matter was non-being, empty space, and yet it had a kind of reality, a resisting power. For Aristotle it had a somewhat more definite character; it was potentiality. But potentiality is a vague conception. It stands opposed to actuality, and yet to have any content at all it must have some, though an inferior, kind of reality. The Platonic and Aristotelian philosophies failed thus to overcome completely the dualism of matter and spirit. Matter with both remained more or less of a recalcitrant factor, and such it continued to be in the later forms of Greek idealism. Plotinus reduced it to an even greater degree of negativity than did Plato, and made souls the active reality behind material phenomena. There was also a tendency in Neoplatonism to find the ultimate source of matter in the ineffable One, the highest form of Deity. But in spite of this, Greek thought as a whole remained to the end haunted by the conception of matter as essentially antithetical to spirit.

Christian philosophy advanced a step nearer to a spiritual monism by its doctrine of creation out of nothing. This doctrine subordinated matter completely to God but it left material things after their creation with a certain metaphysical independence. Not until we come to Leibnitz and Berkeley do we find material objects reduced to pure phenomenality. Metaphysical reality is now conceived wholly in terms of spirit. Matter in both its ancient Platonic and Aristotelian meaning and also in its naturalistic sense is banished from the realm of ultimate being. Spirit only is real, but it exists, according to Berkeley and still more emphatically according to Leibnitz, in a great many independent centers. The finite spirits or monads, it is true, owe their origin to a supreme spirit or monad, but they nevertheless have a substantial reality of their own. In the philosophies of Leibnitz and Berkeley we thus have a qualitative monism but a numerical pluralism, and in the case of Leibnitz an extreme form of pluralism, a kind of spiritual atomism.

As the protagonist of the principle of individuality Leibnitz ascribed to each monad complete independence of every other. No monad receives anything from the others; each is windowless. It acts entirely by virtue of forces resident within itself. There is no such thing as interaction. Each monad exists in absolute self-sufficiency, unfolding its life wholly in accordance with an inner law of its own being, giving nothing and receiving nothing. But such a view, if carried to its logical conclusion, would lead to solipsism. There would be no ground for affirming the existence either of God or the world. For perception on this theory is entirely self-generated; it has no external cause. There is, therefore, no reason for holding to the reality of other monads than oneself. And this manifestly would undermine the credibility of the very perception on which the principle of individuality is based. It is the pluralism of sense-experience that constitutes the real ground of monadism. So, as Bowne used to say, one cannot become a Leibnitzian without trusting perception, and one cannot remain a Leibnitzian without renouncing this trust.

Again, even though we allow the validity of perception so far as the existence of other monads is concerned, the extreme individualism of Leibnitz leaves their orderly relation to one another unaccounted for. To provide for this he had recourse to the theory of a pre-established harmony. According to this theory all finite monads are mutually independent, but they owe their origin, their unique individuality and their harmonious relation to each other to the creative act and purpose of the supreme monad. They are like clocks that have been wound up and that keep time with each other. This theory excludes interaction but it provides for correspondence and thus leaves us with the appearance of an interacting system. It would, however, seem that Leibnitz found it necessary at times to transcend the limits of a merely apparent interaction. He speaks, for instance, of a governing or dominating monad in organisms and even crystals, thus accounting for their inner unity; but this would seem to imply an interaction between the central monad and the other monads held together by it. At least this would be true of the relation of the finite to the infinite. Here we have direct dependence of one upon the other. The infinite acts upon the finite. The finite monads are created by the supreme monad. In this case, therefore, the strict principle of individuality is manifestly transcended. But the chief objection to the theory of pre-established harmony is to be found in its fatalism. It implies determinism; and this, as we have seen, renders impossible the explanation of error and involves both reason and conscience in disaster. Furthermore, the very fact of error negates the harmony which the theory assumes was pre-established. The Leibnitzian attempt to account for the unity of things, consequently, proved unsatisfactory.

Postponing till a little later the further development of the spiritualistic type of monism, we turn to its pantheistic, or Spinozistic, form. Here both the physical and the mental are reduced to phenomenality, and ultimate reality is found in a being or substance that transcends them both. We have anticipations of this type of thought in the Being of Parmenides, the Ideas of Plato, the Forms and active reason of Aristotle, and the transcendent One of Neoplatonism and of the mystics in general. But it was first worked out in a thoroughgoing way and into a clearly articulated system by Spinoza. For him there was one underlying substance with an infinite number of attributes. Of these attributes two are known to us, thought and extension. They manifest themselves in the various concrete psychical and physical modes of existence, revealed to us in our finite experience. These modes are only transitory manifestations of the one substance and have no substantial character of their own. Finite individuality is thus swallowed up in the community or rather unity of being. But the unity on investigation turns out to be purely verbal. To the totality of being the term "substance" is applied, but no proof of the existence of a unitary and transcendent substance is offered. Nor is a glimmer of insight afforded us into the way in which the one substance differentiates itself into the two wholly disparate attributes of thought and extension. The derivation of each is left utterly opaque and so also is the harmony or correspondence of their concrete modes.

The post-Kantian idealists—Fichte, Schelling, Schopenhauer, and Hegel—marked an advance beyond Spinoza in that they overcame the implicit dualism of his system by rejecting the attribute of extension and also in that they sought to prove the reality of an absolute and unitary Being. Insofar as they conceived of this Being as constituted by pure thought or will they attained to both a qualitative and numerical monism. But insofar as they represented the absolute thought or will or self as nonmental or nonpersonal and as completely transcendental in character, they approached the thoroughgoing pantheism of Spinoza with its barren abstractions and its denial of reality to the finite individual. It was this tendency in the Hegelian philosophy that was elaborated in such a striking and impressive way by F. H. Bradley and that called forth the pronounced pluralistic and realistic reaction characteristic of English and American philosophy during the past thirty years. This reaction, while not profound, is widespread, and has created a situation that makes necessary a defense of the idea of the Absolute.

Personalism as the heir of the earlier idealistic spiritualism, consequently, is confronted with a double task. It must defend the principle of individuality against the impersonalism and all engulfing universalism of such a monism as that represented by Spinoza and not a few absolute idealists. On the other hand, it must vindicate the idea of a basal monism against the attacks of pluralists and positivists. It is with the latter problem that we are here concerned. The Leibnitzian method of harmonizing the community of being with its individuality we found unsatisfactory. It had, however, a marked influence for a long time, and no new and significant contribution to the problem was made until we come down to the nineteenth century. Kant in his later years took an agnostic attitude toward the whole problem and, though a theist himself, thought he had for all time demolished all possible attempts to construct a valid theoretical monism. But his criticism only stimulated new and bolder efforts. Those of a pantheistic type we referred to in the preceding paragraph. The most important one, emanating from distinctly theistic circles, is that of Lotze, based on the fact of interaction.

Lotze argued that the interaction of the many can be accounted for only on the assumption of a co-ordinating One. The popular conception of the transference of a state or condition from one independent thing to another is untenable. States, qualities, and conditions are adjectival in nature and cannot be detached from the things to which they belong.   Equally untenable is the idea of an influence passing from one thing to another.   An influence can hardly be thought of as a sort of thing detachable from an object.   The expression is manifestly figurative.   Equally figurative is also the conception of forces playing between things or of spheres of force about them. Forces have no existence apart from acting things.   We cannot, therefore, think of action as "transeunt" or transcendent.   It must be regarded as immanent, and if immanent, the members of an interacting system cannot be conceived of as independent.   They must have their ground in a unitary being which mediates their interaction or of which they are in some sense modes or phases.   Otherwise their systematic interaction would be wholly inexplicable.

F. C. S. Schiller has devoted a chapter in his *Humanism* (pp. 62-84) to a criticism of this argument.   He first contends that Lotze on his own principles is not warranted in seeking an underlying unity of things.   The world is given as an ultimate fact.   Its existence cannot be deduced from anything simpler, but is to be accepted as self-evident.   It is not, therefore, the function of philosophy to explain how the world or how being in general is made.   This truth is one often emphasized by Lotze and it is "one of the most luminous and valuable" of his contributions to philosophy.   But, argues Schiller, there can be no world without coexistence and no coexistence without interaction.   Interaction is, consequently, involved in the very idea of the world, and, since this is so, it does not call for explanation any more than the world itself does.

This objection was anticipated by Bowne in the first edition of his *Metaphysics* (1882) and met in a decisive way. He admitted that action, however conceived, involves as great a mystery as does being itself, and indeed stressed this fact. Neither being nor action can be deduced from simpler elements nor rationally comprehended. They must be accepted as ultimate data of experience. But while this is true of experienced or immanent action, the question of *inter-* or transcendent action constitutes a separate and peculiar problem. Interaction is not a datum of experience. It is a "necessary mental affirmation," and hence the question may legitimately be raised as to how it is to be conceived. Is the necessary interaction of things consistent with their assumed independence and self-sufficiency? Reflection makes it evident that we have here two contradictory conceptions. Necessary interaction implies that nothing is completely independent, but that all things have the grounds of their determinations in others as well as in themselves. We cannot, therefore, hold both to the necessary interaction of things and to a fundamental pluralism. Only as we transcend the independence of things and affirm their common dependence upon a unitary and independent Being can we affirm their interaction. It is not the mystery of interaction between independent things that here constitutes our difficulty but the contradiction involved in it. Action is no doubt as ultimate and inexplicable as being itself. But because being is an ultimate fact is no reason why it should be conceived in a self-contradictory way; and the same holds true of action. Action conceived as the systematic interaction of independent things is self contradictory, and hence must be superseded by the conception of a basal One, in and through whose activity the world is unified. Schiller's first objection to Lotze's monism thus falls to the ground.

Another objection he raises is that Lotze's argument excludes the possibility of such free and independent beings as Lotze himself assumed finite spirits are. If all action is the immanent action of the Absolute, how can human beings have freedom and independence attributed to them? The answer is evident. A distinction must be made between a fundamental pluralism and such a limited and derived pluralism as Lotze and personalists generally affirm. The former is inconsistent with the conception of the world as an interacting system and is the antithesis of a basal monism; but the latter type of pluralism presupposes both. Whatever independence finite spirits may have, they are still part of the world and as such dependent upon the same ultimate cause. How they manage to combine dependence with a measure of independence is indeed a mystery; but the mystery is no greater than that involved in any form of existence, and in any case it involves no contradiction. Furthermore, our possession of a limited freedom is confirmed by our own consciousness and also by the disastrous consequences alike to reason and to conscience that would follow its denial. To be sure, it is possible to conceive of all finite forms of existence as mere modes of the Absolute and hence as devoid of all independence; but this is no necessary element in the Lotzean argument. The argument does not exclude such a conception of the relation of the Absolute to the finite, but it is equally congenial to the conception of the Absolute as a Power which co-ordinates and mediates the interaction of beings that have more or less of independence. For the co-ordination and mediation of the activities of free agents require a unitary world ground quite as much as do the fixed and determined relations of material phenomena. Indeed, the latter, from the idealistic standpoint, are only the media of intercommunion between spirits.

Formally the Lotzean argument starts with the popular scientific conception of the world as a dynamically interacting system. Surprise has been expressed at this on the ground that Lotze's own philosophy is idealistic. But his method and that of Bowne was to begin with a commonly accepted position and then show that it leads necessarily to a profounder view. In this case the current scientific realism, when thought through, requires a basal monism. The conclusion is unavoidable if the premise is granted. But it is possible to call in question the premise. Nature as a unitary and dynamically determined system is not revealed in experience. It is an ideal of the cognitive nature. We assume that there is a reason for everything, and that all things are causally related. But these assumptions are open to question. Cause in the sense of productive causality has been denied, and so also the principle that everything has a reason. These denials, if taken seriously, would leave us with a world of groundless becoming and of chance. They would condemn us to a fundamental "tychism." On this basis things are because they happen to be. There is no necessity, rational or otherwise, lying back of them. There might happen to be a God, but there is nothing in the structure of the universe that requires such a being. This viewpoint makes possible an ultimate pluralism, but it also involves the abnegation of reason.

Reason assumes that everything has a cause, and if this assumption is valid, it is evident that there can be no halting-place short of a fundamental monism. It may be that the universe is not such a closely articulated and exactly balanced whole as dynamic determinism assumes.

But there is at least system; cognition would be impossible without it. And no ultimate system can be made up of independent units. If the system be real, the units must be subordinated to the system. There can be no union without a basal unity. To insist on regarding the union of independent individuals as the ultimate reality is an act of caprice, not of reason. Reason demands a fundamental unity, and this demand cannot be permanently gainsaid. No theory of the externality of relations can long deflect the mind from its monistic bent. This theory, as a matter of fact, is simply a fallacy of abstraction. Eventually reason will have its way. The distinction we make between the possible and the impossible must have its ground in ultimate reality, and this reality we must conceive as one. The logic of interaction requires it.

But while a basal monism is necessary to meet the demands of reason, we have not yet decided how the fundamental unity is to be conceived. We have previously insisted that there is an important truth in the principle of individuality and that this must not be contradicted by the ultimate unity which we affirm. But how these two divergent principles are harmonized in the personalistic philosophy remains to be more fully developed later.

Activity

In addition to recognizing a permanent element of truth both in pluralistic individualism and in monism and seeking to maintain an even balance between them personalism is activistic. It holds that reality consists in the power of action. This view stands opposed to the ordinary sense metaphysics, on the one hand, and to various forms of pantheism and idealism, on the other.

Sense metaphysics raises three objections to activism. First, it says that the mark of being is to be found in its sense qualities, in the fact that it can be seen and touched, not in its activity. Second, it holds that matter is manifestly given as passive and inert. Third, it maintains that a distinction must be made between being and power or matter and force, and that a thing must first *be* before it can act. A criticism of these three views will bring out the necessity of the dynamic or activistic conception of reality, even though we confine ourselves to the realistic or common-sense standpoint.

It is first evident that, if being is differentiated from nonbeing simply by its sense-qualities, we would be driven to a positivistic idealism. Things would exist only insofar as they are perceived. But this is a conclusion which common sense would never countenance. It insists that things exist whether they are perceived or not. The distinguishing mark of their being must, therefore, be found elsewhere than in their perceptibility. It must be found in something that causes them to be perceived, and this causal something manifestly implies that things are in interaction with each other. Otherwise they could not be perceived, nor could any intelligible meaning be attributed to them. Their existence would be both meaningless and groundless. Only as they are thought of from the causal point of view can they have the objectivity ascribed to them by common sense, and only from this point of view do they fulfill any function in the scheme of thought. If out of all causal relation to each other, their existence would be equivalent to nonexistence. Being, if it is to be more than a concept, must not only be definite and determined; it must also be determining.

Nevertheless, common sense replies that matter clearly

is inactive and inert. It is given as such in experience. To this the history of physics is the obvious and decisive response. Physical theory has made it increasingly evident that the passivity of matter is only apparent. The elements of which it consists and which constitute its true being are in ceaseless activity. And it is their activity, not their mere spatial extension, that gives rise to materiality as it appears to us. The mass or lump is not the sum or aggregate of passively existing atoms or electrons but the phenomenal product of their ceaseless activity. Inertia has no place in the ultimate material elements. Such rest and inaction as we observe among the objects of experience are but the resultant of an underlying dynamism. This is the view of matter toward which physics has steadily moved. Any other view would render matter metaphysically superfluous. It could not be acted upon unless it had some power of reaction, nor could it be directly known unless it stood in some sort of interaction with us. So, as Bowne says, it is only on the dynamic theory of matter that its proper existence can be affirmed.

Still, the children of the dragon's teeth, as Plato called sense-bound minds, are not satisfied. They insist that a distinction must be made between matter and force or between being and power. All matter is no doubt active so that we may say with Büchner that there is "no matter without force," but it is equally true, as Büchner says, that there is "no force without matter." Nevertheless, it is claimed that the two are metaphysically distinguishable. Force requires matter, or in more general terms power requires being, as its support, but is not to be identified with it. Being as an entity is distinct from power. Forces inhere in things, but so far as essence is concerned the two are detachable from each other. Being does not account for power nor power for being. The two are disparate, and hence we must retain the idea of inactive being or passive matter. But in all this the sense-bound mind is the dupe of language. We distinguish in thought between being and power and properly so, but in reality they are indistinguishable and inseparable. They are simply different aspects of one and the same being. The reality in every instance is a single and unitary agent. Being or matter as such is an empty abstraction, and is excluded as a metaphysical entity by the principle of individuality which we have already discussed. The same is also true of power or force. The real thing is always an agent acting in certain ways. Apart from the agent there is no activity, and, on the other hand, there is no agent without activity. Activity penetrates to the very core of being, and constitutes its essential nature. Any other view is but "a whim of the imagination," and leaves us with a contentless and superfluous "substance." The idea of substance must be interpreted in causal terms if it is to be retained. Reality is cause. This conclusion must be accepted if common-sense metaphysics is to be made consistent with itself, in spite of the difficulties that it creates for the popular imagination.

It is not, however, only the popular imagination that has resisted the activistic conclusion. The idea of pure or passive being has figured prominently in the history of speculative thought. The earliest striking expression of it is found in the Eleatic philosophy. Parmenides mistook the logical law of identity for a metaphysical principle and so concluded that there could be no such thing as change. Being must always be identical with itself and hence cannot become anything else. It is not, therefore, and cannot be causal in nature, for cause implies change, and change on the Eleatic theory is an illusion. But if so, what is the function of being? As noncausal it explains nothing, not even the illusion of change. Indeed, there is nothing that calls for explanation. All is fixed and changeless. We are thus left with a purely static universe. And of the existence of this universe we have no evidence since it stands in no causal relation to the changing world of experience. Illusory change is all that we directly know. So far as reality itself is concerned, we are, consequently, condemned to agnosticism. This implication of the Eleatic conception of being was early recognized, and hence in subsequent philosophies the attempt has generally been made to account for change. But that this can be done only by adopting a thoroughly activistic view of reality has not been clear to many speculators. The idea of passive being has haunted philosophy throughout most of its history.

To call the Platonic philosophy as a whole "static" is quite misleading. Plato gave a large place in his system to the principle of causality. It appears conspicuously in his conception of the world-soul and the world-creator. He even raises the question as to whether being should not be defined as "simply power."[10] But this was a conclusion that he did not feel able to accept. Rest, he thought, must be provided for in our definition of being, and so we find the Eleatic conception of a changeless substance recurring in his doctrine of Ideas. To what extent he regarded the Ideas as independent and passively existing entities is a question, but insofar as they took on that character and were supposed to "cause neither move-

---

[10] *Sophist*, 247.

ment nor any change" in sensible things, they were, as
Aristotle insisted, a useless appendix to his system.

Another illustration of the survival of the idea of passive being appears in the Platonic conception of matter.
Plato, it is true, denied to matter the character of true
being; he even called it nonbeing, but some sort of existence he allowed that it had. It was, however, formless,
the bare filling of reality, and as such devoid of all definiteness and causal efficiency. The same may also be said
of the Aristotelian conception of matter as potentiality.
Here, too, we have the idea of a vague and impotent sort
of existence, which has no independence of its own and
yet is the presupposition, the raw material, of all concrete
reality. No account of its origin is given, but as the
background or stuff of the universe it seemed to be required by the imagination, and as such it had a marked
influence on speculation down to the time of Descartes.
But in spite of the influence it has exercised the idea of
passive "matter" in both the Platonic and Aristotelian
philosophy is but an empty word.

The nonactivistic conception of reality appears also in
the Neoplatonic, Spinozistic and, to some extent, Hegelian speculations concerning the Absolute. In these speculations true being is often depicted in such transcendental
terms that anything so specific as energy or dynamic
activity cannot be ascribed to it. It is represented as pure
Unity, pure Substance, or pure Thought. Thought, it is
true, may imply activity, but the activity is logical rather
than dynamic. And purely logical activity is nontemporal
—the conclusion is given with the premise—so that this
form of activity is hardly distinguishable from a static
conception of reality. In any case pure Thought is conceived of as transcending the distinction between subject

and object in much the same way as the pure Unity of the Neoplatonists and the pure Substance of Spinoza, and so is allied to that vague conception of the Absolute as undifferentiated being which forms the background of much pantheistic speculation. Being in this sense is nothing more than the bare category of existence. It contains no principle of movement within itself. The world may be said to be a part of it or a logical consequence of its nature, but this is true only in the sense of the logical subordination of the particular to the general. The general term "being" may be applied to all concrete forms of existence, but it implies none of them. There is no possible way of deducing the actual world of experience from being in general. Being as a concept, no matter whether it has its counterpart in reality or not, is motionless. Unity as such cannot differentiate itself into plurality, nor substance as such into attributes. The thoroughfare in this direction is closed by the fact that in logic there can be no more in the conclusion than there is in the premises, and that bare being or unity or substance is an empty notion. It contains no principle of movement. Only as being is dynamic can it account for change and plurality.

The difficulty with most speculation that arrives at the notion of pure or passive being is that it mistakes the analytic processes of thought for the processes of reality. Thought distinguishes between being and action, but in reality the two are inseparable. We think of ultimate or primitive matter or substance as vague and indeterminate in character, but actually it is only our thought that is vague. All reality is definite. A recent writer tells us that it is one thing to occupy position and quite another thing to exercise causal influence. A thing, he says, may quite conceivably have position and yet exercise no influence whatever.[11] In the abstract this is no doubt true. But such a thing would have no place in the universe. It would be both unknowable and unaffirmable. Occupying "position"—an echo of Herbart—is, as a matter of fact, simply the vague notion we form of a thing when its bare existence is abstracted from its own definite and active nature and from the dynamic relations in which it stands to other things. But no such thing is objectively real. There is much in our thinking that has no counterpart in reality. It is a kind of "subjective scaffolding," necessary to the erection of the temple of truth but no part of it. The failure to recognize this has blinded many to the concrete and causal character of all that is metaphysically real.

Back of this error, however, there lies an important difference between the activistic theory of reality and that held by the absolute idealist. The latter regards thought as all-inclusive. For him there is no reality beyond thought; thought is reality. He is, as we have previously noted, an epistemological monist. The activist, on the other hand, distinguishes between thought and reality. For him reality is something other and more than thought. Thought may be expressed in reality but it is not identical with it. Between the two there is an "indefinable," an "ineffable" difference. Reality is deed as well as idea. But how it is constituted we do not know. We may be reasonably certain that it is not made in Platonic fashion by taking an idea and stuffing it with a formless substance. But what the actual process is completely eludes us. There is about reality a mystery that the human mind

[11] John Laird, *Problems of the Self*, p. 76.

can never penetrate. If we start with the idea, we are forced to confess that we do not and cannot know how it is translated into concrete existence. Reality is something we must accept; we cannot deduce it. But if it is to perform its function in the system of thought, and have any definite meaning, it must be conceived of as cause.[12] And this means that it is objective to thought. Thought apprehends it but remains distinct from it. In this sense the activist is a realist by way of distinction from the absolute idealist.

VOLITIONAL CAUSALITY

Having defined reality as causality, or the power of action, we now proceed to determine more precisely how causality is to be conceived. In doing so we discover that personalism differentiates itself rather sharply from other types of activism. Activism as such may take many different forms. It may be dualistic or materialistic or spiritualistic; it may be pluralistic or monistic; it may be realistic or idealistic. In our exposition thus far of personalism as a theory of reality we have found it leaning toward realism, and this remains one of its permanent characteristics as over against absolute idealism. Its activism refuses to be dissolved into a mere thought-process. But as we proceed to a more exact definition of its conception of causality we find personalism taking an idealistic turn, and this, as we shall see in the remainder of this chapter, is the dominant characteristic of its metaphysics. Its idealism, however, is concrete and spiritual rather

---

[12] Professor G. A. Wilson makes the significant remark that "the thinker who can hold himself steadfastly and consistently to the dynamic conception of the given has the key to most of the persistent problems of philosophy." *The Self and Its World*, p. 31. Reprinted by permission of The Macmillan Company, publishers.

than abstract and logical, and so retains a realistic element.

Reality or substantiality, we have insisted, must be interpreted in causal terms. But how is cause itself to be understood? The idea is a complex one and has had a long history. One might almost say with Albert Lang[13] that there are as many conceptions of causality as there have been different philosophic systems. These diverse conceptions may be reduced to three main types: the positivistic, rationalistic, and voluntaristic. Of these the first is very largely a modern development. It has two main sources, Hume and Kant. According to Hume, sensations are the only source of knowledge, and cause is not and cannot be revealed to sense. Hence the principle of causality is an illusion. It owes its origin to the association of ideas, to the regular conjunction of events, to custom or habit. We observe things occurring together or in a certain sequence, and so conclude that there is a permanent causal bond between them. But this conclusion is unwarranted. Empiricism furnishes no basis for the belief in causality in the metaphysical sense of the term. The causal principle must, consequently, be reinterpreted and applied simply to the orderly relations of coexistence and sequence in which phenomena stand to each other. The epistemological basis of this phenomenalism Kant rejected. He insisted that causality is a category of thought and as such is constitutive of experience. But he limited its validity to the phenomenal order, and so agreed with Hume in denying to it metaphysical significance. This positivistic or phenomenalistic conception of causality is the one now dominant in the field of

[13] *Das Kausalproblem. Erster Teil: Geschichte des Kausalproblems*, p. 29.

science, and properly so. Science is not concerned with causation in its dynamic or activistic sense; and, since this is so, it might conduce to clearness of thought if it should surrender the use of the term altogether.

The scientific conception of causality is of no philosophical importance, unless it be interpreted in a positivistic or antimetaphysical sense. And in this sense it not only leaves us with a groundless becoming, a magical series of independent phenomena, but in the form of empiricism contradicts itself by employing the principle of efficient causality as a means of explaining the principle itself away. In the very act of undermining the category of causation it assumes its validity, and builds its argument on that assumption. Nevertheless the theory maintains its popularity. What makes this possible is "the uncritical favor of common sense," as Bowne termed it, the disposition on the part of the average mind to disregard the claims of logical consistency and to lend its support to any speculative theory, no matter how illogical it may be shown to be, provided it flatters the popular taste.

Positivism means the dissolution of causality. Opposed to its superficial and self-contradictory conception of the causal principle stand the two metaphysical modes of conceiving it, the rationalistic and the voluntaristic. Of these the rationalistic is the older. It goes back for its earliest clear formulation to Leucippus, the atomist, and to Plato. "Nothing," says Leucippus, "happens at random, but everything according to reason and of necessity." "Does not everything," asks Plato, "which comes into being of necessity come into being through a cause?" This general principle does not define the nature of cause but simply asserts its rational necessity. At least this is true of

Plato's formulation of the principle. The "necessity" of
which he speaks is rational, not metaphysical. Leucippus, it would seem, used the term in both senses. He
thinks of cause as necessitated. It is "according to reason," but reason implies determinism, it excludes teleology. With Plato, on the other hand, it did not. It
included final cause as an integral factor in the causal
concept. At the very outset we thus have two different
forms of the rationalistic conception of causality, one
deterministic, the other teleological. Both agree in assuming the objectivity of cause and in holding that it conforms with reason, but one ascribes to reason a narrower
range than the other. One identifies reason with impersonal logic, the other ascribes to it a purposive as well as
a purely logical character.

The deterministic form of rationalism has received expression in three great systems of philosophy: in materialism, ancient and modern, in Spinozistic pantheism,
and in Hegelian idealism. These systems may be regarded as three successive stages in the logical unfolding
of the rationalistic idea embodied in them. Materialism
as a distinctive system leaves ultimate reality external to
thought, and, consequently, there is no reason why they
should be parallel to each other. That material causality
operates in a logical way is simply a dogmatic assumption. It has no basis in the nature of matter. Hence
it was a step in advance to carry, as Spinoza did, both
matter and thought back to one underlying substance and
to treat them as attributes of it. Having a common
source it was only natural to suppose that they would
be parallel with each other. And since thought was now
regarded as immanent in ultimate reality and not external
to it, there was no reason why there should be any paral-

lax between them.   But criticism eventually made it clear
that the unity effected by Spinoza was purely verbal.
Though declared to be attributes of a common substance,
matter and thought remained as disparate as ever.   Nor
was there the slightest glimmer of insight given into the
way in which these disparate attributes could be combined
and made immanent in a unitary being.   Furthermore,
since the thought attribute was supposed to be wholly
independent of the material attribute, there was no reason
why the existence of the latter should not be denied outright.   Thought, on Spinoza's principles, would have
gone on the same without it, since there was no direct
relation between the two, not even a "strained" one, as
Bowne says.   The elimination of matter would also remove the unmanageable dualism of thought and thing
from the system.   It was, consequently, a forward step,
from the point of view of logic, when this was done by
the German idealists, especially Hegel.   Reality was now
absorbed by thought, so that there was no longer any
reason why the causal principle of the universe should not
be thoroughly logical.   Indeed, cause lost its externality
altogether and became a thought process.   This process
required a new logic, but it was logical nevertheless.   No
place was left in ultimate reality for cause in its traditional realistic sense.   Causality in this sense was condemned to mere "appearance," and such it remains in the
Hegelian scheme.

In the development of this type of rationalism the tendency, even in the preidealistic period, was to use the
terms "cause" and "reason" as virtually synonymous with
each other.   Cause may have been conceived in the most
realistic fashion, but so close was the parallelism between
it and thought supposed to be that the system of reality

was regarded as an exact mirror of the relations demanded by logic and mathematics. To state, therefore, the cause of a thing or event was also to give its logical ground or reason. Between the two there was no real difference. The causal relation was thus treated as analytic, not synthetic. The effect was thought of as contained in the cause in the same way that a logical conclusion is contained in its premises. Everything is fixed and determined. There is no place for will or purpose. Teleology is excluded and individualism suppressed. The universal and abstract are in the saddle. This was true of the deterministic type of rationalism as a whole, but it was particularly true of Spinoza. For him the ideal in the conception of nature and in philosophy in general was mathematical demonstration. No distinguished thinker ever ruled out freedom more rigorously or identified cause with necessity more completely than he.

The other type of rationalism, which by way of distinction may be called "intellectualism,"[14] goes back to Plato and Aristotle. Its differentiating feature is that it gives purpose a place in reason. In other words, it is teleological. It does not conceive of cause as modeled strictly on the plan of logic or mathematics. It gives the will a certain free play, and thus adds to efficient cause the idea of final cause. But final cause or purpose was regarded as bound up so closely with the intellect that this type of thought is properly called "intellectualistic." Then, too, what we call efficient causality or dynamic determination was broken up into three different elements, and of these one was distinctly logical in character. Aristotle, for instance, distinguished four kinds of cause,

---

[14] See Albert Lang, *Das Kausalproblem*, pp. 35–39.

commonly known as "formal," "material," "efficient"
and "final."[15] Of these the first three had to do with
real or efficient causality, and yet by "formal" cause was
meant the immanent "idea." It constituted the "essence" of things and as such was objectively real, but it
was nevertheless conceptional rather than dynamic in
nature. Here, then, we have a second intellectualistic
factor in the Aristotelian and scholastic conception of
causality. In addition to the view that "final" cause was
largely determined by the intellect, "formal" cause was
regarded as "ideal," an intellectual concept. The result
was that the volitional and dynamic character of causality
did not come to full expression. Rationalistic elements
were intermingled to such a degree that no clear distinction was made between cause and ground or cause and
reason. The effect was supposed to be contained in the
cause in such a way that it could be deduced from it, or,
conversely, an analysis of the effect would reveal the
cause. There was thus a tendency to bring the causal
principle under the logical law of identity and contradiction and to conceive of it as purely analytic. This tendency in the Platonic-Aristotelian philosophy did not gain
the upper hand so completely that it excluded teleology, as
it did in the later Spinozistic philosophy, but it did obscure
the volitional character of causality and also subordinated
to a considerable extent the contingent facts of experience to the necessary laws of reason.

It was Leibnitz who first clearly formulated the law
of causality by way of distinction from the law of identity and contradiction. He called it "the law of the sufficient reason," and explained it as meaning that every-

---

[15] *Metaphysics*, 983a.

thing that is real or true has a sufficient reason why it is
so rather than otherwise. These reasons as a rule lie beyond us. Analysis of contingent truths or truths of fact
can bring us to no end. Yet there must be a "sufficient
reason" for them, and this reason must needs be outside
of them, outside of the sequence or series of contingen-
cies, no matter how infinitely numerous and complex they
may be.[16] In other words, there must be a God in order
to satisfy the demands of the law of the sufficient reason.

The name given to this law by Leibnitz may not be altogether satisfactory, nor his exposition of it. But he
did nevertheless by means of it bring out more clearly
than had previously been done the contingent element
in causality, and thus prepared the way for a recognition
of its synthetic character. Indeed, this was clearly implied in the distinction he made between the law of the
sufficient reason and that of contradiction. The latter is
limited to analysis, and is purely logical. It is not and
cannot be lawgiving for reality in the sense that it determines what reality in the concrete must be. All concrete existence is contingent, and owes its origin to the
divine purpose. It is an act of will. And it is in this
realm of the volitional and dynamic that causality finds its
true meaning. The law of the sufficient reason is, therefore, objective in a sense that the law of contradiction is
not. It has to do with real existence, not merely with
the consistent use of ideas which may or may not have
their counterpart in reality. But while Leibnitz thus made
an important contribution toward differentiating the idea
of cause from that of rational ground, he still remained
essentially intellectualistic in his conception of causality.

---

[16] See *The Monadology*, 32, 37.

Not only did he regard the causal principle as a law of reason instead of a product of experience, but, what is more significant, he thought of the divine will as controlled to no small extent by abstract logic, and denied to the human will all real freedom, so that in his system as a whole there was a pronounced leaning toward intellectual determinism.

Despite this tendency, however, Leibnitz is one of the great names in the history of the voluntaristic theory of causality. He is such not only because of his stress on teleology, individualism, and contingency, but also because of his causal interpretation of substance and particularly because of his spiritual interpretation of cause. To reduce substance to force or power, as he did, is an important step toward freeing the human mind from its bondage to sense and also its bondage to logical abstractions. Passive substance, whether material or immaterial, cannot fulfill the function of reality. Reality must explain appearance, and this it can do only insofar as it is causal in the dynamic sense of the term. But dynamism is invisible. It cannot be represented to the imagination, and it can be given concrete and definite meaning only in the form of volitional causality. This we experience. We are conscious of ourselves as willing and struggling beings. But beyond this experienced fact we have no idea what causality would mean. Impersonal force is to us inconceivable. We must, therefore, think of all force or power or cause as personal or spiritual. This profound insight we owe to Leibnitz. By giving impressive expression to it he laid the foundation of modern voluntarism.

Mediæval voluntarism he rejected. According to it,

the divine will is the arbitrary source of truth or of the
laws of reason. As against this view Leibnitz, we have
seen, was inclined to subordinate the divine will to the
divine reason; and this intellectualistic tendency was still
more pronounced in his conception of man. But in spite
of this rationalistic prejudice, which he failed to overcome, his theory that all force and all reality is of the
nature of spirit, was manifestly voluntaristic in its implications. Spiritual activity, it is true, takes the form
of thought as well as of volition. But the two are really
not separable. Thought-activity is still activity, and as
such involves a conative or volitional element; and this
element is most naturally regarded as fundamental, if
activity is of the essence of being. The activism of Leibnitz thus developed into voluntarism.

We see this clearly in the case of Maine de Biran (1766-
1824), who was a great admirer of Leibnitz and the
founder of the French spiritualist philosophy.[17] He has
been called "the French Kant," and Cousin spoke of him
"as the greatest metaphysician that France has produced
since the time of Malebranche." It was his contention
that activity is the very essence of consciousness. Self-
consciousness for him meant the consciousness of power.
Descartes' "I am" he translated into "I am active"; *"ago"*
with him took the place of *"sum."* In principle this was
also true of Leibnitz's teaching. But with Leibnitz activity or causality was more or less conceptual. It was a
law of reason or a conclusion reached by analysis. With
Maine de Biran, on the other hand, it was a fact of experience, the ultimate and distinctive fact of consciousness.
As such a fact it is incapable of being deduced from any-

---

[17] See Albert Lang, *Maine de Biran und die neuere Philosophie*, 1901;
Franziska Baumgarten, *Die Erkenntnislehre von Maine de Biran*, 1911.

thing simpler. It is the source of the categories, not their product. From it all metaphysical concepts can be derived. The problem of causality is thus "the pivot of metaphysics," and it finds its solution in consciousness itself, which at bottom is a consciousness of voluntary effort. This insight enabled Maine de Biran to overcome the sensationalism of Hume and to transcend the intellectualism of Leibnitz. It led him also to lift the idea of causality to the plane of consciousness more distinctly than Leibnitz had. So important did he himself regard this achievement that he compared its significance to that of the revolutionary discoveries of Lavoisier in the science of chemistry. But significant as was his empirical and voluntaristic conception of causality, it failed to account adequately for the universality of the causal principle. The bare fact that my self-consciousness is a consciousness of power would hardly warrant my making this consciousness normative for the conception of reality as a whole. The causal principle, if it is to be universally valid, must be imbedded more deeply than in the psychological fact of a self-active experience.

It was at this point that Bowne made good the defect in Maine de Biran's teaching by supplementing or, rather, synthesizing it with the Kantian epistemology. According to Kant, causality is a category of thought, but as such it is formal and empty. Its concrete meaning and application can be determined only by experience. But experience Kant conceived of too narrowly. He limited it to physical sensations. Had he extended it so as to include the data of self-consciousness, he might have seen that self-activity is the only form in which causality is actually experienced. In the objective world we assume causality or infer it. But in conscious voluntary effort it is given as a dâtum of experience. In this form, and in this form only, we know what it is and what it means. We may, therefore, accept our own conscious personal agency as the key to the ultimate meaning of the causal category.[18] But the category itself is not derived from our experience. It is rooted in reason, is universal in its application, and stands in its own right. All that experience does is to reveal the concrete form in which the universally valid rational principle manifests itself. In the volitional theory or interpretation of causality we thus have a fusion of apriorism with empiricism. This synthesis was wrought out more thoroughly and more convincingly by Bowne than by any other writer I know.

In arguing for the view that self-determining intelligence is the true and only type of proper causality Bowne points out that there are in popular thought two other great forms of causation, interaction between things and the determination of consequents by antecedents, and then proceeds to show that both of these forms of causation involve contradictions. Interaction, as we have seen, cannot be explained by the theory of a transference of states or by the assumption of a passing influence or of forces playing between things. These are all simply figures of speech. As explanations they are nullified by the fact that states, influences, and forces are adjectival in char-

---

[18] This conclusion, though not connected with the Kantian epistemology, is explicitly and emphatically stated in Bowne's first book, *The Philosophy of Herbert Spencer*. "Self-determination, volition," he there says, "is the essence of the only causation we know; will is the sum total of the dynamic idea; it either stands for that or nothing. . . . Philosophy repudiates the conception of an impersonal force, as involving irrationalities, and declares the great co-ordinating force of nature to be the activity of Him in whom we live, and move, and have our being. I look upon this idea of force as the only mediation between science and religion" (pp. 112, 125).

acter and cannot be separated from the subject to which they belong.   Then, too, the idea of a systematic and necessary interaction of independent things is self-contradictory.   The independence excludes the interaction, and the interaction the independence.   Transeunt or transitive causality must, therefore, be surrendered, and in its place we must put an immanent causality in a fundamental unitary being.   But such a being cannot be spatial, for space is infinitely divisible.   Nor can it be a mechanically constituted or necessitated being, for a being of this character could neither differentiate itself into plurality nor initiate anything new.   It must be eternally identical with itself both qualitatively and quantitatively.   Beginning as a bare unity or simplicity it must, if consistent with itself, forever remain such.   It cannot, therefore, explain the plural and developing world of experience.   We thus see not only that interaction in the form of transeunt causality is untenable but that immanent causality in a basal one is also such, so long as we remain on the plane of necessity.

Equally untenable and self-contradictory is the conception of causality as the determination of consequents by antecedents.   For one thing, causation in this form comes to no end.   It leaves us toiling in the infinite regress. "It is," as Bowne says, "like seeking to support a chain by adding extra links to the upper end, yet without providing any hook for the support of the whole."[19]   On this basis thought is unable to complete itself and is condemned to a Sisyphean task.   In the next place, causation in the form of antecedence and sequence is a logically inconsistent conception.   For on the mechanical plane a

[19] *Personalism*, p. 186. Reprinted by permission of Houghton Mifflin Company, publishers.

thing cannot change and still remain the same thing.
Change, if it is to be accounted for, must be carried into
being itself, and this means that being loses its identity,
that there is nothing in it that abides. The cause gives rise
to the effect, and in so doing is transformed into it.
Metaphysical predication thus becomes impossible. For
the existence of the subject excludes that of the predicate,
and the existence of the predicate excludes that of the
subject. The two cannot coexist, and yet without their
coexistence we can have no real predication. This inner
contradiction it is impossible to escape so long as we remain on the impersonal plane. Again, it may be noted
that the temporal and linear conception of causality makes
no provision for progress. The effect, if it is to be explained, must be contained in the cause. No real development, therefore, is possible on the necessitarian basis.
We may talk about the effect being simply potentially
present in the cause. But potentiality from the mechanical point of view has no definite content. It has a clear
meaning only when it is understood as the self-determination of the free agent.

Our analysis of the popular conception of causation
thus drives us to the conclusion that it is only in its volitional form that causality can be made intelligible and
self-consistent. Two things must be provided for
in any adequate world-view. One is unity and identity,
the other is plurality and change. But on the impersonal
or necessitarian plane there is an impassable gulf between
them, and as a result the causal idea falls into contradiction with itself. In order to explain change we affirm
a permanent thing, but no *thing* can explain change without ceasing to be permanent. Or we affirm the One in

order to explain the many, but no thing-like unity can explain the many without ceasing to be One. This logical *impasse* we can escape only as we rise to the personal plane. There the contradiction in the causal idea is removed by two miraculous powers of the soul, its unifying and self-identifying consciousness and its power of self-determination. How these powers are possible we do not know, but they are manifest facts of experience. We change, we think and do many different things, and yet we remain the same beings. Through consciousness and memory we constitute ourselves one and self-identical, and through the acts of our will we recognize ourselves as free. In the experience of self-determining intelligence we thus overcome the antinomy in causality, and hence conclude that this is its one true type.

Of the two powers of the soul just referred to as constitutive of volitional causality some personalists lay comparatively little stress on the second, that of freedom. Leibnitz denied to man real freedom and Lotze ascribed no special importance to human freedom from the metaphysical point of view. Bowne, however, elevated it to a position of transcendent significance. Without it, he held, reason would be shipwrecked on the problem of error; there would be no truth. Without it the finite spirit would have no independent reality; its consciousness would be merely a dynamic resultant. The very unity and identity that consciousness ascribes to itself would be illusions, for unity and identity cannot be mechanically imposed from without. They are necessarily constituted by the free creative spirit itself, and are unintelligible apart from it. Without freedom also we could neither arrive at a unitary world-view nor could we escape the abyss of the infinite regress. We must, therefore, regard volitional causality not only as psychical or self-conscious in nature but also as free and self-determined.[20]

THE PHENOMENALITY OF MATTER

If reality is causal and causality is volitional, it follows necessarily that not only the passive matter of sense-experience but also the dynamic matter of scientific and materialistic theory is phenomenal. Neither form of matter is ontologically real. In holding this doctrine personalism is idealistic. But idealism has at least three distinct forms: one positivistic, another spiritualistic, and a third absolutistic. As over against absolute idealism personalism or spiritualism is realistic in the sense that it maintains that existence is something other and deeper than thought. To set a thing in reality means more than simply to think it. It implies a deed, a creative act. How creation is possible we do not know, but the term at least brings out the distinctiveness of reality and the mystery that surrounds it. The soul is more than a thought-process; it is the source of thought rather than its product. This holds true of God as well as of man. Real existence is personal, not simply ideational; it is spiritual,

---

[20] In an unpublished dissertation on *The Metaphysics of Personality in the Light of Recent American Philosophy* (1920) Dr. Raymond F. Piper, of Syracuse University, has worked out a very careful comparison of Bowne's theory of personality with that of William James and of R. B. Perry, subjecting each to a thorough criticism. He finds Bowne's theory defective in that it is not sufficiently analytic; and from the psychological point of view this is no doubt true. Had Bowne gone into greater detail in his study of "activity" and other psychical functions, he would probably have appealed to a wider circle of readers, but it is doubtful if he would thereby have materially strengthened his own position. The two aspects of volitional causality above mentioned are the significant ones from the metaphysical standpoint, and neither their reality nor their speculative significance is dependent upon detailed psychological analysis

not merely logical. In thus emphasizing the concrete, the extralogical, the volitional character of reality personalism retains a realistic element that the absolute idealist seeks to dissolve away. It may also be claimed for personalism that it is realistic as over against positivistic idealism in that it holds to a reality other and deeper than that of sense or the passing states of consciousness, a reality that abides through change and that can in a measure be apprehended by the human mind. But while realistic by way of contrast with the two competing forms of idealism, personalism is distinctly idealistic when compared with materialism and with common sense and scientific realism.[21] As opposed to these types of thought it denies all extramental existence and affirms the complete phenomenality of matter.

In taking this position personalism has had the same general aim that the idealistic, as distinguished from the merely mentalistic, movement has had throughout its entire history. Matter is apparently the great foe of the spirit. It seems to reign omnipotent over the life and destiny of men. Hence the human spirit, conscious of its own superior worth and being, has risen in revolt against it and sought to curb its arrogance. This revolt in the field of thought has taken the form of idealism in the broader sense of the term. In the history of this movement, so far as it relates to the conception of matter, three stages may be distinguished.

First, there was the idealism of Plato and Aristotle with its rather obscure and confused view of matter and

---

[21] The clearest and most convincing exposition of the personalistic view of reality in its relation to realism and idealism, of which I know, is to be found in Bowne's *Metaphysics* (1882), pp. 450–487. He there designates his own standpoint as "objective idealism."

the material world. This view, in spite of its defects, exercised a dominant influence in the history of thought for two millenniums, and is not yet wholly obsolete. The key to it is to be found in the logical distinction between form and matter. From one point of view things have form; they are an embodiment of ideas, they express intelligence, while from another point of view they are mere content, formless matter. These two aspects of things belong together, and we should say with Aristotle that they are mere abstractions when separated from each other. But different degrees of worth were nevertheless attached to them, and the distinction made between them to a large degree determined the view of the material world that was formed under the influence of the Platonic and Aristotelian tradition. Insofar as material things "participated" in the Forms or Ideas, or contained them, they reflected a higher mode of existence, and much was said in praise of them and the world constituted by them. But insofar as they merely reflected a higher order and did not truly embody it, much was said in disparagement of the material universe. Matter itself was condemned to virtual nonexistence, so that it became a synonym of unreality. It is, said Plotinus, "merely a phantom or shadow of space, an aspiration toward existence. . . . It is a ghostly thing incapable alike of staying or going since it has drawn no force from the Divine; . . . and so all its pretense of existence is a lie."[22]

But in spite of such negative utterances as these a kind of existence was attributed to matter. It was thought of as the eternal and more or less independent background of the universe, and as such stood more or less

[22] *Enneads*, iii, 6, 7. Translation by Stephen MacKenna.

opposed to the Deity as a resisting force. Neoplatonism sought to overcome this dualism. It developed the doctrine that the higher any cause stands in the scale of being, the lower down do its effects extend; and this was interpreted by Proclus to mean that matter as the lowest form of being was an effect of the transcendent "One" who stood at the other end of the scale.[23] But this device produced only a formal monism; it left the distance between Deity and matter about as great as ever. A marked change was wrought by the introduction of the Christian doctrine of creation. This made matter, at least in principle, the instrument of the divine will. But Christian thought was not sufficiently vigorous and independent to develop the full implications of this position. It remained to a large extent in bondage to the Platonic and Aristotelian tradition. Then, too, the Christian doctrine of redemption had certain points of affinity with Greek dualism, which made it easy to retain the older forms of thought.

It was the idealism of the Cartesian school which first broke in a significant way with Greek tradition and introduced a new stage in the history of idealistic thought. The Aristotelian distinction between form and matter was now given up and in its place was put the distinction between mind and matter. This made possible a more exact definition of matter. Its essence was now found in extension, and the old idea of its formlessness vanished. At the same time a new antithesis was created between mind and matter, and the passivity of matter was emphasized anew. This led to the doctrine of occasionalism and to the conviction that the only primal certainty we

---

[23] See A. E. Taylor, *Platonism and Its Influence*, p. 124.

have is that of the soul's own existence. We may by means of the ontological argument be able to prove the divine existence, but of the existence of the external world we have no direct proof. We infer it from the divine veracity which would not permit of such sense-deception as would be involved in its nonexistence, or we base it on divine revelation. This was Malebranche's view. But on this theory there is no logical ground for retaining the material world at all. If it is completely passive, if there is no interaction between it and the soul, if we see all things in God, we might as well dispense with it altogether. There is a tradition to the effect that Berkeley on a visit to Malebranche pointed this out to him and that the aged philosopher as a result became so agitated that his death was hastened by it. This may be purely legendary, but it is nevertheless true that Berkeley was one of the chief agents in giving the death-blow to the Cartesian system.

Current idealism, which may be regarded as the third stage in the history of idealistic philosophy, took its rise with Berkeley and Leibnitz. The latter showed that extension is the effect of an underlying force, not an ultimate essence; and this force he construed in psychical terms, though he did not do so with complete consistency and in a thoroughly idealistic way. Berkeley, however, identified material objects unequivocally with ideas or presentations, and thus robbed matter of the last shred of extramental existence.[24] What we call the material world is a system of appearances. There is no such thing

---

[24] For an account of a mediæval anticipation of Berkeley's position by an obscure schoolman, Nicholas of Autrecourt, Dean of Metz, see H. Rashdall's *Philosophy and Religion* (p. 12) and his Presidential Address in the *Proceedings of the Aristotelian Society* for 1907.

as matter in the ontological sense of the term. This doctrine was immensely deepened and strengthened by the
Kantian epistemology, and, as we have seen, has taken
several different forms. But in its essential teaching it
has been accepted by all the leading and characteristic
types of modern idealism. The complete phenomenality
of matter is a fundamental tenet of positivistic and of
absolute idealism as well as of personal idealism.

There are, however, two different ways of conceiving
the phenomenality of matter. Both of these appear in
the personalistic camp. We have already referred to
them. One is the panpsychistic, the other the occasionalistic. The former was represented by Leibnitz, who has
had many followers. Indeed, the doctrine in an undeveloped form goes back to Plato and Plotinus, and has
affinities with animism. "Nothing," said Plotinus, "that
is destitute of soul can exist." This also is essentially
Leibnitz' position. Soul is the essence of all existing
things; materiality is simply their phenomenal form.
"There is," says Leibnitz, "a world of creatures, of living
beings, of animals, of entelechies, of souls, in the smallest
particle of matter. Each portion of matter may be conceived as like a garden full of plants and like a pond full
of fish. But each branch of a plant, each member of an
animal, and each drop of the fluids within it, is also such
a garden or such a pond. And although the earth and
the air lying between the plants of the garden, and the
water which is between the fish of the pond, are neither
plant nor fish; yet they nevertheless contain them, though
usually in such minute form as to be imperceptible to us.
Thus there is nothing fallow, or sterile or dead in the
universe, no chaos, no confusion, except in appearance;

very much as it might appear to be in a pond at a distance where one sees a confused movement, and, so to speak, a swarming of fish in the pond without distinguishing the fish themselves."[25]

In favor of this panpsychistic theory it is urged that it gives to nature an independent worth, an existence for itself, so that its being is not exhausted in its being perceived or in its being a vehicle of communication between spirits. It has a reality of its own; and hence the long period of cosmic history before the appearance of the higher forms of conscious life was not without meaning. The theory also, it is claimed, overcomes the dualism of mind and body by making the body the direct phenomenal expression of the mind. But these merits which may be conceded to the theory are more than offset by the difficulties that inhere in it. For one thing, there is no positive evidence in support of it. Appearances are against it. In the next place, it is in a way a reversion to animism or hylozoism and so runs counter to that more sharply defined and purely objective view of the natural order which has been built up through the painstaking labor of the centuries. Again, it leaves the door open to fantastic constructions, akin to the angelology of the past, in which the imagination ran riot without the restraint of fact or the sobering influence of a disciplined reason. And, finally, one wonders what sort of value could possibly attach to so low a grade of mentality as that which might conceivably form the interior life of a material atom. It would seem as though the panpsychistic theory grew out of a vague mystical feeling rather than out of a carefully reasoned attempt to understand the world.

―――――――

[25] *Monadology*, 66–69.

The occasionalistic theory reduces matter in its entirety to a phenomenal product of the divine energizing. Individual things have from this point of view no independent inner life. They are not *real* causes but simply *occasional* causes; that is, they furnish the occasions of the divine activity. The only real cause, so far as the material world is concerned, is God. This viewpoint has its kinship with Aristotle rather than Plato. To Aristotle it seemed inappropriate to extend the notion of soul beyond the realm of living beings and to apply it to the cosmos at large, as Plato did. This also was the view of Berkeley and Bowne, and represents, furthermore, the direction in which modern scientific thought has moved with massive impressiveness. Occasionalism thus finds itself in this respect in accord with the prevailing intellectual temper of the day. It does not see in every material thing the phenomenal manifestation of a soul. For it matter as such is de-animized; it is grounded directly in the divine activity, not in the activity of independent spirits. To the latter it sustains a certain relation of concomitance. Our bodies respond to our wills. But matter is not simply the phenomenal accompaniment of finite minds. It serves other purposes. It is a revelation of the divine thought and will, and as such constitutes an orderly system, objective to ourselves and the necessary condition of our intellectual and moral development. But however objective it may be, it is still to be viewed as phenomenal. It does not contain in itself causal efficiency. It does not fill out the notion of ontological reality. The latter we can find only in intelligent and self-determined beings.

This leads us to the distinction that Bowne made between phenomenal reality and metaphysical reality, to which we have previously referred. Phenomenality does not mean illusion. Material phenomena have an objective causal ground, and in that sense are real. Plotinus said that matter is "a lie," and so it is insofar as it sets up a claim to ontological existence. But Proclus was also justified in adding that it is "a true lie." While not metaphysically real, matter represents an order external to and independent of us, and in this respect is real or "true." And from the practical point of view the importance of knowing this phenomenal order can hardly be exaggerated. This is the field of science, and science, as Bowne said, is "the sum of practical human wisdom." The fullest and freest scope is, therefore, to be given scientific inquiry. But at the same time it is important to remind ourselves that science has to do simply with phenomena, and that there is another order of reality that is not without deep significance for the human spirit. It is, indeed, a matter of special importance in our day that this fact should be enforced. For a new worth is now attached to the physical universe. It supplies, as it did not in earlier times, "an object capable of absorbing the interest and filling the imagination of the greatest among mankind." And this carries with it the peril of a new enslavement. To avoid this peril nothing is more efficacious than to recognize the purely phenomenal character of the physical world. However engrossing and however imposing it may be, it is not ultimate and self-sufficient. Its existence is secondary and instrumental. It serves a spiritual purpose. It may do so imperfectly. It may, like a dome of many-colored glass, stain the white radiance of eternity. But to some extent it transmits it, and in this has its *raison d'être*. To make this clear has been

the aim of the idealistic philosophies throughout their entire history, and this end is best achieved, not by the Platonic degradation of matter, nor the Cartesian insistence
on its passivity, but by such a demonstration of its phenomenality as Bowne has presented. His distinction between phenomenal and metaphysical reality is of permanent value.

With the establishment of the phenomenality of matter
the philosophy of religion has achieved its main purpose,
that of subduing the physical and making it the instrument of the spiritual. Whether from this secure position
it is necessary to advance to a denial of the ontological
reality of space and time is a question on which personalists disagree. The question is not one of special religious
significance, but considerable speculative interest does attach to it. Bowne was unequivocal in his advocacy of the
ideality of both space and time, and this is manifestly the
conclusion to which a thoroughgoing personalism points.

If we start with the Kantian conception of space and
time as forms of the sensibility or categories of thought,
it is evident that we cannot decide the question of their
metaphysical existence by an appeal to intuition. The
problem is one of thought. And here reflection makes it
clear that an ontological space would leave us "lost and
embrangled in inextricable difficulties." Such a conception of space is inconsistent with our idea of reality as
active, since space is not active and cannot be so conceived
without being despatialized. It is inconsistent with the
unity of the world-ground, since any being in a real space
would be divisible. It is also inconsistent with the intellectual demand for an ultimate monism, since a real space
alongside of the world-ground would involve a funda-

mental dualism. We reject, therefore, the metaphysical reality of space and hold that it is as phenomenal as the matter supposed to be contained in it. Apart from experience space has no existence. The spatial world is an effect in us and in thinking beings in general. We need a real space to see things in as little as we need a real space to dream things in. Both the reactions of the sensibility and the activities of the mind are spaceless, and it is these that give rise to the knowledge of space. Space, then, is simply the form of objective experience, and in and by itself is a bare abstraction. Without spatial objects there would be no space. Its phenomenality, therefore, is a corollary of the phenomenality of matter.

The ideality of time is a more difficult conception than that of space, for we have no nontemporal experiences, as we do have nonspatial experiences, to help our thought. But the difficulties involved in the metaphysical reality of time are quite as serious as those connected with space. To be ontologically real, time must be active, but to so regard it is to contradict the time-idea. Then, too, if real, it would leave us with a fundamental dualism, and thus conflict with the mind's demand for a basal monism. Again, time is infinitely divisible, and if metaphysically real, this would mean that nothing can truly exist, for all real existence is in the present, and the present on this assumption would have no duration. It would be simply the bare point or timeless plane which separates the past from the future. Ontological time we, therefore, reject as an inconsistent and self-contradictory conception. The temporal relation, like the spatial, we must regard as merely the form under which we conceive the cosmic process. This process is grounded in the divine activity, but it does not necessarily follow that the divine activity is itself successive. Just as the spatial form of experience has its ground in an immaterial and nonspatial agency, so it is quite possible that the temporal order may be maintained by an activity that has in itself no before and after. Temporality does not require a temporal cause. Indeed, "the successive can exist only for the nonsuccessive."[26] God, we therefore hold, is a nontemporal or supertemporal Being, and yet he founds change.

This is possible because he is a Person. A free being can initiate change without being himself involved in it. This is the mystery of personality and its most distinctive characteristic. In ascribing nontemporality to the Absolute we do not, then, think of him as "a rigid monotony of being but, rather, as the perfect fullness of life, without temporal flow or ebb."[27] What nontemporality means in his case is absolute self-possession or complete self-realization and hence freedom from all those human limitations that grow out of our dependence. The cosmic order may very possibly have for him, as it has for us, the temporal and spatial form. But time and space represent no ultimate realities. They are synonyms for phenomenality. Back of them are power and purpose, and in view of this fact they are not illusory. But what takes place in them has only an instrumental and teleological character; it objectifies and communicates thought. Apart from that there is in the bare temporal or spatial event itself nothing that can be given an intelligible content.

In taking this view of time Bowne allies himself with the Platonic-Augustinian tradition. Plato saw in space

---

[26] B. P. Bowne, *Personalism*, p. 149. Reprinted by permission of Houghton Mifflin Company, publishers.
[27] *Ibid.*, p. 149.

an eternal and indestructible reality, a necessary condition
of existence, but time he regarded as "a moving image
of eternity," as a created being.[28] This way of conceiving time was adopted by Augustine and formulated in
the well-known saying that "God made the world not *in*
time but *with* time." The temporal relation is thus coexistent with the cosmic process, but unreal apart from it.
This, as we have seen, is also Bowne's view. But he
grounded it in a deeper epistemology and a profounder
conception of personality. His Kantian theory of thought
made it possible for him to give to time a more ideal
character than did Plato and Augustine, and his individualistic and voluntaristic conception of personality furnished him with the key to the solution of the age-old
antinomy between change and identity and also between
time and eternity. It is, indeed, the thoroughness with
which he has elaborated this solution and worked out its
wide-reaching implications, that constitutes his chief
claim to a place in the history of philosophy.

PERSONALITY

The metaphysics of personalism may be summed up in
the statement that personality is the key to reality. All
that has thus far been said about the individuality of the
real, about a basal unity, about causality, and about the
phenomenality of space and time, has pointed toward this
truth. It is in personality that individuality finds its only
adequate realization. It is personality alone that has the
characteristics necessary to a basal unity. It is in personal agency that we have the source of the idea of causality and its only self-consistent embodiment. It is the

---

[28] *Timaeus*, 52, 37, 38.

reality of personality that constitutes the foil to the phenomenality of matter, space, and time and renders it intelligible.   From every point of view it is thus evident that in personality we have the crown of the personalistic system, the keystone in its arch, the masterlight of all our metaphysical seeing.

This conception of personality is, of course, not wholly new.   It is really implicit in theism.   Indeed, the history of theism may be regarded as the gradual and logical unfolding of its personalistic implications.   To trace this development in outline will be a help to the understanding of what is distinctive in modern personalism.   In doing so it will be well to distinguish between ancient and mediæval theism, on the one hand, and modern theism, on the other.   Ancient and mediæval theism took its cue to a large extent from Plato, who was not only the first philosophical theist and the first systematic theologian but also the greatest of this entire period. Aristotle, Plotinus, Augustine, and Thomas Aquinas were all to a considerable degree his disciples, so that a certain unity characterizes the theistic type of thought current down to the modern era.

Theism by its very nature assimilates ultimate reality to the finite mind or to some aspect of personal intelligence, and this, of course was recognized by the ancient as well as by modern theists.   "Know thyself" was not only a counsel of practical wisdom but also a guide to metaphysical insight.   "One that seeks to penetrate the nature of the divine Mind," said Plotinus, "must see deeply into the nature of his own soul, into the divinest part of himself."   But in addition to this general conviction, the full import of which lay beyond the mental horizon of the ancient and mediæval world, there were other elements in the Platonic, Aristotelian, and Augustinian philosophy that pointed toward the unique reality of the self. Several of these may be noted.

First, the immateriality of the soul was taught. This marked an extremely significant step in the direction of a spiritualistic metaphysics, a step that represents a permanent gain to philosophy. It may be that Plato and Plotinus were mistaken in concluding that because the soul is immaterial it must be simple in structure, hence indissoluble, and, therefore, immortal. But by differentiating it from every form of material existence and by lifting it above the purely phenomenal level they gave it a unique distinction and established between it and the physical a gulf which no materialistic theory has since been able successfully to bridge. The immateriality of the soul implies both its uniqueness and its possession of a higher form of reality.

Another point to be noted is the stress that was laid on the soul as the source of motion. Plato emphasized in particular the idea that the soul has the power of self-motion. He defined the soul as "the motion that moves itself"; and to him this seemed a most significant fact. "The motion," he said, "which is able to move itself is ten thousand times superior to all others."[29] Again, he says that "self-motion is the very idea and essence of the soul. But if the soul be truly affirmed to be the self-moving, then must she also be without beginning and immortal."[30] Essentially the same view appears also in Plotinus. The soul, he said, "is the starting-point of motion and becomes the leader and provider of motion to

[29] *Laws*, 894. Translation by B. Jowett.
[30] *Phaedrus*, 245c.

all else." It "lives not in the sense of potential reception of life but by its own energy; and this can be no cause of dissolution."[31]   Aristotle, it is true, rejected the Platonic idea of a "self-moving motion" and substituted for it the idea of an "unmoved mover." But in so doing he took a more limited view of "movement" than did Plato, excluding mental activity from it. "The soul," he said, "is not in motion; but if it is not in motion, it is clear that it is not self-moved."[32]   Then, too, by movement he understood transition from a state of potentiality to one of actuality and this he felt could not properly be ascribed to the "prime mover." Furthermore, self-movement, taken strictly and absolutely, implies that a thing is both actual and potential at the same time and in the same sense; and this, from Aristotle's point of view, was self-contradictory. He did, however, ascribe a self-originated thinking activity to the "unmoved mover," and so there was probably no essential difference between his view and that of Plato. Nevertheless, Plato's method of expression is more distinctly personalistic than Aristotle's. It recognizes in the soul a truly independent and creative activity, a power that transcends the distinction between potentiality and actuality and combines them both in its own unique and transcendent life. To it, therefore, reality in the fullest sense belongs.

A third significant quality attributed to the soul was that of combining unity with plurality and serving as a mediator between them. This was a point especially emphasized by Plotinus. "The nature," he says, "at once divisible and indivisible, which we affirm to be soul has not the unity of an extended thing: it does not consist of

[31] *Enneads* iv, 7, 9, 12.
[32] *De Anima*, 408b.

separate sections; its divisibility lies in its presence at
every point of the recipient, but it is indivisible as dwelling
entire in the total and entire in any part. To have penetrated this idea is to know the greatness of the soul and
its power, the divinity and wonder of its being, as a nature transcending the sphere of Things."[33] In this and
other similar statements that might be quoted from
Plotinus we have a remarkable anticipation of the modern
personalistic conception of the self. But the soul's synthesis of unity and plurality did not have the same metaphysical significance for Plotinus that it has for us. We
see in it the key to ultimate reality. But for him it denoted an intermediate being, since he thought of the highest form of reality as the One or pure unity and looked
upon plurality as characteristic of matter and the lower
forms of existence. A being that combined both unity
and plurality was thus regarded as lower than the One,
but at the same time it transcended the material realm of
the Many, and this gave to the soul in Plotinus' system
a unique pre-eminence.

Still another important conclusion with reference to the
soul appeared in ancient philosophy. Augustine, as we
have previously noted, taught that the soul is more certain of its own existence than it is of the existence of
anything else. In this fact he saw an absolutely conclusive response to the skeptic, and by his insistence upon it
anticipated in a striking way the subjectivism of modern
philosophy. But the idea, profound and significant as
it was, bore no immediate fruit. Augustine also taught
in a new and original way the freedom of the will. This
teaching served as a corrective of the intellectual deter-

[33] *Enneads*, iv, 2, 1. Translation by Stephen MacKenna.

minism, more or less characteristic of Greek thought, but
it might also have been combined with Plato's conception
of the soul as self-moving and thus have led to the personalistic conclusion that causality finds its highest and
only true exemplification in the free activity of the spirit.
This combination, however, was not made and no new
and important metaphysical insight resulted from Augustine's indeterminism.

We thus see that there were several doctrines laid down
in ancient philosophy that pointed in the direction of the
personalistic theory of reality—namely, the immateriality
of the soul, its unique power of self-motion and its freedom, its synthesis of unity and plurality, and the primacy
of its self-certainty.   But for various reasons these doctrines were left in a state of arrested development.   For
one thing, the objectivity of thought was interpreted in
a crude realistic sense and obstinately adhered to, so that
the primacy attributed by Augustine to the soul's certainty of its own existence was not allowed to work itself
out to its logical conclusion.   In the next place, ancient
and mediæval philosophy was unduly rationalistic.   Subjective, logical processes were often mistaken for the order of reality.   The result was that the unity and individuality of the soul and of being in general were not
clearly apprehended.   Aristotle, for instance, made substance individual, but he at the same time made the universal the essence of the individual, and thus obscured,
if he did not destroy, the true unity of the self.   The distinction he made between form and matter also militated
against the metaphysical independence of the soul.   He
and other ancient and mediæval thinkers failed to see that
concrete reality is not a compound.   It cannot be made

by taking an Idea and filling it with a formless substance. The concrete individual things come first. The aspects of their being that we abstract from them have no objective existence. Unity, intelligence, and soul—the Neoplatonic trinity—are not distinct or independent realities, as Plotinus held. They are simply abstractions from the unitary and conscious life of the self. And the self, too, is not a compound of consciousness and life. Its life, as a matter of fact, is its consciousness, and its consciousness is its life; and only in its living consciousness do we have true reality. But this insight was withheld from ancient and mediæval thought because of its rationalistic prejudices and its realistic assumptions.

In modern times, however, these restraints were gradually removed. The Augustinian stress on the supreme certainty of self-existence was revived by Descartes and carried to its logical idealistic conclusion by later thinkers. "I should like to know," said Leibnitz, "how we could attain to a knowledge of reality if we or our soul were not real." "However it may be," said Fichte, "with the reality of a sensible world external to me, I myself am real; I take hold on reality here; it lies in me, and is there at home." It was this deep-seated conviction, with which modern philosophy began, that led to the immaterialism of Leibnitz, Berkeley, Fichte and other idealists. These men saw that, if the soul is the true type of reality, things cannot be real in the same sense.

This conclusion was further strengthened by a more exact definition of the nature of the soul. Leibnitz, for instance, brought out more distinctly its individuality. He pointed out that individuality penetrates to the very core of being, so that the essence of the soul cannot be

constituted by any universal idea or substance, but must
be something unique, something into whose inmost nature
logical analysis cannot penetrate, something that must be
experienced in order to be known.   To some extent this
conception of individuality was implied in Descartes' definition of mind as *thinking* substance, but it was developed
much more fully by Leibnitz and made still more distinct
by Kant, Fichte, Maine de Biran, and Lotze, who identified the reality of the self more completely with its own
self-conscious unity and freedom.   This more exact definition of the self tended yet further to accentuate the difference between it and impersonal things, and to make
its type of reality the one true norm of being.

It was this line of development that resulted in the formulation of the central and most characteristic doctrine
of personalism, namely, that personality is the key to
reality.

This doctrine is fundamentally empiricistic.   Personality is something given.   We do not create it, nor do we
know how it is created.   It is an ultimate fact, but as
such it contains the "key to the whole puzzle about reality," so far as this puzzle admits of solution.   The basal
problem connected with reality is how it can combine
unity with diversity and identity with change.   The response is that the combination is actually effected in personality.   Our self-experience presents us with a solution
of the problem.   To this F. H. Bradley objects on the
ground that, while our experience of self-identity is "indubitable," it does not make our sameness "intelligible."
It does not enable us to *understand* the way in which
diversity is harmonized."[34]   To this we freely assent.   We

---

[34] *Appearance and Reality*, p. 104.

do not know how selves are made and how they succeed in overcoming the antinomy between unity and identity, on the one hand, and plurality and change, on the other. The *understanding* throws no light on the process. But this in no way discredits the fact. The fact is given in experience, and no matter how mysterious it may be, it is conclusive evidence that in reality the problem of unity and diversity is somehow solved. Our self-experience, and it alone, gives us the solution. It is, therefore, no "arbitrary refuge" to which we resort when we make personality our ultimate and irreducible datum.[35] Experience, through which alone reality is revealed, justifies it.

But while the central doctrine of personalism thus has an empirical basis it is important to note that it is also grounded in the Kantian epistemology. Professor Ralph B. Perry seems to think that these two standpoints are inconsistent with each other. Personal idealism, he says, by its insistence on the intuition of individual self-existence, escapes the Hegelian Absolute, but in so doing it loses the important support of the Kantian theory of knowledge.[36] The latter, he thinks, leads necessarily to absolute idealism. But this is to overlook one of its most characteristic features. It was Kant's claim that the categories of thought are in themselves purely formal and that they derive their meaning and content from concrete experience. Apart from the objects of a real or possible experience they have no application; they are "utterly vacuous." And if this be so, it is manifestly only a logical application of the Kantian theory when we find in personal experience the key to the interpretation of the categories and hence the key to reality. If we wish to know

[35] See B. Bosanquet, *The Principle of Individuality*, p. 13.
[36] *The Present Conflict of Ideals*, p. 218.

246 THE PHILOSOPHY OF PERSONALISM

what unity, identity and causality really mean we must turn to our own experience. In free intelligence itself, which is the source of all the categories, we have at once their living embodiment and their only adequate explanation. This doctrine, instead of being inconsistent with the Kantian epistemology, is the direct outgrowth of it.

We have heard not a little in recent years about "the ego-centric predicament."[37] By this is meant the fact that nothing can exist for us except as we think it, and that, consequently, we cannot know anything as it is in itself, apart from its relation to an apprehending intelligence. From this fact many have drawn an idealistic conclusion, but this the neo-realist rightly insists is unwarranted. That we have to think a thing in order to know it is no evidence that the thing has no existence apart from thought. The difficulty connected with the subjectivity of perception vanishes as soon as we recognize its true nature. The ego-centric predicament, however, goes much deeper than this, much deeper than the neo-realist realizes. Not only is the ego necessarily involved in all knowledge of reality, but it is in the ego that all the fundamental principles of thought have their seat and find their meaning. Abstracted from their living source in the self and applied to impersonal beings, they fall into contradiction with each other and cease to be intelligible. Only as reality is lifted to the personal plane does it become amenable to the demands of reason. It is the clearness with which Bowne apprehended this truth and the systematic thoroughness with which he elaborated it that makes his philosophy one of the most strikingly individual creations in the history of metaphysics in America.

---

[37] See R. B. Perry, *Present Philosophical Tendencies*, pp. 129ff.

CHAPTER IV

PERSONALISM AND RELIGIOUS BELIEF

PERSONALISM is in a pre-eminent sense the philosophy of religion of our day. It may indeed be said to be the most thoroughgoing philosophical expression that Christianity has yet received. This does not, however, mean that every Christian must be a personalist in philosophy. The relation of the Christian religion to philosophy has been a varied one. To many the two have seemed necessarily hostile to each other. One as the embodiment of reason and the other as the embodiment of faith have seemed to be moving in opposite directions. Much has consequently been said by theologians such as Tertullian of the Fathers and Luther among the Reformers in disparagement of philosophy and of reason. Even Ritschl, the most influential theologian of the past seventy-five years, expressed himself in a similar way concerning natural theology. And this is a rather popular point of view at present. It follows naturally from the pragmatistic and voluntaristic tendencies in current philosophy. If the intellect is secondary and purely instrumental in character, it could hardly serve as a key to the riddle of the universe. For such a key we must in that case turn elsewhere or renounce the quest altogether.

This is perhaps the common feeling to-day. It is also the position that has often been taken by theologians in support of ecclesiastical or biblical authority. The inadequacy of reason has been made the chief reason for be-

248 THE PHILOSOPHY OF PERSONALISM

lieving in an authoritative revelation. Religious faith has
been founded on philosophical skepticism. But while this
method has been effective with the popular mind and
while there is some justification for it, it is not a method
that we can accept as ultimately valid. No doubt, logically, skepticism is as fatal to materialism as to idealism,
but to refute materialism by means of skepticism would
be, as Dean Inge has said, to cast out devils by Beelzebub.
For no matter how antithetical philosophical skepticism
may formally be to dogmatic materialism, in spirit it is
akin to it, and in its current positivistic form it is often
nothing more than a thin disguise for a materialistic naturalism. To substitute skepticism for materialism means
thus usually simply a change of name. Between the two
there is no real conflict. The devils of materialism may
be more uncouth and aggressive than the Beelzebub of
positivistic skepticism, but the latter is at bottom no more
hospitable to religion than the former. In this respect
both are essentially alike, and to use one to dislodge the
other would be no particular advantage. The skeptical
mood is as hostile to faith as is that of dogmatic negation.
To base religion, then, on philosophical skepticism is to
rest on a bruised reed which pierces the hand that leans
upon it. An un-Christian head cannot be made the friend
of a Christian heart.

This in the long run has usually come to be recognized
as true, and so in spite of skeptical outbursts in the ancient and mediæval church and in spite of the wavering
attitude of the Lutheran schools the main tendency in
Christian thought has been to link up religious faith with
faith in reason and to find in reason a support of religion.
But reason itself is a changing quantity. It embodies

itself in different philosophies from age to age; and it is the union of Christianity with these changing philosophies that has produced our Christian theology in all its varied forms.

Taking the history of the church as a whole we may distinguish four great systems of philosophy with which the Christian faith has successively made alliances: Neoplatonism, Aristotelianism, Cartesianism and the idealism of Berkeley, Kant, and Hegel. These successive alliances, however, do not mean that the earlier alliances have been completely displaced by the later. Neoplatonism, though supplanted by Aristotelianism in the thirteenth century, is still an influential factor in Christian thought. Dean Inge, for instance, takes the position that there is no other philosophy that can work harmoniously with Christian theology,[1] and even Troeltsch expressed the opinion that the future of Christian philosophy depended on the renewal of its alliance with Neoplatonism. Aristotelianism, although indissolubly bound up with mediæval scholasticism, is still the official philosophy of the Roman Catholic Church and in that body is so dominant that its triumph in the thirteenth century has with some plausibility been declared to be the only instance, in the entire history of the church, of a modernist movement that succeeded. Cartesianism, which initiated the modern break with Aristotelianism, still lingers in a modified form in the common sense realism of our day, which in recent years has undergone somewhat of a revival in professional circles.

It is, then, evident that the statement at the beginning of this chapter is not one to which general assent would

---

[1] *The Philosophy of Plotinus*, i, p. 12.

be given. Personal idealism in neither its Berkeleian, Kantian, nor Hegelian form, nor in all of them together, has so completely established itself as to be entitled to be called in an exclusive sense *the* Christian philosophy of our day. But that it has during the last century been the most powerful ally of religion and that, at least in Protestant lands, it has almost alone defended the citadel of religious faith against the attacks of a materialistic and positivistic naturalism, is conceded even by its foes.[2] For it the claim may, therefore, fairly be made that it is the type of philosophy with which Christian thought most naturally allies itself at the present time.

The personalistic attitude toward the religious problem has four characteristic features. First, personalism maintains the uniqueness and independence of religion, or, in other words, its autonomous validity. Second, it distinguishes so clearly and sharply between science and religion that logically there is and can be no real conflict between them. Third, it holds that religion necessarily has its philosophical implications and that these implications can be shown to be better grounded logically and otherwise than those of any competing world-view. Fourth, it regards religion as something richer and deeper than its philosophical content, and hence rejects the idea that there can ever be a rationalistic substitute for historic Christianity. The latter implies and receives powerful support from philosophical theism but can never be displaced by it. Its own unique doctrines stand in their own right.

Of these characteristic features of the personalistic

<hr>

[2] See R. B. Perry, *Present Philosophical Tendencies*, p. 192.

view of religion it is the third with which we are chiefly concerned in this chapter. What we here in the main aim to do is to expound and evaluate from the personalistic standpoint the various arguments in support of the two cardinal beliefs of religion, the belief in God and the belief in immortality. But a brief preliminary statement should be made with reference to the other points.

The autonomous validity of religion follows naturally from the apriorism of personalism and from its assumption that life is deeper than logic. If the universal vital interests of men are deeper and more controlling than the theoretical reason, it may fairly be concluded that they are in their essential nature independent of it, and that religion, for instance, does not derive its right to exist from the intellect. It stands in its own right; and this right is not a freak of nature. It is as valid as the *a priori* principles of thought. Empiricists, it is true, have denied the existence of such principles, but in the very act of denying them they have assumed them. Without logical norms there could be no rational thought. And as norms are required and assumed by the theoretical reason, so also is it in the field of art, of morals and of religion. There is a religious *a priori* as well as a theoretical *a priori;* that is, the human need or capacity, expressed in religion, is not an accident of human development but is structural in the human reason or spirit as such, and consequently, carries its validity in itself. Religious experience, in other words, is as ultimate as any form of experience; and since it is such, it can neither be created nor destroyed by logic. The function of logic is regulative, not constitutive. It may and should guide the development of our fundamental instincts, but it can neither call them into being nor eliminate them.   They are given to us; we do not make them, we find them. This is as true of religion as of any other basal interest or structural principle of the human mind.   There is, therefore, an *a priori* presupposition in favor of its validity.   To cast doubt upon its trustworthiness would be to discredit all the higher faiths of men.   Religion may then be accepted as autonomously valid.

This position with reference to religion is logically impregnable.   The only possible way in which it could be refuted would be by the permanent decay of the religious sentiment.   And when this comes, if it ever does, there will not be enough interest in religion left even to raise a serious question as to its truth.   Religion in the last analysis justifies itself, and apart from this self-justification every attempted proof of it is formal and empty. Vital religious experience is the presupposition of every effective apologetic.   What gives dynamic to all argument in defense of religion is the unreasoned faith that lies back of it. This does not mean that such argument is necessarily valueless. F. H. Bradley has said that "metaphysics is the finding of bad reasons for what we believe upon instinct."   "But," he added, "to find these reasons is no less an instinct."[3]   Religion, in spite of its instinctive character and its autonomous validity, needs intellectual defense; and this need itself is instinctive.   The whole history of theology is evidence of this fact.   Nevertheless, it is important to recognize the truth that religion is so deeply grounded in human nature or in the human reason that it is as fully justified in validating itself as is the perceptual or the logical faculty.   In elaborating this posi-

---

[3] *Appearance and Reality*, p. xiv.

tion personalism has rendered an important service to religious apologetics.

The second characteristic, above noted, of the personalistic treatment of the religious problem was its sharp distinction between the province of religion and that of science and its contention that, when this distinction is properly understood, there is no valid ground for conflict between them. The distinction here referred to is that between phenomenal and ontological reality. The long warfare between science and theology, which has been creditable to neither side and has been a particularly humiliating chapter in the history of the church, has been due largely to a failure to understand this distinction or to appreciate its significance. If both scientists and theologians had understood that science is by its very nature confined to the phenomenal realm and that religion by its nature is concerned simply with the ultimate power and purpose that lie back of phenomena, most of the conflicts between them in the past would have been avoided. It was the philosophical unpreparedness of both groups that led to the struggle between them. This was particularly evident in the debate of fifty years or so ago, occasioned by the Darwinian theory of evolution, and holds true also of the recent belated and benighted controversy between "Fundamentalists" and "Modernists." In this connection it is worthy of note that the large religious communion with which Bowne was identified has been almost entirely free from this controversy while some of its leading sister communions have been well-nigh rent asunder by it. This striking fact is due in large part to Bowne's influence, which because of his long connection with Boston University has been much greater within his own denomination than elsewhere. He perhaps more

clearly than any man of his generation saw the real difficulty facing the popular religious thought of his day and
dealt in a fundamental and conclusive way with it.   For
anyone who sat at his feet or studied his books the conflict between science and religion became a thing of the
past.

The fourth point we mentioned in our analysis of the
personalistic attitude toward religion was the preference
shown for historical Christianity over its rationalistic
substitutes.   This preference is characteristic of personalism only to a limited degree.   It holds as against the
Hegelian tendency to depersonalize the Absolute and to
find the essence of Christianity in a principle rather than
in a Person.   Personalism is unequivocally in accord with
the faith of the church insofar as the latter insists on the
personality of God and on the view that the highest revelation of divine truth is to be found in the person of Christ
rather than in his oral teaching.   The magic word "personality," by virtue of the new insight it gives us into
the nature of reality and into the conditions of knowledge, binds together historical Christianity and the personalistic philosophy.   But while this is true, it is also
true that personalism is a modernist movement.   It stands
intimately related to the latest and most significant developments of modern speculative thought.   It is charged
throughout with the spirit of modernity, and as such cannot but be out of harmony with certain aspects of traditional Christianity. The point at which conservative criticism is particularly leveled is the exclusiveness or impervi-
ousness of personality, as taught by personal idealists.
This, it is urged, is out of accord with the deep strain of
mysticism that runs through historical Christianity, and
also at variance with its cardinal doctrines, such as the

Trinity, the Incarnation, and the Atonement. That this criticism has some justification is not to be denied. The older Christian theology and older type of Christian experience were closely bound up with metaphysical realism or universalism, and to sever this bond would naturally have a disturbing effect upon them. But it is at least an open question whether the essential truth in them cannot be conserved as well or even better on the present personalistic than on the older realistic basis. This, however, is a subject to which I shall revert for fuller discussion toward the close of the chapter.

Here I wish simply to direct attention to the fact that personalism recognizes the distinction between philosophical theism and the Christian faith or between what used to be called Natural Theology[4] and Revealed Theology. It does not seek to reduce Christianity to the dimensions of a theistic philosophy. This charge might perhaps be brought with some justice against such a personalist as Renouvier. But the great body of personalists see in the Christian faith something which transcends their own personalism. They recognize in it a unique content that owes its origin to revelation or history or some other extralogical source. But this unique content and its doctrinal formulation they refuse to regard as so super-

---

[4] The term "Natural Theology" did not originate by way of contrast with Revealed Theology. It may be traced back to Marcus Terentius Varro, a contemporary of Cicero, who distinguished three kinds of theology: "poetical," "civil," and "natural." "Poetical theology" had to do with the stories or myths related by the poets concerning the gods, and "civil theology" with the cultus prescribed by the state. Neither was concerned with the truth of religion. That was the field of "Natural" or philosophical theology. The contrast with "Revealed Theology" did not arise until the mediæval period. The earliest book to bear the title "Natural Theology" seems to have been written by the late Spanish schoolman, Raymond of Sebonde, who died about 1434. See C. C. J. Webb, *Studies in the History of Natural Theology*, pp. 9, 18.

rational that it lies completely beyond the range of the human intellect and is to be accepted simply on the ground of external authority. This viewpoint was introduced by Albertus Magnus and Thomas Aquinas in the thirteenth century, when the official philosophy of the church changed from Platonism to Aristotelianism. The Aristotelian philosophy assigned to the human reason a more limited range than did the Platonic. It restricted its activity to abstraction and generalization based on sense-data. But reason so restricted could not justify the unique doctrines of Christianity. Hence another basis had to be found for them, and thus arose the distinction between Revealed Theology, based on authority, and Natural Theology, based on reason. This distinction was carried over into Protestant dogmatics, and down to comparatively recent times was generally accepted by orthodox theologians.

Before the time of Albert and Thomas it was, of course, recognized that there was a distinction between philosophy and Christian theology in the narrower sense of the term. But the latter, though more directly based on revelation than the former, was still regarded as a rational science. Anselm, for instance, sought to prove the doctrines of the Trinity and the Incarnation in the same way that he sought to establish the existence of God, namely by "reason." He thus accorded to reason a wider scope than did the Aristotelians, and so did the Platonists in general. It is to this broader Platonic standpoint that personalism reverts. It recognizes the unique content of the Christian faith and allows it a place of pre-eminent importance in the human quest after truth, but it declines to admit that it is immune to rational criticism or entirely beyond the reach of rational construction. The distinctive doctrines of the church grew originally out of attempts to construe rationally the mysteries of the divine grace, and since they had such an origin they are, of course, open to criticism and to revision. There is no inner core of Christian teaching so different from the general body of religious truth that it rests upon an entirely different basis and is to be accepted on totally different grounds. The distinction between Natural and Revealed Theology in its old form thus vanishes. All theology is from one point of view revealed, and from another point of view it is natural. But this by no means cancels the uniqueness and supreme worth of the Christian revelation. Religion is an historical growth, and to attempt to displace the positive forms in which it has manifested itself in the past by some sort of philosophical theism would be absurd.

But while personalism is thus favorable to historical Christianity it is itself primarily interested in the philosophical foundation of religion in general. This is the third of the four characteristics of the personalistic attitude toward religion above mentioned, and from our point of view the most significant. In this respect personalism represents a reaction against the agnostic tendency of much post-Kantian thought and a return to the Platonic and Aristotelian tradition. Both in theological and philosophical circles it has been widely assumed that Kant completely destroyed the traditional arguments for the divine existence and that to repeat them any further is a sign of a belated intelligence. But this assumption is hasty and superficial. No doubt the traditional theistic arguments attempted to prove too much, and none of them were demonstrations in the strict sense of the term. But they still had their value, and are of permanent worth.

Kant was right in according primacy to the practical reason, and it may with good ground be maintained that the religious argument should be based chiefly upon it. But to institute a sharp and radical distinction between the theoretical and the practical reason and to insist that religion must be based exclusively on the latter, is to do violence to the unity of human nature. What the heart requires and what the head affirms cannot be matters of mutual indifference; they must ultimately conform to each other. And if so, it is evident that the Platonic-Aristotelian attempt to ground the belief in God and immortality in the intellect as well as in conscience cannot be mistaken. In any case this is the position taken by personalism, and to its treatment of the theistic argument we now pass.

Kant, as is well known, reduced the arguments for the divine existence drawn from the speculative reason to three: the ontological, the cosmological, and the physico-theological or teleological. To these he added, and laid chief stress upon, the argument drawn from our moral nature. This classification has commonly been accepted since his day, and much can be said in support of it. But it seems to me that the cosmological and teleological arguments are at bottom one, since they are both based upon the same principle, namely, that of causality. It also seems to me that by putting the speculative arguments in a class by themselves Kant distinguished too sharply between them and the moral or practical argument. Hence I venture to suggest another classification, one that is somewhat simpler and more comprehensive. All the theistic arguments, including the practical, I should group under three heads: the conceptual, the causal, and the valuational. The first of these corresponds roughly with the ontological argument, the second with the cosmological and physico-theological, and the third with the moral. Of these three arguments it is worth noting that the first flourished under Platonic influence and was perhaps emphasized most in the period down to 1200 A. D.; that the second was supported by the Aristotelian philosophy and was most prominent from the thirteenth to the eighteenth centuries; and that the third was put into the foreground by Kant and has on the whole maintained that position since his time. These arguments, however, are not mutually exclusive. They, rather, imply each other, and as a matter of fact all of them have coexisted since the time of Plato. They have simply been emphasized differently by different types of philosophy, and hence we have the three stages in the history of theistic thought to which I have just referred. We now pass to a study of each of these arguments in the light of its historical development.

THE CONCEPTUAL ARGUMENT

This argument is bound up with Platonic realism. It received its purest and most famous expression in the ontological proof which we owe to Anselm (d. 1109). Although the most abstract of all, this proof was the first to be clearly and sharply formulated. It is, at least in its intention, a purely *a priori* argument. It takes no account of experience or of the existence of other things or beings. Out of the bare idea of God it seeks to deduce his existence. The form of the argument is familiar. God is defined as "a being than which nothing greater can be conceived." But "that, than which nothing greater can be conceived, cannot exist in the understanding alone. For, suppose it exists in the understanding alone: then it can be conceived to exist in reality; which is greater.

Therefore, if that, than which nothing greater can be conceived, exists in the understanding alone, the very being, than which nothing greater can be conceived, is one, than which a greater can be conceived. But obviously this is impossible. Hence, there is no doubt that there exists a being, than which nothing greater can be conceived, and it exists both in the understanding and in reality."[5] This argument may be reduced to the simple statement that the idea of the perfect implies its existence. That God exists is an analytic judgment. It is involved in the definition of God, and hence is a necessary truth of reason. One could not, said Descartes, conceive of a supremely perfect being without attributing existence to him any more than one could conceive a mountain without a valley.[6] The very concept we have of God contains in itself the proof that he exists.

Of this proof, if it may be called such, Bowne says that it does not possess a shadow of cogency. All that it does is to point out that the idea of the perfect, if it is to be self-consistent, must include the idea of existence, but that the self-consistent idea represents an objective reality is not and cannot be proved by a mere analysis of the idea. Between idea and reality there is a gulf which mere logic cannot bridge. Reality is revealed to us only in experience, and apart from experience there is nothing substantial on which thought can lay hold. Thought is purely formal. By virtue of its categories it gives us the framework within which reality must be conceived. But the concreteness and individuality of being, without which

[5] Anselm's *Proslogium*, chap. ii. Translation by Sidney Norton Deane. Reprinted by permission of The Open Court Publishing Company.
[6] *Meditations*, v.

there would be nothing real, is given to us only in experience. There is, therefore, and can be no high *a priori* road leading from idea to reality. This applies to the idea of God as well as to every other idea. From reality as revealed in experience we may proceed to the idea of a perfect being; but this is a one-way road. We cannot travel in the reverse direction. Even if we could prove that the idea of God is as necessary and as universal as a category of thought, we would not have translated it into reality, for the categories are simply the formal conditions of thought. In and of themselves they are devoid of content. And so also it would be with the idea of God without the filling furnished by experience. The idea as idea would simply express an abstract possibility. The objective existence of the corresponding reality cannot by any wizardry of logic be extracted from it. Thought apart from experience is necessarily shut up within itself. Struggle and agonize as it may, it cannot leap across the chasm that separates it from the metaphysically real. This limitation it may itself be loth to accept. It may protest against it, as it does in an extreme form in the ontological argument. But the protest is vain. Reality remains external to formal thought, and since this is so, it is possible to conceive of the perfect Being, even though he be a necessity of thought, as nonexistent. There can, therefore, be no purely conceptual proof of the divine existence.

But while this is clear and decisive from the personalistic point of view, it is nevertheless true that the ontological argument has had a notable history. Though rejected by Thomas Aquinas, it was revived by Descartes and Leibnitz, and then after its repudiation by Kant,

Hegel sought again to rehabilitate it, declaring it to be the only true proof.[7] It has thus appealed to some of the greatest intellects in the world's history, and the question, consequently, arises as to how this could be. In seeking an answer to this question we are led back to Platonic realism, out of which the ontological argument grew and of which it is the most important product. The argument itself was original with Anselm. It is not to be found in Plato or in any of the Neoplatonists. But whatever cogency it has had it derived from its realistic background. Indeed, it is its Platonic presuppositions that alone make it really intelligible. And here it is that we meet with the conceptual argument in the broader sense of the term.

The difference between the Anselmic and the broader form of the conceptual argument is found in their relation to experience and to the principle of causality. Anselm took no account of the world of experience. He did not in any way make it the basis of his argument. He simply disregarded it. Clement of Alexandria complained of some of the philosophizing of his day that it "touched earth with only one foot,"[8] but Anselm did not even do that. He kept aloof from the earth altogether, arguing from the mere idea of an absolute Being to its existence. Actually he had acquired the idea of God from his religious faith and from what might be called the cosmological argument, but having once acquired it he kicked away the scaffolding by means of which he had attained to it and tried to make the idea itself self-sufficient. This *a priori* method had its root in the Platonic theory of

---

[7] *Lectures on the Philosophy of Religion*, iii, p. 361.
[8] Quoted by Charles Bigg, *The Christian Platonists of Alexandria*, p. 94.

Ideas. Ideas, or concepts, according to Plato, were real, but they were not real, so to speak, in their own right alone. They stood in more or less of a causal or constitutive relation to material phenomena, and it was through this relation that their existence was revealed to men. The ideas as such did not carry with them their own objective reality. They might exist apart from things, but this independent existence on their part was an inference from sense experience. It was their embodiment in the sensible world that led to the affirmation that there was a realm of immaterial ideas. The argument by which this conclusion was reached was thus of the cosmological rather than the strictly ontological type.

But there is an important difference between this form of the cosmological argument and that which we will consider later under what I call the causal argument. The principle of causality was involved in the Platonic and Neoplatonic theory of ideas, but it did not in that connection come to clear and independent expression. It was to a large extent identified with the principle of logical subordination. Reality was ascribed to concepts according to the degree of their generality, and then as a sort of afterthought they were represented as causes. The causal principle was thus quite secondary, a kind of appendix to metaphysical conceptualism. What gave reality to the ideas was primarily their universality, not their causal agency. The latter was, rather, an inference from their reality than a constitutive element of it. Hence causes were thought of as descending in efficacy as they descended in generality. According to the principle of logical subordination, the greater the universality of an idea the greater was its reality; and with this the causal

principle was made to conform.[9]   It was for this reason
also that individual things were represented, not as
the effects of ideas, but as "participating" in them.
F. M. Cornford has attempted to explain the
Platonic idea of "participation" (*methexis*) by the
theory that the Ideas were originally group-souls and that
as such they communicated themselves to the individual
members of the group who in their mystery-rites partook
of or "participated" in them.[10]   But whatever may be said
of the theory that Plato's ideas were simply desiccated
group-souls, it is evident that he himself, insofar as he
gave any definite meaning to the term at all, interpreted
"participation" in a logical sense.   The individual participated in the Idea in the same way that the particular
participates in the universal.   And this was also the prevailing view in Neoplatonism, though more or less of the
mystical was intermingled with it.   It is for this reason
that I apply the term "conceptual," rather than the term
"causal," to that more or less indefinite argument for the
divine existence which before the time of Anselm was
connected with the Platonic theory of ideas.

In this general conceptual argument we may distinguish several lines of thought which were more or less
directly connected with the more specific ontological argument.   One of these we have already dwelt upon.   It is
that universality and reality are terms of parallel import.
The more universal an idea is, the more real it also is. It
follows from this that God as the most universal and,
indeed, absolutely universal Being must be the most real,
indeed, the absolutely real Being, the *ens realissimum.*

---

[9] Compare Thomas Whittaker, *The Neo-Platonists*, pp. 170ff.
[10] *From Religion to Philosophy*, p. 254.

It was this presupposition that lay back of the Anselmic argument and constituted its true rationale.

From this universalistic conception of reality it also followed that there is a logical gradation of being from more to most or, in the realm of value, from better to best. The existence of the imperfect points, therefore, to the existence of the best. We find this argument for a Supreme Good or God in Augustine,[11] and it is also attributed to Aristotle, who is reported as saying, "Where there is a better, there is a best; now among existing things one is better than another; therefore there is a best, which must be divine." In fact, this line of thought is implied in the Aristotelian distinction between matter and form or potentiality and actuality. Beings are all graded according to the relative degree of form and actuality embodied in them, and this, when logically carried out, leads to pure form or pure actuality at the apex of the universe. The argument is not wholly *a priori*. It presupposes the world. But it is based on a conceptual analysis of the existing order rather than on the principle of causality, and so bears a certain kinship to the ontological proof, indeed is presupposed by it.

A somewhat more specific form of the conceptual argument appears in Augustine's epistemological application of it. This was his most characteristic theistic proof. It consisted in pointing out that there are certain fundamental ideas and laws of thought common to all minds, and that this community of thought can be accounted for only on the assumption that there is a universal Truth, in which all individual minds share and in whose Light the intelligible world is revealed to reason in much the

11 *De Trinitate*, viii, iii, 4, 5.

same way that the sensible world is made manifest to the eye. The human mind cannot be its own light. For its source of illumination it must turn to a supreme Being, who is himself the Truth and the Light. Apart from such a being the light that is in us might be darkness, and in any case its community would be wholly unintelligible. The validity of reason thus requires the existence of God, who as the supreme Reason imparts himself to all finite minds. Back of this line of thought lies no doubt the ancient assumption that the human mind in the knowing process is passive, but more important than this assumption is the implied conceptual view of reality. Augustine fails to distinguish between truth as a general concept and truth as objectively real. For him "to be true is the same as to be."[12] The idea of Truth implies its reality.

Akin to this Augustinian argument, though developed in a somewhat different way, was Descartes' attempt to justify the ontological proof on the ground that the idea of the Infinite requires the Infinite as its source or cause.[13] The founder of modern philosophy here apparently transforms the conceptual argument into a causal argument, but it is only apparently that he does so. For he conceives of causality in the Neoplatonic fashion. It is a relation of "participation" or "imitation." The effect is contained in the cause in much the same way as the particular in the universal. It is determined in its inner being by it, and resembles it, though imperfectly. Hence an idea such as that of the Infinite, which lies beyond our own imaginative or creative power to produce, must have as its cause a being which has in it at least as much of perfection as is contained in the idea viewed from the

[12] *De Trinitate*, viii, 2.
[13] *Meditation*, iii.

standpoint of its objective reference. The idea itself thus serves, "as it were, for the mark of the workman impressed on his work." It is this Neoplatonic or conceptual interpretation of causality that alone gives any cogency to Descartes' supplement to the ontological proof. The idea of the Infinite as effect no more requires the existence of the Infinite than it does as pure concept. If the latter is invalid, so also is the former.

The foregoing analysis of the conceptual argument has made it clear that there were certain elements in Platonic realism that led naturally to the ontological proof in its Anselmic form. If universals are real and if there is a logical gradation of being from the lowest to the highest, it is evident that the most universal and the most perfect concept must not only be real but must represent the highest degree of reality. But these assumptions have no valid basis. We have repeatedly pointed out the error in them. They fail to take adequate account of the subjective element in thought and the objective element in reality. The classifying processes of our thought have no double in reality. The analysis of ideas and their logical arrangement do not necessarily give us true metaphysical insight. No doubt our thought must be valid for reality, if knowledge is to be possible at all. But this does not mean that our general ideas and our logical analyses have their counterparts in reality, nor does it mean that thought so completely apprehends the real object that the two are virtually identical with each other. It is at this point that much of ancient rationalism and much of modern idealism has erred, and it is this error that has made possible the ontological argument. This argument, as C. C. J. Webb says, is "the concentrated ex-

pression of confidence in the power of thought to apprehend reality as it is in itself." The ancient and mediæval
rationalist did not deny to reality a certain externality
to and independence of thought, but he failed to recognize the large subjective element in our thinking. He
naïvely assumed that the parallelism between thought and
thing is so complete that the analytic processes of thought
have their counterpart in the objective order. Hence it
seemed to him possible to pass from the bare idea to
existence itself. Reality, while other and more than
thought, was regarded as so open to thought as to be in
a sense embraced within it. There was, consequently, no
inherent difficulty in passing with apodictic certainty from
reason to reality.

The modern absolute idealist has been still bolder. He
has denied outright the otherness of reality, thus not only
bringing it within the range of thought but identifying
it with thought. This position is known as epistemological monism. We have already discussed it at some
length.[14] If sound, it would justify the ontological proof.
Hegel's attempt to rehabilitate the latter is, therefore, not
strange. "The Notion," he said, "and still more the absolute Notion, the Notion-in-and-for-itself, the Notion
of God, is to be taken for itself, and this Notion contains
Being as a determinate characteristic."[15] Between notion
and being there is thus no line of division. The middle
wall of separation between them is broken down. The
two are one. The idea of the perfect not only points to
or implies its existence, but is itself the objectively real
and perfect being. This idealistic identification of idea

---

[14] See chap. ii, subsection entitled "The Dualism of Thought and
Thing."
[15] *The Philosophy of Religion*, iii, p. 355.

and reality marks an advance beyond the older form of
the ontological argument, but the principle underlying it
is the same. Reason is the key to reality; it either completely mirrors it or is identical with it. The objections
to the latter view we have already stated. It fails to account for the dualism in our human knowing, it founders
on the problem of error, it offers no explanation of the
given element in experience, and it is blind to the unique
objectivity of reality. In modern absolute idealism with
its epistemological monism we consequently find a no
more satisfactory justification of the ontological proof
than in the extreme form of ancient and mediæval rationalism with its implicit epistemological dualism. The
decisive objections to this proof are to be found in the
undeniable subjective element in human thought and in
the unique objective element in real existence as implied
in its necessary concreteness and individuality.

What the mediæval rationalist and the modern absolute idealist have aimed at is clear enough. They have
wanted to translate the subjective certainty of religious
faith into a logical demonstration of the divine existence.
But in this they have attempted the impossible. If reality
is truly objective and individual, there is no way of
reaching it except by an act of faith. But in view of
this it may seem strange that Leibnitz, the individualist,
should have indorsed the ontological argument. The explanation is that he endeavored to combine his individualism with a thoroughgoing rationalism, and that
it was in the latter that he found the basis of his
a priori proof. "Truths of fact" he regarded as
ultimately reducible to "truths of reason"; but in taking this position he virtually, though not intentionally, re-

nounced his metaphysical individualism. The latter doctrine implies that reality is something other and deeper than thought, and from this point of view it is manifestly impossible ever to identify the two or to throw a logical bridge from thought to reality. Only faith can leap across the gulf that separates them. It alone is "saltatory"; logic is necessarily "ambulatory."

Personalism, consequently, rejects the ontological proof, but not without recognizing certain elements of truth in it and in the broader conceptual argument. First, as Lotze pointed out, there is in the human mind a deep, irrepressible faith in the reality of its ideals, and it is this faith that lies at the foundation of the ontological proof. With us "it is an immediate certainty that what is greatest, most beautiful, most worthy is not a mere thought, but must be a reality, because it would be intolerable to believe of our ideal that it is an idea produced by the action of thought but having no existence, no power, and no validity in the world of reality. . . . If what is greatest did not *exist,* then what is *greatest* would not be, and it is impossible that that which is the greatest of all conceivable things should *not* be."[16]   Eduard von Hartmann in his critique of Lotze's philosophy dismissed this consideration as a mere personal feeling on Lotze's part and devoid of any philosophical significance. But the point is not one that can be so easily disposed of. Immediate faith in the ideal is not peculiar to any individual or group of individuals but is structural in human nature[17] and

---

[16] *Microcosmus,* ii, 670.

[17] Lotze assumes the validity of the argument made prominent by the Stoics, the *consensus gentium.* Indeed, he virtually transforms the ontological proof into the Stoic argument. There is, however, this difference that he based his conclusion on an analysis of human nature rather than on the universality of the belief in God.

constitutes the real driving power in the higher life of the soul. It cannot be logically deduced from experience, and it is a mistake to attempt to give it a demonstrable logical form, as the ontological proof does. But it is nevertheless a great and significant human fact, which no serious inquiry into the conditions of knowledge can disregard. It grows out of the assumption that the human mind stands in an organic relation to the universe and is at home in it; and thus viewed it may be regarded as the, presupposition of our entire spiritual life. Though incapable of demonstration, it is everywhere implied. But when reduced to this faith, the ontological proof, it is evident, ceases to be a "conceptual" argument and becomes a form of the valuational argument.

Augustine, as we have seen, sought to deduce the existence of God from the conception of truth. Truth, he argued, is common to many minds and hence must be an objective reality in which we share. Only on this basis can our thought be valid. But so conceived, Truth is identical with God. Therefore, God exists. In this form the argument presupposes Platonic realism and is fallacious. But put in a different way it is both valid and weighty. Truth for us requires a parallelism of the thought series and the thing series, but such a parallelism can be accounted for only on the basis of a theistic monism. If an intelligent Being created finite minds in his own image and also cast things in the mould of thought, the harmony between them is intelligible, but otherwise no explanation of it is possible. Knowledge, therefore, if it is to be rationally accounted for, requires the existence of God.

Underlying Platonic realism was the conviction that

the intelligibility of the world is not extraneous to it but is structural within it. Hence the ideas which express the rationality of the world were said to be "real," and intelligence was thus carried into reality itself. The particular form in which this conclusion or conviction was expressed is, as we have frequently pointed out, untenable. But the conviction itself is sound. The intelligibility of the world requires that there be intelligence in the world or back of it. Speech has meaning only insofar as it is the expression of an intelligent being. Apart from that it would be mere noise. And so it is with the world. It has meaning and is intelligible, simply because it expresses the thought of a thinker.[18] Without that assumption "all is opacity and darkness."

Again, we have seen how the Platonist by his reflections on the permanence of the real was led to the conclusion that only ideas are truly real and that the supreme reality is to be found in the Idea of the Good or the perfect Idea. The considerations adduced in support of this conclusion we have found defective. And the conclusion itself leaves us with an abstract and vague notion of what reality is. Reality must no doubt be permanent, but it must also provide for change. It must not only be One, it must also produce the many. It must be causal and active. But how can it be active and change and yet be identical with itself? Nothing in the Idea itself can solve this problem. But if we rise above the Idea to the plane of personality, we have a solution. Here

[18] It may be a matter of interest to note that the very last sentence written or dictated by Professor Bowne for publication was a statement of this truth: "The problem of knowledge implies thought at both ends—thought at the further end to make nature the bearer of meanings, and thought at the nearer end to receive and rethink the meaning." See the *Methodist Review*, May, 1922, p. 369.

unity and plurality, identity and change, permanence and causality are all combined in the experience of free intelligence. On the impersonal plane such a combination is impossible. The personal, and it only, is, therefore, truly real. The analysis of the idea of reality leads to this conclusion.

We thus see that there are in the old conceptual argument important elements of truth that in one way or another are conserved in modern personalism. The ontological proof is logically invalid, but lying back of it as its driving force is the mind's instinctive faith in the reality of the ideal. This faith is implicit in the entire life of the soul. The validity of knowledge does not require the objective existence of an absolute Truth in which our minds in some mystical way participate, but it does require a parallelism of thought and thing which can be provided for only by a theistic monism. The intelligibility of the world does not imply that ideas are objectively real in the same way that things are supposed to be, but it does imply that there is a thinker back of the meaning or ideas expressed in the world. The notion of reality is not satisfied by the mere element of permanence that the ideas of reason have as over against the passing phenomena of sense, but this idealistic conception of the real is an important step in the direction of that profounder insight which sees in the concrete life of the spirit the one true type of reality. There are thus certain concepts, such as that of reality, of the intelligibility of the world, and of the validity of knowledge, which, when thought through, require the idea of God. But these concepts are all mediated by experience and presuppose the world. Only faith can leap from the ideal to the real.

The Causal Argument

There are two different ways of viewing the world. We may regard it either as an expression of meaning or as an effect produced by a cause. In the former case we put back of it the divine intelligence, and in the latter case the divine will. It is this fact that lies back of and constitutes the difference betwen the conceptual and the causal arguments. The conceptual argument does not necessarily ignore the world. In its extreme "ontological" form it seeks to do so, but in its broader and more general form it takes its start from the world. What it does is simply to direct attention to the meaning expressed by the world, to its intelligibility and what is implied in it. It does not exclude the causal principle. It, rather, assumes it. But it subordinates it to the logical connection of ideas. It gives to it an intellectualistic interpretation. It talks about "participation" and "imitation" more than about causal efficiency, and when it speaks of the latter it is rather in a derived sense. The reality of the ideas comes first. Their causal power is more or less of an inference from their reality, it is not regarded as constitutive of it. It is for this reason that the conceptual argument is to be distinguished from the causal argument. The latter stresses the world as a fact, as an existence, as an effect, which as such requires the divine will for its explanation. The divine will does not, of course, exclude the divine reason but it is something other and more than the mere logical or rational connection of ideas. It involves a dynamic element, and this element transcends the purely conceptual plane. It introduces us to the realm of causal self-determination which is the realm of true ontological reality. In this sense the causal argument is deeper than the conceptual argument. Indeed, without it we would not be able to pass from the world of appearance to that of reality. We affirm ontological reality because we need a causal ground of the phenomenal order. A purely conceptual world would be static. It would provide for no motion and account for no change. It is only as dynamic agency is surreptitiously introduced into it that such a world can be given even the semblance of an adequate explanation of the existing order. And it is only in this way also that it can escape the charge of being a barren abstraction. Ultimate reality must be causal, or the very idea of such a reality must be rejected as superfluous. At bottom the theistic argument is, therefore, necessarily a causal argument.

The causal argument has taken two main forms, the cosmological and the physico-theological or teleological. The distinction that Kant draws between these is that the first rests on "indefinite experience only, that is, on any sort of existence empirically given," while the second takes its start "from definite experience and the special constitution of the sense-world thus revealed to us."[19] In other words, the cosmological argument is based on the bare fact of the world's existence, while the physico-theological argument has to do with such concrete features of the world as its orderliness, the apparent design in it, the existence of finite minds, and other facts that point to an intelligent Author. The line of demarcation between the two arguments, however, is not one that can be sharply maintained. For the bare existence of the world is an empty abstraction apart from the concrete forms in

---

[19] *Critique of Pure Reason,* p. 476.

which it manifests itself.   The cosmological argument consequently tends to pass over into the physico-theological, or at least to include elements that belong in it, such as the fact of order.   Whether it is worth while trying to maintain the distinction between the two arguments is open to question.   Bowne rejected the traditional classification as "unedifying."   In its place he put, first, the argument for the unity of the world ground, and, second, the argument for its intelligence.   The latter he divided into an inductive argument, based on the fact of order, of design, and of the existence of finite intelligence, and a speculative argument, based on epistemological and metaphysical considerations.   He then dealt separately with the question of the personality of God and his ethical character.   This method of presenting the theistic argument has manifest advantages over that current in the past.   But the two methods are not entirely out of harmony with each other; and from the historical point of view it will help to an understanding of the causal argument, if we retain the traditional distinction between its cosmological and its teleological form.

In view of what has been said of the relation of the conceptual argument to Platonic realism, it may seem a little strange to be now told that the causal argument also is to be traced back to Plato.   Indeed, the realistic conception of ideas was not employed by Plato himself as a theistic proof.   It had that significance for later thinkers, but for him the "Ideas" or "Forms" were external or objective to God.   God used them as patterns in the making of heaven and earth, and so in a sense they were metaphysically prior to himself.   So far as he himself was concerned, Plato thought of him primarily in causal terms. He was a soul, and soul for Plato meant "motion that moves itself." God was thus the great self-mover, "the eldest and mightiest principle of change," "the origin and beginning of motion." The only direct proof that Plato anywhere offers of the divine existence is essentially what I have called the causal argument.[20] In it he assumes that everything must have a cause, that there cannot be an infinite regress in the causal series, and that the cosmic movements as a whole are orderly. These assumptions, when thought through, lead logically to the conclusion that there is an original or first cause of the world—a self-moving soul—and that this soul is "good" in the sense that it is the source of the order and providential arrangement of the cosmos. The argument, as presented by Plato, contains elements of both the cosmological and teleological proofs. Though developed only once in a formal way in his writings, there can be no doubt, as John Burnet has said, that he himself regarded it as of vital importance and as expressing the central thing in his philosophy.[21]

It is customary to connect the cosmological proof more directly with Aristotle than Plato; and it is true not only that Aristotle elaborated the argument more fully than Plato but that it was the revival of Aristotelianism in the thirteenth century that led to its more precise formulation by the scholastics and its adoption by them as the chief theistic proof. Aristotle expounds the argument at considerable length both in the eighth book of his *Physics* and in the twelfth book of his *Metaphysics*. He agrees with Plato in distinguishing between communicated and original motion and in regarding the soul as the one

[20] *Laws*, book x.
[21] *Greek Philosophy*, p. 335.

source of the latter. But he is not able to accept the idea
of self-motion as ultimate. He analyzes it and finds that,
if taken in an absolute way, it is self-contradictory. For
motion, he held, means change from potentiality to actuality, and this is something that must be referred to an
external agent. The soul as self-mover would be its own
creator, and this would be a contradiction in terms. It
would imply that the soul existed as a creative agent before it really existed. Or, in Aristotelian terms, it would
imply that it was both actual and potential at the same
time and in the same respect, which would involve a formal contradiction. The soul is, therefore, not self-moving in the strict sense of the term. It has a desire for
some objective good, and thus becomes the source of motion. But the desire is not self-originated. It is due to
another and higher source, to which the soul thus comes
to stand in a potential relation. And so, again, this higher
source presupposes a yet higher, and thus, if no new principle were introduced, the regress would continue indefi-
nitely. Consequently, to escape it Aristotle held that we
must assume an ultimate unmoved mover instead of the
Platonic self-mover.

The unmoved mover is pure actuality. It awakens desire in others, but it has no desire itself. Its action is not
of the dynamic type; it does not go forth from itself and
create other beings or things. It is pure final cause, and
as such produces motion by virtue of the love it evokes;
and that which is thus moved in turn imparts motion to
other things.[22] But how this love is awakened is not
stated. Aristotle seems to endow matter with an original
capacity to respond to and struggle toward an ideal form

[22] See Aristotle, *Metaphysics*, 1072b.

of existence; and this would suggest a hylozoistic or even panpsychistic view of the world. Indeed, we read in Aristotle that "the soul is in a certain sense all things."[23] But this is not to be understood as meaning that all reality is psychical in nature. It rather means that the soul is a microcosm, mirroring the entire world. What kind of inner being, if any, Aristotle ascribed to material things is not clear. Matter with him was largely a negative and abstract conception, and the capacity for desire, attributed to it, must have been of the passive sort. It was not regarded as self-operative. It had to be evoked by a superior good, and the activity of this good again by one superior to it, and so on until the supreme good was reached, which was itself unmoved because there was nothing superior to it, but which itself was still the source of all motion. All being thus had its face directed upward except the supreme being, who could do nothing but turn his gaze upon himself. He was thus thought of as pure self-consciousness, as "a thinking of thinking," living so far as he himself was concerned in complete isolation. F. M. Cornford speaks of him as a "monistic and self-hypnotized abstraction." Both from the religious point of view and from the standpoint of efficient causality he stood unrelated to the world. The world was bound to him, but there was no reciprocal tie that united him to the world.

Such a deity manifestly fulfilled neither an adequate practical nor an adequate theoretical function. In both respects he fell far short of the Platonic deity. But this does not mean that the Aristotelian argument is in principle unsound and that it is necessarily bound up with

---

[23] *De Anima*, 431b.

such an inadequate view of God.[24] Its main contention is
that movement and change in the world must ultimately
be referred to a cause that lies outside of the physical
series itself.   In this respect it reproduces the Platonic
argument and may be accepted as valid.   It is no necessary part of the argument that the prime mover be
thought of as purely a final cause or that he be represented as entirely self-centered and devoid of interest in
the world.   These are rather excrescences that may be removed without impairing the argument.   Indeed, the
argument would be strengthened by their removal; and
this was what was done in the thirteenth century when
Aristotelianism became the philosophy of the church.   It
was then that the causal argument was first developed into
a complete theistic proof.

Aristotelianism in its original form was distinctly less
satisfactory as a religious philosophy than Platonism.
Indeed, it degenerated into a simple naturalism within
fifty years after the death of Aristotle.   It may then seem
strange that it should have triumphed over Platonism or
Neoplatonism in the mediæval period when the church
was at the height of its power.   Various reasons contributed to this result.   Of these the extrareligious were
probably the decisive ones.   The Aristotelian physics was
distinctly superior to the Neoplatonic, and its triumph
could hardly have been stayed even if the church had desired it.[25]   Theologians consequently set themselves the
task of Christianizing Aristotle, and this they did with
admirable thoroughness and success.   But in carrying
out this plan they were not simply making a virtue of

[24] On the Aristotelian argument see *"Der Alte Gottesbeweis und das
moderne Denken"* (1914), by Dr. Guill. Pletschette.
[25] Étienne Gilson, *The Philosophy of St. Thomas Aquinas*, pp. 14ff.

necessity. There were elements in Aristotelianism that served the purposes of Christian apologetics better than Neoplatonism, and of these the most fundamental and the most important was the more distinctly transcendental and causal character it ascribed to the Deity.

Neoplatonism was infected with the virus of an extreme realism. The individual was subordinated to the universal, cause was made secondary to concept, and volition to logic. The result was a marked tendency toward pantheism, against which the Christian tradition was forced to struggle. To think of God in Aristotelian terms as "the prime mover" seemed, therefore, a relief to Christian faith. It distinguished more clearly than did Neoplatonism between God and the world and tended also to accentuate the volitional and active side of his being. As "mover" God stood apart from his works. He did not, like a logical universal, embrace them; he, rather, by the exercise of his will called them into being and directed them. The original Aristotelian expression, "unmoved mover," or "prime mover," had, it is true, certain nonreligious associations. It excluded creation, productive causality on the part of the Deity, and his interest in the world. It was deistic in its implications. But these associations or refinements of the term were easily overlooked or set aside; and the term came to be accepted as virtually equivalent to the Christian idea of a Creator. Aristotelianism thus seemed to have a more distinctly theistic cast than Neoplatonism with its pantheistic leaning. This was probably the main reason why it proved more acceptable to the church as a philosophy.

With this change of philosophy it was inevitable that the theistic argument should be recast. "Cause" rather than "concept" now became the ultimate category, and in accordance with this change the theistic proof became fundamentally causal rather than conceptual. The distinction between the causal and the conceptual or logical relation was not made as clear by the mediæval Aristotelians as it ought to have been; they did not completely break away from Platonic realism. But they at least gave to the causal idea greater independence than the Neoplatonists had done. In their fundamental thinking they stressed causal agency more than they did conceptual or logical inclusiveness. This resulted naturally from the individualism and empiricism which they had inherited from Aristotle, and manifests itself clearly in the way in which they developed the theistic proof. The new form of this argument received its classic expression from Thomas Aquinas,[26] and it was in no small measure due to the weight of his influence that its predominance was established and was maintained down to the time of Kant.

Thomas explicitly rejected the ontological proof.[27] He did so on the ground that all human knowledge is derived from sense-experience, and that it is consequently impossible for us to pass from the mere idea of God to his existence. We may infer his existence from the data of experience but we cannot deduce it from any *a priori* conception that we have of him. The theistic argument must, therefore, be *a posteriori;* it must rest on the principle of causality; it must be an inference from the effects of the divine activity.

The argument, as it was analyzed and outlined by

---

[26] *Summa Theologica*, part i, Ques. ii; *Summa Contra Gentiles*, book i, chap. xiii.
[27] *Summa Contra Gentiles*, i, 10, 11.

Thomas, took five different forms.[28] The first was the argument from motion to a First Mover; the second the argument from efficient causation to a First Cause; the third the argument "from possibility or necessity," commonly known as the argument from the contingency of the world; the fourth the argument from "the gradation to be found in things," the assumption being that the existence of lower degrees of perfection implies the existence of a perfect Being; and the fifth the argument from "the governance of the world." Of these the last is the physico-theological or teleological proof, to which we shall revert later. The fourth is similar to the conceptual argument which we have already found in Augustine and Aristotle. The only difference is that Thomas stresses the causal element in the argument more than his predecessors had done. He expressly says that "what is most complete in any genus is the cause of all in that genus; as fire, which is the most complete form of heat, is the cause whereby all things are made hot. Therefore there must also be something which is to all beings the cause of their being, goodness, and every other perfection; and this we call God." But the use of the term "cause" does not really alter the character of the argument. We have here a lapse into Neoplatonic realism. The general idea is real, and the more general it is the more real it is. That it is also causal, is an inference from its reality rather than the ground of it. The causal idea is secondary. At bottom the argument is of the conceptual type.

The three remaining arguments—those from motion, efficient causation, and the contingency of the world—are all variations of the cosmological proof and contain es-

---

[28] For a good modern exposition and defense of Thomistic or scholastic theism see *Principles of Natural Theology*, by George H. Joyce, S. J.

sentially the same idea. They start with the world as manifestly an incomplete and dependent form of existence, and argue from it to the existence of an independent and self-sufficient Being. The most abstract form of the argument is the one from the contingency of the world, and this later became its typical form. But the idea of contingency, when it is thought through, implies both the ideas of "motion" and "causation," so that the three arguments amount to virtually the same thing. The world is contingent, because it is not self-existent; it is a "moving" or developing thing, and as such it cannot be its own cause. It must have a cause exterior to itself, of which it is the effect. Effect, motion, and contingency are thus practically equivalent terms; at least they denote in the cosmological argument the same general aspect of the world, its dependent character.

Thomas Aquinas assigned the first place to the argument from motion, treating the other four arguments in the *Summa Contra Gentiles*[29] as hardly more than appendices to it. This would seem to indicate that he regarded it as the most fundamental and the most convincing, though the influence of Aristotle may have had something to do with the pre-eminence given it. The argument in its Aristotelian form we have already set forth. Thomas repeats it in its essential features. "By 'motion'," he says, "we mean nothing else than the reduction of something from a state of potentiality into a state of actuality. . . . Whatever is in motion must be put in motion by another. . . . This cannot go on to infinity. . . . Therefore it is necessary to arrive at a First Mover, put in motion by no other; and this everyone understands

[29] Book i, chap. xii.

to be God."[30]   The motor power of God is not limited
by Thomas, as it apparently is by Aristotle, to that of
a final cause; but otherwise the argument presented by
both is virtually the same.   It may also be noted that
Thomas held that the difference between the Aristotelian
and Platonic conceptions of the first mover was largely
verbal.   Movement according to Aristotle did not include understanding and thinking, while with Plato it did.
Hence, says Thomas, "it makes no difference whether
with Plato we come to a first mover that moves itself,
or with Aristotle to something first which is altogether
immovable."[31]

The argument from the world as effect or from the
fact of efficient causation to a first cause is parallel to
that from motion to a first mover.   It, too, had its source
in Aristotle,[32] but it was not employed by him as a theistic argument.   Others, however, had so used it before
the time of Thomas.[33]   It marks an advance beyond the
argument from motion in that it brings out more distinctly the creative activity of God.   Here not simply the
movement of the world but its very existence is referred
to a divine agent.   This argument has at times been interpreted in a temporal sense, as though secondary causes
sufficed at present, but an infinite series of causes and
effects would be repugnant to reason and hence we must
affirm a first cause at the beginning of things.   Such an
interpretation of the argument, however, is not necessary.   Aristotle held to the eternity of the world, and

---

[30] *Summa Theologica*, part i, Ques. ii, art. 3.   Translation by the
English Dominican Fathers.
[31] *Summa Contra Gentiles*, book i, chap. xiii.
[32] *Metaphysics*, ii, 2.
[33] See Étienne Gilson, *The Philosophy of St. Thomas Aquinas*,
pp. 60f.

Thomas maintained that this view was philosophically tenable. There is nothing in the notion of a first cause that is inconsistent with the idea of eternal creation. A spring would be just as necessary to keep a watch running forever as to keep it running for a brief span of time; and so it is with the first cause in its relation to the world. It is to be sought "intensively" rather than as a temporal antecedent.

The argument from contingency rests on the distinction between the possible and the necessary. Things that come and go are only possible. They may exist or they may not. Existence is not one of their essential predicates. But if they may not exist and if everything that can cease to exist must have had a beginning, "then at one time there could have been nothing in existence." But "if this were true, even now there would be nothing in existence, because that which does not exist only begins to exist by something already existing. Therefore, if at one time nothing was in existence, it would have been impossible for anything to have begun to exist; and thus even now nothing would be in existence—which is absurd. Therefore, not all beings are merely possible, but there must exist something the existence of which is necessary."[34] If there were no self-existent or necessary being, nothing would be possible. Possibility requires as its background necessary existence of some kind and would be meaningless without it. In saying that a thing is possible or contingent we mean that it does not have the ground of its existence in itself. The sufficient reason for its being must then be found in a cause external to itself, and this cause must ultimately be self-sufficient and nec-

[34] Thomas Aquinas, *Summa Theologica*, part i, Ques. ii, art. 3. Translation by the English Dominican Fathers.

essary, if we are to escape the infinite regress. The world as contingent might be eternal but this would not obviate the necessity of a necessary being upon which it depends. The dependence is causal, and this does not necessarily involve temporal succession.

The three cosmological arguments which we have just outlined—from contingency, from causation, and from motion—are, as we have said, at bottom one. The differences between them are almost entirely verbal. "First mover," "first cause," and "necessary being" all mean essentially the same thing, and so also do the terms, "movement," "contingency," and causal dependence, applied to finite objects. The one argument, expressed in these three different ways, rests on two assumptions: the ontological validity of the causal principle and the impossibility of the infinite regress. It is taken for granted that the principle of causality is universally valid, and that it requires a completed system, an infinite regress running counter to its essential nature; and from this it is concluded that there must be an uncaused cause, an unmoved mover or a necessary being. If the assumptions are granted, as they commonly were down to the eighteenth century, the conclusion logically follows. But since the time of Hume and Kant the assumptions have been called in question. Kant rejected them both, limiting the category of causality to the phenomenal realm and denying that it could legitimately be made the basis for inferring the existence of a transcendental being.[35] This undermined the cosmological argument completely, and hence Kant repudiated it as wholly unsound. Earlier in his life he had accepted it, had treated it as "the only possible proof of the being

[35] *Critique of Pure Reason*, pp. 486ff.

of God,"[36] and had developed it in a unique way by stress-
ing the fact that the range of the possible and the very
distinction between the possible and the impossible must
have their ground in actual existence.   But all this he
later rejected under the influence of his "critical" or
"formal" rationalism.   Since the categories for him were
now simply the empty "forms" of experience, he concluded that they could not mediate the knowledge of
things-in-themselves.   Necessary being and ontological
cause of every kind, consequently, lay entirely beyond human ken. But this agnosticism has been repeatedly shown
to be inconsistent with other elements in the Kantian system and to be in itself unwarranted.   In our own self-
experience we have direct acquaintance with causal
agency, and what we find within ourselves we are justified
in seeking in the objective world.   The human mind will
not and cannot dispense with the principle of causality;
and insofar as its universal validity is recognized the cosmological argument, as presented by Thomas Aquinas,
is sound. The contingent must find its ultimate explanation in the necessary; "movement" or development points
logically to a prime mover; and "secondary" causes presuppose a first cause.

But the language employed by Thomas and others in
their exposition of the argument is to our ears strange.
"Motion" and "prime mover" had with them certain
Aristotelian associations that they now lack and without
which the argument loses much of its force.   "Contingent" and "necessary" are highly abstract terms that do
not at once convey to us the precise meaning they originally had in the argument.   "First cause" and "secondary

---

[36] The title of one of his essays, published in 1763.

causes" also had formerly connotations more or less re-
mote from our present ways of thinking. The result is
that the argument in its traditional form does not have
the cogency it once had.

Then, too, more was read into the conclusion than was
warranted by the argument itself. From the world as
contingent may be inferred a necessary being as cause.
But beyond its being uncaused nothing can logically
be deduced concerning its nature from the mere fact of
the contingency of the world. Even the conclusion that it
is One would, as Lotze said, be "an altogether arbitrary
leap." It might be conceived as consisting of independent
and self-existing atoms. Such a pluralism, it is true,
would involve serious difficulties, but it would supply the
one essential element of unconditioned being. If we are
to pass beyond this abstract conception to that of a unitary being and an *ens realissimum,* we must start with
something more than the mere contingent existence of
the world. We must assume that it is a systematic whole.
More or less surreptitiously this was done by earlier exponents of the cosmological proof. In no other way could
they have established the unity of the necessary being,
and on no other ground could they have ascribed to the
necessary being the character of the *ens realissimum.* It
is only because the necessary being is the single and sole
cause of the world, that it can be thought of as the "most
real" being. The unity of the world is, therefore, an essential element in the premise, from which the cosmological argument takes its start; and this needs to be more
distinctly recognized than it was in the past.

Furthermore, it was not only supposed that the unity
of the necessary being could be deduced from the con-

tingency of the world. The identification of this being
with the God of theism was also supposed to be warranted by the same deduction. But this is very far from
being the case. Such an identification can be effected only
by the introduction of purely valuational elements to which
no strictly logical character can properly be ascribed.
That this was not clearly recognized by the older theists,
may seem strange. One thing that no doubt blinded them
to it was the certainty with which they held the theistic
faith. So immediately was God given to them in their
Christian consciousness that the identification of him
with the *ens realissimum* or necessary being of philosophical speculation was made almost automatically. This
is evident from the way that Thomas Aquinas ends each
of his five arguments by saying, without more ado, that
everyone gives the name of God to the particular kind of
ultimate being to which each argument leads. But there
was also another reason why he and others failed to see
that they put much more into the conclusion than the cosmological argument itself warranted. In the background
of their thought lay the Platonic-Aristotelian conception
of a hierarchically ordered universe. This was more or
less axiomatic with them, as much so as the scientific conception of the reign of law is with us. They, consequently,
simply took it for granted that the ultimate being of speculation was also ethically the perfect being and hence
identical with the God of religious faith. No argument
to establish this conclusion was felt to be necessary. This
was also true of the unity of the necessary being. It also
was implicit in the Platonic-Aristotelian realism. So no
special stress needed to be placed upon it. It was assumed. Only as we bear this in mind can we understand

the range and the cogency attributed by earlier thinkers to the cosmological argument.

This fact also will help us to understand more fully the dissatisfaction of the modern world with the argument in its traditional form. The philosophical presuppositions which gave to it its rational urge have in large part been abandoned. Metaphysical individualism has been gradually supplanting the Platonic-Aristotelian realism. The sharp distinction between soul and body introduced by Descartes has to no small degree rendered obsolete the Platonic-Aristotelian conception of a logically graded order of reality, based on the distinction between form and matter. And the new scientific world view with its stress on the reign of law and efficient causation has given a quite different complexion to the unity of the world from what it had in the Platonic-Aristotelian philosophy. The bond of union is now found in dynamic determination rather than in any purely logical or teleological cement. The existence of the latter may perhaps be established by speculation, but it cannot be assumed as a self-evident truth on which to base a speculative proof of the existence of God.

In view of these significant changes in the philosophical orientation of the Western world it is not surprising that a demand arose that the cosmological proof either be abandoned or be interpreted in terms more acceptable and more convincing to the modern mind. The distinction of having worked out such a reinterpretation and reformulation of the argument belongs to Lotze. The argument, as he presents it, we have already discussed.[37] It centers about the idea of systematic interaction. Such

---

[37] See the preceding chapter, subsection entitled "Unity."

interaction is impossible between independent things. The ideas of independence and of necessary interaction contradict each other. Things that belong to an interacting system by that very fact surrender their independence. They become dependent either upon each other or upon an underlying being which mediates their interaction or of which they are modes or phases. The attempt, however, to think through a purely interdependent system, where things are mutually dependent upon each other, breaks down. There is no way of conceiving interaction as transcendent. Forces, influences, and states cannot be detached from the objects to which they belong. We must, therefore, ground all interaction in the immanent action of a co-ordinating One.

This argument has several advantages over the traditional form of the cosmological proof. First, it defines contingency more precisely by making it consist in dynamic dependence. Second, it adds the idea of systematic interaction and thus falls in line with modern science, surrendering the old conception of a logically graded scale of beings.[38] Third, it frankly recognizes that the idea of the world as an interacting system, with which it starts, is an assumption. It cannot be proved to be a fact. It is an ideal of the cognitive nature. The argument based upon it consequently cannot have the character of a demonstration. It is hypothetical in nature and theoretically leaves the door open to skepticism, but this commends it to sober critical thought rather than otherwise. Fourth, it limits itself to the establishment of a unitary

---

[38] It should, however, be noted that modern dynamism or activism does not exclude the idea of an *ens realissimum* or of different degrees of reality but, rather, implies it. This idea, from the personalistic point of view, was developed in a suggestive and helpful way by Bishop McConnell in his first book, entitled *The Diviner Immanence*.

world-ground. Here, too, its logical restraint is a source of strength. From an interacting system we may legitimately argue to a co-ordinating One. But beyond this logic does not carry us. What the nature of the One is, is left open to be determined in other ways. Hence Bowne, who here follows Lotze, makes the first stage of the theistic argument consist simply in the attempt to establish the unity of the world-ground.[39] This conclusion does not in and of itself exclude materialism or pantheism. But it does exclude positivism and pluralism, and these at present are the chief menace to a theistic world-view. To show the necessity of a unitary world-ground or of an Absolute, is, therefore, under existing conditions of thought, a vitally essential and a long step toward establishing the theistic position. And this initial step we owe to the cosmological proof in its modern Lotzean form.

The next step in the theistic argument consists in the attempt to prove the intelligence of the world-ground; and for this we turn to the physico-theological or teleological proof. This proof, like the cosmological, rests entirely upon the principle of causality. It differs from the latter, according to Kant, in that it begins with the world of concrete experience rather than with an abstract and indefinite aspect of it such as its contingency. But while this distinction holds for the arguments in their traditional form, it manifestly does not apply so clearly to them in the modified form that they have in more recent years received. The fact of an interacting system, for instance, is as concrete as is the fact of order and of

---

[39] *Theism*, pp. 44–63.

design. Indeed, an interacting system implies order. Without it interaction would be lawless. There would be no system to it, and without system there would be no need of an underlying One. The fact or facts, with which the modern cosmological and teleological arguments begin, are thus the same. The two arguments simply view the same fact or facts from different angles. The cosmological argument treats the fact of interaction from the standpoint of dynamic determination and concludes to a *unitary* Cause. The teleological argument treats the same fact, that is, the fact of order, from the standpoint of the reason or intelligence revealed in it, and hence concludes to an *intelligent* Cause. But it is the same objective fact in both cases.

One might, it is true, limit the teleological or physico-theological argument to the evidences of design in the organic world. Indeed, it has not infrequently been given a purely anthropomorphic interpretation. The world has been represented as primarily adapted in its various details to our individual convenience. Hegel, for instance, tells of someone who held that God created the corktree in order that we might have stoppers. But more commonly the teleological argument has been restricted to the unique contrivances and complex adaptations found in the organic realm. A distinction has, consequently, been made between the argument from order and that from design. We find this in Bowne. Order is cosmic, it holds in the universe as a whole. Purpose, on the other hand, appears clearly only in animate nature. With it the design argument is, therefore, more particularly concerned. But while thus distinguishing this argument from that based on the fact of cosmic order, Bowne admits that there is no sharp separation between them. The intelligence manifest in the cosmic order must be purposive. There is no such thing as a nonpurposive intelligence. Hence it is a mistake to limit the design argument to any particular class of facts. The important thing in it is the convergence of a number of different factors toward a common end; and this is essentially the same whether seen in the details of the individual organism, in the whole system of animate nature, or in the vast movement of the cosmos itself. The only difference between these realms is that purpose is more easily traceable in the first two than the last. In principle there is no difference between them.

Cosmic order, it should also be noted, is as much of an empirical fact as is the apparent design in animate nature. If, therefore, Kant is right in making the characteristic thing in the physico-theological proof the fact that it is based on *definite* experience, it is evident that the argument from order belongs to it rather than to the cosmological proof. But as indicated above the Kantian distinction between the two proofs really breaks down at this point. The true difference between them does not lie in this that one takes its start from *indefinite* and the other from *definite* experience, but, rather, in this, that one deals with those aspects of experience that point to the *unity* of the world-ground and the other with those aspects of experience that point to its *intelligence*. The three inductive arguments, consequently, that Bowne elaborates —those from order, design, and finite intelligence—are all really different phases of the one teleological proof. The essential thing in this proof is what Plato understood it to be, namely, that the intelligibility of the world and the presence of intelligence in it require for their explanation intelligence in its producing and sustaining cause. Nevertheless, it is true that the most striking evidences of intelligence in the world are to be found in the adaptations of means to ends in the organic realm. Hence, it is only natural that in the development of the teleological argument the main interest should have centered in facts of this kind.

Socrates, Plato, and Aristotle were all greatly impressed with the theory of Anaxagoras that reason or intelligence (*nous*) was an ultimate, distinct, and constitutive element in the universe. Plato represents Socrates as saying, "Then I heard someone who had a book of Anaxagoras, as he said, out of which he read that mind was the disposer and cause of all, and I was delighted at the notion of this, which appeared admirable";[40] and Aristotle, referring to Anaxagoras, says, "When someone said that it is the presence of Mind which is the cause of all order and arrangement in the universe at large, just as it is in the animal organism, he seemed, by contrast with his predecessors, like a sober man compared with idle babblers."[41] But both Socrates and Aristotle were disappointed with the use that Anaxagoras made of the spiritual principle which he had been the first clearly to recognize. According to Plato, Socrates said, "As I went on to read further, I found my philosopher altogether forsaking mind or any other principle of order, but having recourse to air, and ether, and water, and other monstrosities";[42] Aristotle echoes the same criti-

---

[40] *Phaedo*, 97.
[41] *Metaphysics*, i, 984b. Translation by A. E. Taylor in *Aristotle on His Predecessors*. Reprinted by permission of The Open Court Publishing Company.
[42] *Phaedo*, 98.

cism, saying that "Anaxagoras . . . uses his 'Mind' as a mechanical device for the production of order in nature, and when he is at a loss to say by what cause some result is necessitated, then he drags in Mind as a last resource, but in all other cases he assigns anything and everything rather than Mind as the cause of what occurs."[43]

What the three great Greek idealists found defective in the method of Anaxagoras they sought to make good in their own philosophy. This is particularly true of Plato and Aristotle, in whose systems the teleological principle was fundamental. That Socrates also held essentially the same view of the world, is evident from what Xenophon reports concerning his teaching as well as from what Plato attributes to him. But he did not develop his ideas in this field into a system as his two great successors did. It is, however, worthy of note that he formulated quite distinctively the teleological proof of the divine existence.[44] Everywhere in the world he saw providential adaptations to human need, and this he made so clear to his interlocutor, Euthydemus, that the latter finally exclaimed, "I begin to doubt whether after all the gods are occupied in any other work than the service of man." This general idea appears also in Plato, who speaks often of the divine providence. But he broadens the argument, as we have previously indicated, so as to include the cosmic order as a whole. "The earth and the sun, and the stars and the universe, and the fair order of the seasons, and the division of them into years and months"—all of these, he says, furnish proofs of the existence of God or the gods.[45] He calls this "an argument from the order of

[43] *Ibid.*, i, 985a.
[44] Xenophon, *Memorabilia* i, 4, 4ff.; iv, 3, 3ff.
[45] *Laws* x, 886.

motion of the heavens, and of all things of which the
mind that ordered the universe is the author."[46]

   With Aristotle, who has little or nothing to say about
the divine providence, the teleological argument in the
narrower sense of the term hardly appears, though in
some of his earlier writings he seems to have given expression to it.   His system, as a whole, however, was
fundamentally teleological, but in a different sense from
that of Plato and theists in general.   God, according to
Aristotle, was pure final cause, so exclusively such that his
own direct connection with efficient causality was broken.
He was the ultimate and necessary source of motion, but
he was such not by virtue of any forthgoing of his own
energy but by virtue of the aspiration which his own
"unmoved" existence evoked in finite beings.   The spiritual activity that produced motion and that connected the
world with God was, therefore, to be found in the world
rather than in God.   It was purposive, but the purpose
was mundane.   It was directed by the world toward God,
not by God toward the world.[47]   It owed its origin, it is
true, to God, in the sense that without him it would have
had no object and so would not have come into being.
But the attractive power of the Divine Object was not
creative or causal in the efficient sense of the term, nor
was it purposive.   Intentional causality had no place in

---

[46] *Laws*, xii, 966.
[47] An interesting modification of the Aristotelian conception of God
and the world appears in the Gifford Lectures, entitled *Space, Time
and Deity*, by the neo-realist, S. Alexander.   Professor Alexander
identifies God, insofar as he is an actual existent, with the struggling
and aspiring world or with the world viewed as a nisus toward deity.
Deity in the Aristotelian sense of the term he regards as purely ideal
or conceptual.   There is no infinite God who is the source of the
world's motion or aspiration.   The purposiveness of the world is itself
the only truly existent deity.   Alexander's view consequently might
be described as a decapitated Aristotelianism.

the Aristotelian Deity. Intention or purpose, whether conscious or unconscious, existed only in the world, and as such was no necessary indication of the divine intelligence. The intelligence of God might, on the Aristotelian basis, be inferred from the graded scale of being, extending from pure matter to pure form, of which he was supposed to be the crown. But the bare facts of order and apparent design in and of themselves would not warrant this conclusion. Only the principle of efficient causation makes possible a direct inference from the intelligibility of the world to the intelligence of God; and this is lacking in the Aristotelian conception of the relation of God to the world. Aristotle, therefore, really leaves no place for the teleological argument in its inductive and historical sense. He eliminates the dynamic bond between God and the world upon which the argument is based, and, furthermore, cuts the spiritual nerve of the argument by virtually denying the divine providence. If there be no providential governance of the world, it matters little whether the cosmic order and the organic adaptation of means to ends point to a divine intelligence or not.

With the revival of Aristotelianism in the thirteenth century its exclusively finalistic conception of the Deity was abandoned. As a result of Christian influence God was now thought of as efficient cause and Creator. This opened the door to the teleological argument, and it took its place among the Aristotelians alongside of the various forms of the cosmological argument. Primacy, however, was at first accorded the latter. In Thomas Aquinas' list of five arguments the teleological came last. This was due in part to the influence of tradition. Both the Platonic and Aristotelian philosophies favored the more abstract type of thought when it came to the question of theism.   This type, which approached the mathematical, seemed more conclusive than the inductive method.   The empirical sciences were as yet undeveloped, and hence the appeal to the concrete facts of the organic world did not have the cogency that came later to be attached to it.   But the logical validity of the appeal was generally admitted.

With the development of modern science a new interest in the design argument arose.   Biology and physiology furnished the student with a profusion of illustrations that could be used with telling effect in popular expositions of the argument.   But in addition to this two circumstances contributed to a special interest in it.

One was the rise of a mechanistic view of the universe under the fostering influence of the physical sciences. Nature came to be looked upon as a self-running mechanism, driven from behind by virtue of forces resident within itself.   It needed no outside "Mover" or "First Cause," nor did it need a governing intelligence.   It had laws of its own, and these accounted for the fact of cosmic order.   As for final cause it needed and permitted none.   This type of thought had a double effect upon the teleological argument.   First, it tended to limit it to the organic realm.   Order was supposed to be furnished by the material elements themselves, and so required no backlying intelligence for its explanation. If indications of intelligence were anywhere to be found in nature, they must be in the purpose-like adaptations connected with the life of organic and intelligent beings.   Hence the theistic argument naturally concentrated attention upon facts of this character, and the teleological proof was restricted almost entirely to them. A second way in which the modern mechanistic view of the world affected the design argument was by denying its validity even in the organic realm. This stimulated interest in it and made it one of the hot-spots of theological controversy. Indeed, the fate of the whole theistic argument seemed for a time to be involved in it.

The other circumstance above referred to as contributing to a new interest in the design argument was the Darwinian theory of evolution. As popularly understood, this was simply a specification under the broader mechanistic view of nature. But it had its own limited and definite field and was supported by such an array of new facts that it made a powerful impression both upon religious and antireligious thought and so is deserving of special mention. Many believed that the new theory gave the quietus once for all to the teleological proof. Now for the first time a genuinely scientific explanation of the purpose-like adaptations of nature was offered. They were accounted for by the law of natural selection and the survival of the fittest. These laws, operating through untold ages without purpose of any kind, were supposed to have produced all the apparent instances of design that we have in the vegetable and animal world. The naturalistic assumptions upon which the theory was based and its shallowness from the metaphysical standpoint escaped for a time the attention of many, and the result was not a little alarm among religionists, premature rejoicing in the camp of their enemies, and much misdirected argument on both sides. The fact, of course, is, as Bowne pointed out, that the Darwinian theory leaves the argument from design essentially where it was before. The really sig-

nificant question, as he says, has to do not with the survival of the fittest but with their "arrival," and this on
the Darwinian theory remains as much of a mystery as
ever.   Slowness in its realization by no means excludes
purpose.   Indeed, a purpose pursued faithfully and persistently through the ages is far more impressive and
significant than one which is brought to completion in a
day.   But these facts were not at first understood or appreciated, and hence during the past generation there was
a quickened and widespread interest in the fate of the
design argument.

Kant subjected this argument as he did the ontological
and cosmological to a searching criticism, but he dealt
more gently with it.   It deserves, he says, "to be always
mentioned with respect.   It is the oldest, the clearest,
and the best adapted to the common human reason."[48]
What he objects to in it is the "apodictic certainty" associated with it.   He points out, what is manifestly true,
that the argument, insofar as it is based on inductive
data, does not warrant us in concluding to the absolute
unity and omnipotence of the designing intelligence. "An
architect of the world" would meet all the needs of the
case. Indeed, it is a question whether a number of "archi-
tects" might not explain the facts quite as satisfactorily
as a single one.   "The teleological argument," says Lotze,
"was wrecked by the fact that it was unable, with sufficient certainty and to a sufficient extent, to prove empirically the empirical datum, which it assumed to make its
point of departure, namely, the world's conformity to an
end."[49]   This conformity was assumed by the Platonic
and Aristotelian philosophies.   It was structural in them;

---

[48] *Critique of Pure Reason*, p. 502.
[49] *Outlines of the Philosophy of Religion*, p. 25.

and this may be a reason, additional to those already given, why the teleological argument was not more fully developed under their direct influence. Its main principle was taken for granted. But this was no longer possible after the development of the modern mechanistic view of the world. Empirical evidence of purpose was now required and it could not be furnished to an extent sufficient to maintain the weight of the conclusion previously deduced from the teleological argument. Lotze's statement, however, with reference to the wrecking of the argument holds of it only as an independent and self-sufficient proof of the existence of God. As a supplement to the cosmological argument it is valid. Indeed, the two arguments belong together; one implies the other. They are two different aspects of one and the same causal argument. By means of one we prove a Cause of the world and by means of the other we prove an intentional or intelligent Cause of it.

The latter proof, as we have previously noted, is subdivided by Bowne into a threefold proof—one based on cosmic order, the other on design in the organic world, and the third on the finite spirit. Order is the great mark of intelligence. We find it legislated into the very structure of the material world. Hence we infer intelligence as its source. In the organic realm there are many marvelous adaptations of means to ends such as the eye to seeing and the ear to hearing. But ends, as such, can exist only in a preconceiving intelligence. Hence we assume such an intelligence as the source of the multitudinous purposes that seem to be realized in nature. The human spirit has its roots in the universe and must somehow be accounted for. But in logic there is no way of passing from nonintelligence to intelligence. "Only verbal transits are possible." Hence we must assume intelligence in the world-ground as the source of human intelligence.

> He that planted the ear, shall he not hear?
> He that formed the eye, shall he not see?

In a similar way we may argue to the ethical character of the world-ground from the existence of our own moral nature, from the moral structure of human society, and from the moral forces that have manifestly been operative in the course of human history. The argument here is less conclusive than that for the intelligence of the Absolute, because it rests to a larger degree upon subjective factors and upon data that are open to question. Intelligence is more evident in the universe than goodness. But in principle the causal argument for the goodness of the world-ground is as sound as the corresponding argument for its intelligence.

The causal argument, as we have thus far expounded it, is based on objective data, on the world of experience, and the indications of intelligence and purpose in it. As such it is irrefutable. But it may be considerably strengthened by speculative considerations borrowed from epistemology and metaphysics. Two of these may be mentioned. The first is that knowledge implies a parallelism of the thought-series and the thing-series and that this parallelism requires for its explanation a purposive intelligence. When one considers the amazing complexity and the infinite detail involved in this parallelism, one cannot but see in it the supreme instance of design in the world. The other consideration grows out of the nature of causality. Metaphysics, as we have seen, makes it

clear that causality remains a self-contradictory idea until
it is lifted to the personal plane. Only on the plane of free
intelligence can the elements of permanence and change
implied in causality be harmonized with each other. If
there be, therefore, a unitary cause of the world, this
cause must be intelligent and personal. Speculative considerations of this kind may be too abstract and difficult
to have much weight with the average mind, but logically
they are more conclusive than arguments of a purely
inductive character.

The line of demarcation between the causal and the
conceptual arguments is not one that can be sharply
drawn. In its most extreme form, that of the ontological
proof, the conceptual argument seeks to dispense with the
causal idea altogether. But the moment the world is
taken account of, the causal idea obtrudes itself. The
only way that this could be avoided would be by a fundamental pluralism or monadism, and this, when it is logical, is, as Bertrand Russell remarks, "necessarily
atheistic."[50] If there be a God, he must stand in a causal
relation to the world. Otherwise there would be no
ground for affirming his existence. Even the ontological
argument implies this relation in its definition of God.
A being than which nothing greater can be conceived
must be the cause of the world, for as cause of the world
he would be greater than if he were not such. Causality
is thus implicit even in the ontological proof, and in the
broader form of the conceptual argument it becomes, as
we have seen, explicit. The difference at this point between the conceptual and causal arguments is that the
former has a Neoplatonic while the latter has an Aristote-

[50] *The Philosophy of Leibnitz*, p. 172.

lian background. The former argues to a supreme intelligence which is also cause, the latter to a fundamental
cause which is also intelligent. Cause, however, is somewhat differently conceived in the two cases. In the one it
is assimilated to the process of logical subordination, in
the other it takes the form of dynamic determination.[51]
The latter is the standpoint represented by personalism.
Hence with it the causal argument is basal, and the conceptual supplementary.

The Valuational Argument

Professor Hocking says, rather paradoxically, that the
cosmological and teleological arguments reason from the
existence of the world to the existence of God, while the
ontological argument reasons from the nonexistence of
the world to the existence of God.[52] The first part of this
statement is clear enough. It is because the world is in
some sense real that we are warranted in holding that it
must have a cause proportionate to it, equal to producing
it. But the other part of the statement is not so clear.
Strictly the ontological argument says that God exists,
no matter whether the world does or not. Not the denial
of the world but indifference to it is the motive that lies
back of its affirmation of God. Between these two standpoints there is a considerable difference. To say that God
exists, regardless of whether there is a world or not, is to
assert the complete self-sufficiency both of his being and
of the argument by means of which his being is affirmed;
the concept of God implies his existence. But to base his

[51] In his very valuable article on "Theism" in the *Encyclopedia of
Religion and Ethics*, to which reference has already been made, A. E.
Taylor does not seem to me to distinguish as clearly as he might between these two conceptions of cause.
[52] *The Meaning of God in Human Experience*, p. 312.

existence on the negation of the world is to forsake the field of logic and enter the realm of feeling. And this is what Professor Hocking here does. He gives us a valuational interpretation of the ontological argument. The argument for him means that we affirm God because of the emptiness and negativity of the world. It fails to satisfy us, and so we turn to him. He alone is, and he is, because the world is not. It is his contrast with the world that makes it clear that he alone fills out the notion of true being; and the contrast is one, not of logical inclusiveness nor of dynamic determination, but of value. Worth is the key to reality.

It is this conviction that constitutes the essence of what I call the valuational argument. Whether this argument, commonly known as the "moral" or "practical" argument, is really an argument at all, may be open to question. In strict logic one cannot pass from what ought to be to what is or from subjective interests to objective fact. But in actual life the transition is made, and it is made in one form or another by everyone. Believer and unbeliever, saint and sinner, theologian and scientist, philosopher and traditionalist—all have to some degree an instinctive faith in the ideal, and all to some degree practice it. They cannot avoid it. In spite of ourselves the ideals of life assert themselves. They become determining factors in belief. No matter how great devotees we may be of disinterested logic, the element of value creeps into our rational processes, and we cannot completely exorcise it. It stands in its own right, and before its bar every philosophic system must in some way justify itself. A philosophy of despair, it is true, need not be false. Complete skepticism might conceivably be war-

ranted.   But such a philosophy would have against it
the weight of a profound human conviction.   Men will
not allow the element of worth to be eliminated from
their world-view.   Consciously or unconsciously they
concede to it a certain degree of authority.   And hence
virtually every system of philosophy seeks to make provision for what it regards as the true ideals of life.   If it
fails to make such provision, if it tends to wreck these
ideals, it is certain to that extent to be discredited.   On
the other hand, if it sustains life's highest ideals, and in-
spires men to realize them, the weight of human optimism
will inevitably be thrown in its favor.   It is this fact on
which the valuational argument is based.   It seeks to
show that without the belief in God our ideals would collapse or would be made unattainable and the springs of
action would be broken.   Such a consideration as this is
not a proof of theism in the logical sense of the term,
but, if justified, it would be a weighty factor in determining human belief, and in this sense we may speak of it as
a theistic "proof" or "argument."

This argument was first given a recognized place in
philosophic theism by Kant, and since his time it has been
a favorite with religious apologists.   In popular treatises
on theism it has to a considerable degree supplanted the
traditional conceptual and causal arguments, so that it
may be said to be the dominant and characteristic argument of the age in which we live.   But while not clearly
formulated as an independent "proof" before the time of
Kant, it was implicit in theistic speculation from the beginning, as it has been also in religious faith.

In the Platonic-Aristotelian philosophy it was assumed
that the universe was constructed on a hierarchical plan.

There was an ascending scale of being from the lowest to the highest. The gradation was determined by the logical subordination of the individual to the universal, and this was interpreted as carrying with it the relation of causal dependence. But along with the principle of universality and causality went that of worth. The highest Idea or universal, according to Plato, was the Good,[53] and the Prime Mover of Aristotle was a perfect Being. In both cases the conceptions of worth and of being were inseparably fused together. The same was true of the Neoplatonic world-view. Plotinus held that the hierarchies of existence and of value must ultimately correspond. This conviction also underlay Anselm's ontological proof, and but for the fact that it was tacitly assumed by Thomas Aquinas his cosmological and teleological proofs would have been seen to be quite inadequate. The traditional theistic arguments took it for granted that reality and worth went together and that one implied the other. This assumption was a corollary of such a teleological world-view as we have in the Platonic-Aristotelian philosophy. But it was not made the subject of special investigation. It remained an intuition rather than a carefully reasoned faith.

Not until Kant took the problem in hand was a sharp distinction made between existence and value, between the natural order and the moral order, between the world as it is and the world as it ought to be. Kant argued that on the basis of the natural order or from the standpoint of the theoretical reason no firmly grounded conclusion with reference to the existence of God could be reached. The possibility of his existence was left open. But the

[53] *Republic*, 509.

final decision of the question, he held, must be turned over to the practical reason. The moral nature would fall into contradiction with itself if there were no God. For it requires us not only to seek the highest good but to believe that it is realizable; and this we know from the constitution of the world it could not be without a supreme moral will. To satisfy the demands of conscience there must, therefore, be a God. So Kant argued. The argument is based on the assumption that moral values are absolute, and derives its entire cogency from the strength of this conviction. Where moral conviction is lacking, the moral argument collapses. But moral conviction is not a matter of individual caprice. It is structural in the human reason, it has an *a priori* foundation. Unlike, however, the *a priori* principles of the theoretical reason it is not limited to the phenomenal realm. Its categorical imperative is a court of final appeal; its postulates hold for ultimate reality. We may, therefore, safely trust them as an adequate foundation for our belief in God.

The valuational argument, as Kant thus developed it, was restricted too exclusively to the moral nature. Kant did not give adequate recognition to the independent worth of religious experience. Indeed, religious experience as an immediate apprehension of the Divine he rejected as fanatical. For him experience had necessarily a sensible content, and hence there could be no experience of God. God was purely a postulate of the moral nature, and as such was beyond the reach both of demonstration and of intuition. But while Kant took too narrow a view of experience and of the ideal values of life, his argument for the existence of God, based on the moral nature, was in principle sound. And since his time the argument has been expanded, elaborated, and given a more convincing expression by Lotze, Bowne, Sorley, Pringle-Pattison and others.

In the form in which Bowne developed the valuational argument we may distinguish two lines of thought. First, he justifies this type of argument by showing that it is not peculiar to religion. Science as well as religion rests ultimately on value-judgments, on faith in an ideal. It assumes that the world is intelligible and that we are able to understand it. But neither assumption is capable of demonstration. Both are affirmations of faith. They are "subjective ideals," "idols of the human tribe." Yet we accept them without serious question. Our cognitive interests require it, and we follow their lead. Facts to some degree confirm our assumptions, but only to a very limited extent; yet we adhere to them. It is so also in the moral and religious realms. Here under the influence of subjective interests we also form ideals, and these ideals we cling to, even though it is difficult and in some cases impossible to bring the facts of experience into harmony with them.

The same method is thus followed both in religion and in science; and if it is valid in the latter field, there is no reason why it should not be in the former. Truth is a value quite as certainly as is goodness or God, and it is because it is a value that we hold it to be grounded in reality and accessible to us. Existence cannot be separated from worth. Science is not *wertfrei* in the sense that it makes no assumptions and eliminates altogether the ideal from its conception of the real. It assumes that the real is rational, and this involves a large ideal element. Indeed, apart from the ideal it is difficult, if not impossible, for us to construe the real. Our own existence is indissolubly bound up with the experience of value, and hence there is, as Pringle-Pattison says,[54] a kind of "moral impossibility" about conceiving anything as ultimately real that is devoid of value. This is probably the fundamental reason why matter or extramental existence has been repudiated by the world's profoundest thinkers as essentially unreal. Ultimate reality carries with it the idea of intrinsic worth. We cannot separate the two. Science as well as religion presupposes their union. The basis on which the valuational argument rests must, therefore, be admitted to be sound.

The second line of thought adopted in this argument consists in showing that the rejection of the belief in God would have disastrous consequences for the higher spiritual interests of men. In this connection stress is usually laid on the evil moral effects of atheism. As a necessitarian system it undermines the sense of responsibility, leaves men without ethical ideals, and deprives life of inspiration. Against it, consequently, the moral nature revolts, and in its own self-defense affirms a theistic world-view. Theism is thus an implication of conscience. This line of argument is accepted as valid by Bowne and developed in a most effective way by him, but along with it he also emphasizes, as does no other theist whom I know, the suicidal effect of atheism upon knowledge.[55] A necessitarian system makes knowledge quite as impossible as it does morality. Without freedom there can be

---

[54] *The Idea of God*, p. 200.

[55] Eduard von Hartmann calls Lotze "the epistemologist of the speculative theism of the nineteenth century" (*Lotze's Philosophie*, p. vii). This characterization would apply still more truly to Bowne.

no distinction between truth and error. One is as necessary as the other and there is no standard by which one can be differentiated from the other; and even if there were, we as necessitated beings would be unable to use it. Atheism thus overthrows knowledge and in the general overthrow destroys itself. This fact, it is true, does not demonstrate theism, but it does show that it is the only type of metaphysics that can save us from speculative disaster. Metaphysical necessitarianism in every form is suicidal. Our conclusion must, then, be either theism or nothing.

The possibility of "nothing," of a world devoid of rationality and of all ideals, cannot be gainsaid. It lingers with us and haunts our noblest moods. But it is in itself utterly barren; and if translated into a positive conviction, wrecks both science and conscience. To see this and to see that life's real worth consists in faith and knowledge is a great insight; and to help men to this insight is the chief function of the theistic argument. This argument should not be confined to any one line of thought. To make it either wholly practical or wholly theoretical is a mistake. The universe presents itself to us in three distinct aspects. From one point of view it is a system of concepts, from another a system of causes, and from a third a system of values. Each of these has its own independent significance, and yet none is truly real in abstraction from the others. The system of concepts, when thought through, points to a Supreme Reason, the system of causes to a Supreme Will, and the system of values to a Supreme Good. But Reason, Will and Goodness have no existence apart from the Supreme Person, in whom they have their perfect embodiment. To make this clear and to expound in a convincing manner the different lines of thought which lead to this conclusion is the task of theism. One type of philosophy will naturally lay its chief stress on one line of thought, and another on another. Personalism seeks to do justice to each of the three main arguments, and to some extent it utilizes them all. But by its very nature it, too, has its preferences. It begins with the valuational argument. This is the most fundamental. Without faith the mind could not lay hold of reality at all. But having the world as a datum personalism puts its main stress on the causal argument. The order, apparent design, and intelligent beings that we see about us point to a Supreme Intelligence for their explanation. This argument with most minds will always have the greatest logical cogency. To the conceptual argument in its traditional form personalism concedes very litle weight, but modified in such a way as to be an argument from the general fact of knowledge and of the intelligibility of the world to a Supreme Knower it has its value. In the development of these different arguments many of the greatest minds in the world's history have had a part and each age has made its contribution to them. I myself know no one who in the past generation summed them up more effectively and expounded them more victoriously than Bowne. His *Theism* is, to my mind, the classic treatise on that subject.

IMMORTALITY

We now pass to the second of the two cardinal beliefs of religion—the belief in the immortality of the soul. This belief, like the belief in God, was first introduced into philosophy by Plato. He was the first to develop and formulate a rational defense of it, though some of his ideas on the subject were probably derived from Socrates and others. The argument he presents in support of it is elaborated in his writings more fully than is the theistic proof. Indeed, there is a saying to the effect that nothing new has been said in favor of a future life since Plato and nothing new against it since Epicurus. We begin, therefore, our brief historical survey of the argument with Plato.

Many different proofs of the soul's immortality are to be found in his writings. Janet and Seailles[56] mention ten, and to these still others might be added. But however many there may be, they may perhaps be reduced to three, which correspond roughly with the three fundamental theistic arguments which we have expounded. These three proofs of immortality, according to Edward Caird,[57] represent successive stages in the development of Plato's thought. In the *Phaedo* stress is laid on the relation of the soul to the Ideas. The Ideas are eternal, and hence the soul, which shares in them, recalls them and resembles them, must also be eternal. Particular importance in this connection is attached to the doctrine that "knowledge is simply recollection." This doctrine "necessarily implies a previous time in which we learned that which we now recollect. But this would be impossible unless our soul was in some place before existing in the human form."[58] So knowledge implies pre-existence, and it also implies kinship with the Ideas. They are immaterial and incorruptible, and hence the soul, which knows and participates in them, must be such. The soul

---

[56] *A History of the Problems of Philosophy*, ii, p. 353ff.
[57] *The Evolution of Theology in the Greek Philosophers*, i, p. 200ff.
[58] *Phaedo*, 72.

THE PHILOSOPHY OF PERSONALISM

"existed before we were born, then our souls must have
existed before we were born, and if not the ideas, then
not the souls."[59]   This line of thought might be called
Plato's conceptual argument for immortality.   There is
also in the *Phaedo* a more extreme form of the argument
which resembles the ontological proof of the divine existence.   Plato argues that life is an alienable characteristic of the soul and that the soul, consequently, cannot
die.   Just as the idea of the perfect Being includes or
implies its existence, so the idea of the soul includes that
of life. "To her belongs the essence of which the very
name implies existence."[60]   The soul, therefore, cannot
have come to be nor can it cease to be.   It is eternal and
immortal.   This argument is logically no more valid than
is the corresponding argument for theism.   Both arguments involve the fallacy of the universal.   But the deduction of the soul's immortality from its relation to the
Ideas had, nevertheless, one very significant consequence.
It led to the conception of the soul as an immaterial substance.   This conception marked a very important advance beyond earlier thought and has had a permanent
and profound influence upon subsequent speculation.   It
implied that the soul is not necessarily dependent on the
body for its existence and that it is not necessarily subject
to dissolution as is the body.   The *possibility* of its immortality was thus established.

The second Platonic argument in support of the belief
in a future life bears a resemblance to the causal argument in theism, and may itself be so designated.   It is
anticipated in *Phaedo,* but receives its most distinct ex-

[59] *Phaedo*, 76.
[60] *Ibid.*, 92.

pression in *Phaedrus*. The essential point to it is that the
soul is self-moved or self-determined and, therefore, immortal. It does not derive its immortality, as in the preceding argument, from the fact that it shares in the *idea*
of life but from the fact that as self-moving it is itself
the principle of life and of all substantial reality. "The
soul," we are told, "is immortal, for that is immortal
which is ever in motion; but that which moves and is
moved by another, in ceasing to move ceases also to live.
Therefore, only that which is self-moving, never failing
of self, never ceases to move, and is the fountain and beginning of motion to all that moves besides. . . . The
self-moving is the beginning of motion; and this can
neither be destroyed nor forgotten, for in that case the
whole heavens and all generation would collapse and stand
still, and never again have motion or birth. But if the
self-moving is immortal, he who affirms that self-motion
is the very idea and essence of the soul will not be put to
confusion. For the body which is moved from without
is soulless; but that which is moved from within has a
soul, and this is involved in the nature of the soul. But
if the soul be truly affirmed to be self-moving, then must
she also be without beginning, and immortal."[61] In other
words, self-motion is the distinctive mark of ultimate
reality. It is, as Plato says in *Laws* (894), "ten thousand times superior to all the others." And since it is the
essential characteristic of the soul, the soul must itself
be ontologically real and immortal. In this argument
Plato has in mind chiefly the soul of the world, but since
human souls share in the nature of the world-soul it applies also to them. They "rule and govern" the bodies

---

[61] *Phaedrus*, 245. Translation by B. Jowett.

with which they are united, and hence we may conclude that they are "in the very likeness of the divine, and immortal."[62] This argument is not so conclusive as Plato seemed to think, but it does make an advance beyond the preceding argument. By showing that the soul, in addition to being fundamentally different from the body, possesses that power of self-determination which is characteristic of ultimate reality, it not only establishes the possibility of immortality but creates a certain presumption in its favor. If the soul is self-active and, therefore, metaphysically real, there is a certain inherent probability that it will survive death.

Plato's third argument is found in *Timaeus* and by way of implication in *Philebus* and *Laws*. It differs from the preceding arguments in that it surrenders what may be called the natural immortality of the soul, and bases the belief in a future life on the divine will. God here appears as Creator. To his goodness all souls owe their present existence, and to his goodness they will owe their existence hereafter. But this need not awaken doubt about the future. "My creations," says the Creator of the universe, "are indissoluble, if so I will. All that is bound may be dissolved, but only an evil being would wish to dissolve that which is harmonious and happy. And although being created, ye are not altogether immortal and indissoluble, ye shall certainly not be dissolved, nor be liable to the fate of death; having in my will a greater and mightier bond than those which bound you when ye were created."[63] This argument is based on the worth of the human spirit and the place that it occupies in the di-

---

[62] *Phaedo*, 80.
[63] *Timaeus*, 41.

vine plan. It is thus a valuational argument and so corresponds to the third of our theistic proofs.

The question has been raised as to whether Plato taught personal immortality. He distinguishes between a lower and a higher soul and ascribes immortality only to the latter, the rational soul.[64] How, then, is the rational soul to be conceived? Did Plato think of it as an impersonal principle or as personal in our sense of the term? He probably never set himself the problem in quite the way we do. Indeed, he disclaims the ability to determine which part of the soul is human and which divine. But his stress on the soul's power of self-determination and on its intrinsic worth points strongly in the direction of what we call personal immortality; and this, I think we may safely say, would almost certainly have been his conclusion had the question been put to him in its modern form.

When it comes to Aristotle, however, the matter is not so clear. He introduced a new conception of the soul, interpreting it in terms of its organic relations. For him the soul was the form or entelechy of the body, its efficient, formal, and final cause, that which brings its latent capacities into activity and actuality. In other words, it was the immanent principle of unity in an organic being, and as such necessarily varied with the nature of the organism so that there were different kinds of souls. Aristotle distinguished three: the vegetable or nutritive soul, the animal or sensitive (also conative and locomotive) soul, and the human or rational soul, the last taking up into itself and unifying the two inferior souls and their functions. The relation of the soul to the organism

---

[64] *Ibid.*, 69–72.

in each case was in principle the same. The two were bound together so that neither could exist without the other. Indeed, one by its very definition implies the other. Hence there could in the nature of the case be no independent existence of the soul. It must perish with the body.

But clear and conclusive as this seems to be, there is another side to the case. Aristotle distinguished within the human or rational soul between a passive and an active reason, and to the latter he explicitly ascribed immortality while denying it to the former. "With regard to reason and the faculty of thought," he says, "we have as yet no conclusive evidence. But reason would seem to be a different type of soul from all others, and it alone can exist in a state of separation from the body, as the eternal from the perishable. This creative reason is not intermittent in its thinking; but it is only when separated from the body that it becomes its true self; and this it is that alone is immortal and eternal."[65] What Aristotle, however, meant by the active reason has long been a matter of dispute. Some think that he identified it with God; others hold that he regarded it as a superhuman intelligence, one of the highest members of the hierarchy of being, but subordinate to God; and still others maintain that he regarded it as a part of the human soul, our true self. Much can be said in favor of each of these views. If we adopt the last, it is quite possible that Aristotle believed in personal immortality, nor is the belief necessarily excluded by the other two. The active reason might be a superhuman intelligence, either divine or subdivine, and yet the human soul might stand in such a relation to it

---

[65] *De Anima*, 413b; 430a.

as to share in its immortality. That was essentially Plato's view; only he spoke of a world-soul instead of an active reason. The main difference between him and Aristotle was that the latter was more intellectualistic in his conception of God and of the divine element in human life. He deified the theoretical reason, and relegated the other more distinctly personal faculties of the soul, the emotional and the volitional, to a lower and mortal plane. Hence it is a question whether the Aristotelian God, even though self-conscious, can properly be spoken of as personal, and a question also whether Aristotle's immortal active reason, even though conceived of as individual, was truly personal. A clear-cut doctrine of personal immortality we at least do not have in Aristotle, and even in Plato the matter is not so clear as to have been wholly free from question.

But whatever uncertainty may attach to the Aristotelian and even the Platonic teaching concerning immortality, no uncertainty on this point is to be found in the two great synthesizers of Plato and Aristotle, namely, Plotinus and Thomas Aquinas. Of these the former leaned toward Plato and the latter toward Aristotle, but both affirmed what we would call individual or personal immortality. "If it is pretended," says Plotinus, "that one kind of soul, our own for example, is mortal, and another, that of the All, let us suppose, is immortal, we demand to know the reason of the difference alleged. Each is a principle of motion, each is self-living, . . . each is seeking to win to what is essential being. . . . The soul is one and simplex, living not in the sense of potential reception of life but by its own energy; and this can be no cause of dissolution. . . . Nothing from the realm of

real being shall pass away."[66]   Thomas Aquinas, as a
Christian theologian, was naturally equally explicit on
this subject.   But he was more of an Aristotelian than a
Platonist and so held to a closer relation of the soul to the
body than did Plotinus.   The soul, said the latter, "is
not present as form is in matter; for the form as in matter is inseparable, and, further, is something superim-
posed upon an already existing thing; soul, on the contrary, is that which engenders the form residing within
the matter and therefore is not the form."[67]   Thomas, on
the other hand, rejected the Platonic view "that the soul
is in the body as a sailor in a boat,"[68] and adopted the
Aristotelian conception of the soul as the form or entelechy of the body.[69]   This conception furnished a better
philosophic basis for the Christian doctrine of the resurrection of the body; and it is probable that this fact
contributed not a little to the triumph of Aristotelianism
over Platonism which Thomas did much to bring about.
He insisted, however, that the soul, though the form of
the body, could exist independently of it, and that Aristotle's active reason was to be interpreted individualisti-
cally as "part of the soul."[70]   Both Thomas and Plotinus
held that the human soul is immaterial and incorruptible,
but they differed with reference to the immortality of
animal souls and the origin of souls in general.   Plotinus
held that "nothing that really is can ever perish," that
all souls have existed from eternity, and that the souls
of animals are immortal.   Thomas, on the other hand,
denied immortality to the animal soul and maintained that

[66] *Enneads*, iv, 2, 12, 14.   Translation by Stephen MacKenna.
[67] *Ibid.*, iv, 3, 20.
[68] *Summa Contra Gentiles*, ii, 57.
[69] *Ibid.*, ii, 68–72.
[70] *Ibid.*, ii, 76.

the human as well as the animal soul was created by God and began to exist with the body.

Three difficulties inhered in the Thomistic proof of the soul's immortality. One had to do with the distinction drawn between the human and the animal soul; another with the individuality of the soul; and the third with its substantiality. Each of these was given special attention by a distinguished modern philosopher. Descartes dealt with the first, Leibnitz with the second, and Kant with the third. With respect to the first there was a feeling that on the Aristotelian basis the human soul was not differentiated sharply enough from the animal soul to warrant its immortality, in case immortality was denied the latter. Hence Descartes denied that animals have souls in the proper sense of the term; their actions are automatic.[71] Soul he defined as "a thinking substance." This excluded the Aristotelian conception of a vegetable or nutritive soul and of an animal or sensitive soul. At the same time it established a sharper distinction between mind and matter and between soul and body than had heretofore been made. Thought was now regarded as constituting the essence of mind or soul, and so constituted, the mind stood distinctly opposed to extended matter and the soul to the divisible and perishable body. As thought the soul was the most certain object of knowledge. It was also "a pure substance," maintaining its identity through change as the body could not do, and hence was to be considered as "in its own nature immortal."

While Thomas asserted the individuality of the human soul, he was prevented by his Aristotelian inheritance from adequately defining and protecting it. He did, it is

---

[71] This view Bowne sharply rejected. See *Metaphysics* (1882), pp. 340f.

true, show that the Aristotelian conception of the active reason and of the soul as the form of the body could be interpreted in such a way as to be consonant with the belief in the soul's immortality, but as commonly understood those conceptions were not favorable to the true individuality and immortality of the soul. Leibnitz consequently introduced a new view of the independence of the individual soul. He held that each soul or monad was entirely independent of every other. It could not by natural means be either created or annihilated. God might call it into being or destroy it, but he alone could. In and of itself as a part of the natural order the individual soul was eternal and immortal. It might undergo change, metamorphoses; that is what birth and death are. But in and of itself the soul persists; and insofar as it is intelligent, it is assured of a conscious immortality. It does not derive its existence from any superhuman being in whose substance it shares, nor does it depend for its existence on an external material organism. It exists in its own right, and by virtue of its own inner constitution may be expected to grow eternally from more to more.

The third difficulty in Thomas' proof of immortality had to do with the idea of substance. That the soul was an immaterial substance was accepted by Descartes and Leibnitz as well as by Thomas, though they differed somewhat in their conception of the nature of this substance. But the idea of substance itself was open to question. It had been assumed by Descartes and Leibnitz that the soul's consciousness of its own identity carried with it the persistence of some kind of soul substance, and that in the persistence of this substance was to be found the guarantee of its immortality. Kant, however, dissented from this view. He showed that the unity and identity of the soul are matters of conscious experience, and that as such they are independent of any underlying simple and self-existent spiritual entity. The latter conception he rejected altogether as lying beyond the reach of human knowledge, and with it went apparently the main traditional argument in support of the soul's immortality. That the soul is immortal, Kant continued to believe, but he based his belief on practical instead of theoretical grounds. The moral nature, he held, has an infinite task, and hence must have an endless time in which to fulfill it. Immortality is thus a postulate of the practical reason. It is a faith grounded in the idea of the worth of personality.[72]

With the conclusions reached by Kant on this subject personalism is to a considerable degree in accord, but by no means entirely so. It rejects explicitly the distinction he drew between the empirical and the real self. For it the self of experience is the true ontological self. The failure of Kant to realize this shows that he unconsciously remained in bondage to the old conception of substantiality which he himself did much to discredit. The real contribution that he made to the doctrine of the soul was not his supposed disproof of its substantiality but the incentive he gave to a reinterpretation of the idea of substance. As a result of his criticism of the traditional idea, substance came to be thought of in personal terms, in terms of self-consciousness and self-determination. The unity and identity of the soul as conscious experiences ceased to be regarded as mere effects, as a kind of

[72] An admirable putting of this argument together with a valuable historical treatment of the subject as a whole will be found in *The Problem of Immortality* (1924), by Professor Radoslav A. Tsanoff.

"harmony" produced by an underlying substance.   It came now to be seen that they were themselves constitutive of the soul's reality.[73]   The despised empirical self thus turned out to be as real and as substantial as ever the soul was conceived to be from the time of Plato to that of Leibnitz.   The only difference was that substantiality was now interpreted in personal instead of impersonal terms.

Having rejected the Kantian distinction between the empirical and transcendental self, personalism sees no need of throwing overboard completely the traditional metaphysical argument for the soul's immortality.   It may be maintained as confidently to-day as ever that the body is no analytically necessary factor of our inner life. So far as we can see by an analysis of mental data they might conceivably go on independently of the body.   The facts of mental dependence upon physical conditions leave the question as to the relation of the two series to each other undetermined.   The spiritualistic view is at least quite as possible as the materialistic.   We have no more warrant for limiting conscious life to present physiological conditions "than an unborn philosopher would have for declaring the antenatal life to be the only one possible."[74]   Again, while we are not justified in holding that the soul is a simple and incorruptible substance and, therefore, immortal, there is, as we have seen, good ground

---

[73] On this point Bowne seems not to have thought himself through to a definite conclusion at the time when he wrote the first edition of his *Metaphysics* (1882).   On page 51 he represents the conscious life of the soul as the outcome of its basal spontaneous and ceaseless activity, while on pages 97–98 he declares that consciousness is the only basis of the soul's permanence and identity.   Later he distinguished clearly between the real and conscious existence of the soul for itself and its possible unconscious and phenomenal existence for God.

[74] B. P. Bowne, *North American Review*, 1910, p. 102.

for maintaining that it is a real agent, that it fills out the notion of true being more completely than any other form of finite existence, and that there is, therefore, at least a presumption in favor of its continued existence after death.

This, however, does not warrant the conclusion that the soul is by nature immortal. However akin we may be to the Supreme Person, we are dependent beings and in the last analysis our future rests with him. It is our place in the divine plan and our worth in the total scheme of things that will decide our destiny. Beyond this we cannot go; nor is there any good reason why we should desire anything more certain than the divine will. For God is a God of the living, not of the dead. To him we may, therefore, safely trust the future, confident that the highest spiritual values will find their realization in what he wills. No demonstration of the future life is possible. An extreme personalistic pluralism here deceives itself; and so also does that form of absolute idealism which seeks logically to deduce the future life from the being and character of God. Kant was right in basing the belief in immortality chiefly on the moral nature; but so also was Plato in teaching that a theoretical as well as a practical basis for the belief is to be found in the nature of the soul and in the nature of God.

CHRISTIANITY

Personalism, as we have already pointed out, does not set itself up as a substitute for positive religion. It recognizes that religion is a natural growth and that it is only in its historical forms that its true nature is revealed. What it seeks to do, so far as religion is concerned, is to present a view of the world in which it as well as science will be at home. It seeks to provide religion with a philosophical underpinning, to give it a cosmic framework in which it will fit, to create for it an intellectual atmosphere in which it will thrive. It is, therefore, primarily concerned with the more general and more fundamental aspects of religion such as the belief in God and the belief in immortality. But these are only parts of a larger whole. The living faith of the Western world is not an abstract philosophical theism but that complex body of belief known as Christianity. It is this larger whole that makes theism vital, and not the reverse. Without historical Christianity theism would languish; it is second, not first. This is frankly recognized by personalism, and hence its attitude toward the unique and characteristic elements in Christianity is favorable. But this fact does not prevent it from being critical, and so the question arises as to its more definite relation to the historic faith and practice of the church. Only two or three general aspects of this question can here be considered.

So far as the Christian and personalistic views of the world are concerned, it will, I think, be admitted that there is no serious discord between them. In the course of the church's history there have been five questions relative to the world that have been the subject of earnest controversy.

The first had to do with the relation of the world to God. Is it an emanation from God or a creation of his will? This was a point of conflict between Neoplatonism and Christianity. Christian philosophy as well as Christian tradition decided in favor of creation, and with this conclusion personalism is in emphatic accord.

The second was concerned with the origin of the world. Is the world eternal? Or did it have a temporal beginning? The controversy over this point was precipitated by the mediæval revival of Aristotelianism, and the decision reached was that, while revelation required belief in a temporal creation, there was no adequate rational ground for rejecting the eternity of the world. With the latter part of this conclusion personalism also agrees.

The third disturbing question had reference to the Copernican astronomy, and here the consensus of scientific opinion finally forced the church into acquiescence with the newer view in spite of a hostile Christian tradition.

The fourth had to do with miracles. This was a more serious matter, since it seemed to involve the question of God's free relation to the world as well as the historical credibility of Scripture. So far as the church is concerned, the problem cannot yet be regarded as settled. Christian opinion is agreed in rejecting the mechanical view of nature and in holding to the possibility of miracle, but as to the historicity of the biblical miracles it is divided. Such in substance may also be said to be the view represented by personalism. It insists on God's free relation to the world, and thus leaves the door open to belief in the biblical miracles without, however, deciding the question of fact one way or the other.[75]

The fifth question concerning nature that has agitated the church is that with reference to biological evolution. That the Darwinian theory in its main outline will come to be generally accepted in much the same way as the Copernican astronomy, is probable. In any case, there

---

[75] Bowne's last discussion of this subject is to be found in an essay entitled *"Concerning Miracle"* in the *Harvard Theological Review* for 1910, pp. 143-166.

is no conflict at this point between personalism and Christianity.

It is coming to be more and more generally agreed that Christianity has nothing to fear from science, and that there is no reason why it should hesitate to accept any well-established scientific conclusion. Occasionally this is interpreted as a surrender on the part of Christianity. It is likened to the method adopted by "a man who disarms the robber by going naked."[76] But this is to misunderstand the true nature both of religion and of science. Science has to do simply with the phenomenal order, while religion is concerned with the power world. In Ritschlian circles it was customary to say that science consisted of existential judgments, while religion was based on judgments of value. But this method of distinguishing science and religion from each other is misleading. It suggests that existence can be separated altogether from value. Dean Inge, for instance, says that this separation forms the basis of the Ritschlian theology.[77] In this he is mistaken. Ritschl and his followers held to Kant's primacy of the practical reason and regarded value as determinative for our view of ultimate reality. But their phraseology naturally gave rise to such a misunderstanding as Dean Inge reflects. It is far better to adopt Bowne's distinction between phenomenal and ontological reality, and then to say that science is concerned with the former and religion with the latter. This allows for the Ritschlian distinction between the predominantly factual character of science and the predominantly valuational character of religion without giving rise to the erroneous impression that existence is indifferent and foreign to

---

[76] C. Bigg, *Neoplatonism* (1895), p. 140.
[77] *The Philosophy of Plotinus*, i, 133.

values and that values have no significance for our conception of fundamental reality. The distinction, in any
case, however we may phrase it, is a valid one, and should
obviate hereafter any clash between pure science and pure
religion.

When it comes to such characteristic doctrines as those
of the Trinity, the Incarnation and the Atonement, the
accord between personalism and Christianity is not so
evident. Dean Inge expresses himself in very pronounced
terms on the subject.[78] He declares that personalism
translates Christian theology into an alien dialect and introduces enormous difficulties into the region of Christian
faith. It mutilates, he says, and distorts the whole body
of Christian theology, making of the doctrine of the
Trinity "an incomprehensible and manifestly self-contradictory piece of word-jugglery." The main ground on
which this indictment is based is the modern conception
of a person as one who cannot share his being with another. This notion of impervious spiritual atoms, we are
told, runs directly counter to the absolutely fluid conception of personality that we have in the New Testament
and is flatly contrary to Christianity.

In response to this charge several considerations may
be urged. For one thing, Dean Inge exaggerates the
separateness and exclusiveness attributed to personality
by the personal idealist. Spiritual atomism is too strong
a term to apply to a view that holds to a fundamental
monism. However independent finite persons may be of
each other, they are all dependent upon a Supreme Person, and this common dependence breaks down their supposed atomic separateness. They do stand in a certain

---

[78] *Personal Idealism and Mysticism*, pp. 93ff.

relation to each other and they do to some extent share each other's life. But this relationship is to be interpreted in spiritual terms. It does not involve any fusion of soul substances. No doubt it is made possible by the relation of causal dependence in which all souls stand to the world-ground, but it does not consist in any metaphysical interpenetration of being. It is a spiritual act, which presupposes mutual independence as well as a common dependence. Without the common dependence on God intercommunion, so far as we can see, would be impossible, and without the mutual independence it would cease to be *inter*communion and would vanish into an unintelligible feeling of oneness. True participation in the life of another presupposes, therefore, rather than excludes a measure of metaphysical separateness.

Again, it should be noted that the doctrine of the Trinity does not owe its incomprehensibility to the personalistic philosophy. Since the time of Thomas Aquinas it has been the established teaching of the church that the Trinity is a supernatural mystery which the human reason can never hope to comprehend. Malebranche advanced the interesting theory that the persistence of the doctrine in the face of this fact was an evidence of the special intervention of Divine Providence. If it were not, he said, for the watchful care of Christ over his church, the Unitarians would before long outnumber the true Catholics,[79] since their opinions are manifestly more acceptable to the natural reason. Philosophy has for six centuries past been out of accord with the doctrine of the Trinity, at least more so than the earlier Platonic philosophy. It was Platonism that furnished the intellectual soil out of

[79] See *Dialogues on Metaphysics and Religion*, xiv, 1. Translated by Morris Ginsberg.

which the doctrine grew; and it is from that standpoint that the doctrine is most easily understood. But it does not follow from this that it is not in need of revision from the standpoint of later thought or that it is necessarily devoid of meaning to a different type of philosophy. It is quite possible to give to the doctrine of the Trinity a personalistic interpretation. One might say with Bowne that it is simply pantheism applied to the Godhead—a case of organic unity combined with numerical plurality, which is at least a legitimate conception. This view fits in with the social interpretation of the Trinity which has been known to the church since the time of Augustine.[80] Or one might adopt the psychological interpretation of the Trinity, which is also to be found in Augustine.[81] This interpretation is perhaps less true to the original genius of the Trinitarian doctrine than the social interpretation. But neither is altogether satisfactory, and while personalism may seem naturally more favorable to the psychological than the social analogy it is not necessarily inconsistent with either. In its essential teaching it is in harmony with the main motives that have underlain the Trinitarian doctrine as a whole. It emphatically excludes pantheism, and yet holds strictly to the absoluteness of God in the sense that no limitations are imposed upon him from without. It also attributes to him an inexhaustible richness of life, and thus conserves the basal religious truth in the doctrine of the Trinity. To say then with Dean Inge that personalism is

[80] Compare H. M. Gwatkin, *The Knowledge of God*, ii, 298.

[81] The psychological interpretation of the Trinity finds in the unitary consciousness or self-consciousness with its threefold activity an analogy to the Trinity, while the social interpretation implies three distinct centers of consciousness.

necessarily shut up either to an abstract monotheism or to a form of finitism, is quite unwarranted.[82]

Personalism is also criticized because of its supposed bearing on the Christian life. The charge is made that it eliminates the mystical element in religion by denying the actual presence of Christ or of the Divine Spirit in the believer. The metaphysical otherness which it attributes to all spiritual beings excludes, it is claimed, that direct participation of the human in the divine which is implied in the language of Christian piety. From the personalistic point of view religion is reduced to a relation of wills and becomes a dry and colorless moralism. It loses the depth of mystical feeling which grows out of the sense of oneness with God. This charge was occasionally brought against Bowne's view of religion. It was said to be rationalistic. But this rested upon a misunderstanding. He did, it is true, emphasize in a striking way the ethical element in religion. He felt that the prevailing emotionalism in the religious communion with which he was connected, called for this emphasis as a corrective. But fundamentally his conception of religion was mystical. In the causal dependence of the soul on God he found a sufficient basis for the language of mysticism. This language was to be interpreted metaphorically rather than metaphysically, but the union it affirmed between the human and the divine was on that account none the less real; nor was it any the less real because it was construed in terms of mutual understanding, of love and of obedience, rather than in terms of fusion or absorption. The latter is the language of a mystical pantheism. Christian mysticism finds its true expression in such a *conscious*

---

[82] See Francis J. McConnell, *Is God Limited?* pp. 243–282.

relation of dependence and devotion as grows naturally out of the personalistic conception of the mutual otherness of the finite and the infinite. It is, therefore, a serious mistake to charge personalism with reducing the New Testament language about the solidaric relation of believers to Christ to a "fantastic and misleading metaphor." Such mystical language, from the personalistic point of view, finds its ample justification in the spirit of worship and the consciousness of fellowship which bind the human to the divine.

CHAPTER V

MILITANT PERSONALISM

THE preceding chapters have been devoted to the definition of personalism and to the exposition of its fundamental principles in the light of their historical development. Incidentally, opposing views have been criticized and the personalistic position has been defended against attacks made upon it. But the polemic aspects of the subject have not been dealt with in a systematic way. No attempt has been made to sum up the arguments against rival systems or to gather together the various objections to personalism and to meet them. This is the task we have set ourselves in the present chapter. Here personalism appears on the offensive and the defensive; it becomes militant.

Karl Marx, speaking of his own philosophy, said, "Here is truth, kneel down here!"[1] No such dogmatic temper characterizes the personalist. He may be profoundly convinced of the truth of his own world-view, but he knows that the conditions under which it and every world-view is arrived at are not such as to warrant haughtiness of spirit. When it comes to questions of ultimate reality the answers are not determined by an iron law of logic to which every mind must bow. Personal factors enter in that we cannot escape, and it is these that usually cast the deciding vote. One's character determines one's philosophy. We choose our world-view. Not

[1] Quoted by J. W. Scott, *Syndicalism and Philosophic Realism*, pp. 21f.

rational necessity but moral necessity is the final arbiter between competing systems, and moral necessity involves a volitional element. It implies an ideal that lies beyond the reach of pure logic, an ideal that we voluntarily recognize. This ideal does not coerce us, it does not compel assent. All that it can do is to present itself to our free spirits and then await their response. The response actually given is determined by ethical as well as purely logical considerations.

No ultimate world-view can be sun-clear to a finite mind. Every philosophy involves unfathomable mysteries. But this does not warrant complete agnosticism. There is a choice between mysteries. Some are less repugnant to reason than others. Some, if accepted, throw a flood of light over life as a whole, while others involve us in yet greater darkness. The fundamental question, consequently, with reference to any philosophy is not as to whether it is logically demonstrable—no philosophy is that—but as to whether it offers to the mind the line of least resistance. The latter is the claim that personalism makes for itself. It does not set itself up as the absolute philosophy. It frankly recognizes that there are limits to human knowledge, that all knowledge in the last analysis is based on faith. It frankly admits that there are difficulties in its own view of the world and of ultimate reality. It cannot, for example, explain creation. It can neither tell us how souls are made nor how the divine energizing gives rise to the spatial and temporal order. All this remains a mystery, and so for the most part also does the Divine Providence and the inner thought life of the Infinite. Of the latter we can have only "the vaguest apprehension." And yet in spite of these fundamental mysteries personalism is confident that as a philosophy it represents the line of least resistance. Other philosophies are involved in far greater difficulties. This the personalist seeks to make clear, and insofar as he succeeds in doing so he establishes his position as securely as any philosophy can be established.

In dealing with the other philosophies it will be convenient to divide them into two groups: one predominantly metaphysical and the other predominantly epistemological and positivistic. To the first belong materialism, "natural" realism, and absolute idealism; to the second empiricism, pragmatism, and neorealism. Each of these systems, if they all may be called such, will be briefly considered, after which we will take up the objections to personalism.

MATERIALISM

Materialism is the antithesis of personalism; it is the one pure form of impersonalism. As an ontology it denies the ultimate reality of spirit, as a psychology it denies the independent existence of the human spirit, and as an ethics it denies its independent worth. It stands thus as the negation of all that personalism represents. It is with materialism as an ontology that we are here chiefly concerned. A philosophy might agree with materialism in its psychology and ethics and yet not be materialistic in its metaphysics. Metaphysical materialism, on the other hand, carries with it both psychological and ethical materialism, and hence is the fundamental and characteristic form of this type of philosophy.

At present materialism as a metaphysics is in disrepute in professional circles. This at least is true of the word. Occasionally a teacher of philosophy professes himself a

materialist or a "neo-materialist,"[2] but as a rule he conceals his materialism, if such be his actual philosophy,
under some other name such as "agnosticism," "naturalism," or "realism." Since this is so, many seem to think
that materialism is an obsolete type of philosophy and
that one who is up to date in his thinking need take no
account of it. But this is a hasty and superficial conclusion. Materialism in its essential nature is one of the
persistent forms of speculative thought. It is, as F. A.
Lange says, "the first, the lowest, but also comparatively
the firmest stage in philosophy."[3] It may disappear for a
moment, but if so, it is only to reappear in new disguise.
There are tendencies in human nature, both practical and
theoretical, that almost inevitably lead to materialistic
modes of thought, and these tendencies have been to a
considerable degree strengthened by the physical sciences.
Materialism is not, therefore, a type of thought that can
be disposed of once for all. It is like a cloud on a mountain peak, driven away by the cold wind and yet constantly reformed by the warm, vapor-laden air from beneath. Each generation produces its own materialistic
philosophy, and it is only as the winds of criticism blow
it away that it is kept within manageable bounds. In and
of itself it stands as a perpetual threat against the higher
interests of men, and hence the arguments directed
against it are always timely and pertinent. No thinker
has won the right to a spiritual world-view who has not
for himself slain the materialistic dragon.

Etymologically materialism is easily defined. It is the
doctrine that the ultimate source of all the facts of experience is to be found in matter. But "matter" unfortu-

---

[2] See, for instance, R. W. Sellars, *Critical Realism*, p. vii.
[3] *History of Materialism*, iii, p. 335.

nately is "Protean in form and chameleon in hue." What its exact nature is has never been agreed upon, not even by materialists. A great many different theories have been proposed, and it is not easy to classify them in a satisfactory way. For our purposes the most important distinction is that between atomistic and hylozoistic or pantheistic materialism. This distinction arose early in the history of Greek thought. Atomism is the more clearly defined theory; indeed, it is the only sharply differentiated form of materialism. Hylozoistic and pantheistic materialism attributes to matter capacities or qualities that are nonmaterial, and so vitiates the purity of its own materialism. "Matter" is still the ultimate reality, but it is not the crude matter of common sense or even that of the atomic theory. It is something other and more; it is matter endowed with the mystic properties of life and consciousness. Such a theory may still be called materialism, since the impersonal and extramental factor predominates in its view of matter. But it leaves a place for the psychical in its conception of ultimate reality, and this breaks down to some extent its inner consistency as a system. Atomism, on the other hand, denies consciousness in any form to the ultimate metaphysical units. These units by their combinations produce mental phenomena but in and of themselves they are purely material. This is true whether with ancient materialists we regard the soul as corporeal or with modern materialists deny the reality of the soul and conceive of the mind as a mere function of the body.

From the scientific point of view atomism because of its more precise definition of matter represented a distinct advance beyond hylozoism, and in modern times it has been accepted as the basis of the physical sciences. But from the metaphysical standpoint it was less satisfactory. It could give no better account of the mental life than that it was due to an accidental collocation of atoms. Hence there has during the past century been a return on the part of many materialists to hylozoism. The older "brickbat" or "billiard-ball" theory is scornfully rejected. It is, in the words of Professor Tyndall, "absurd, monstrous, and fit only for the intellectual gibbet." Life and thought must be included in any adequate definition of matter. Matter, when properly understood, has in it "the promise and potency of all terrestrial life." This is sometimes called the "higher" materialism. It may be either pluralistic or monistic in its conception of matter; it may ally itself either with atomism or Spinozism. Often it does not define itself on this point, but in either case it endows matter with vital and psychical properties. We may, then, distinguish three different forms of materialism: the lower atomistic materialism, the higher pluralistic materialism, and the higher monistic materialism. With each of these we will deal, but our argument will be directed against materialism as a whole rather than any particular form of it.

Materialism often claims to have this advantage over spiritualism that it is based on immediate experience. Matter, it fancies, is something given. We see it, and see that it is a real cause. Spirit, on the other hand, is hypothetical. We have no direct perception of it as an objective cause of phenomena. We merely assume it where matter fails. But since matter has explained so much, there is good ground to believe that with advancing knowledge it will explain more and more until finally it

342 THE PHILOSOPHY OF PERSONALISM

will come to be recognized as the universal principle of explanation. In any case its causal efficiency is real. We know it at first hand. Matter is not a cause whose existence we merely infer. We see it at work about us. It is revealed in experience. Materialism is, therefore, empirical in a sense that theism cannot be. It is based on direct observation, while theism is purely a speculative theory. Hence there is presumptive evidence in its favor. Why duplicate causes, adding one of a hypothetical nature? Matter as cause we know. It is proving itself more and more adequate to the task of explaining the world. Why not, then, obey the law of parsimony and be content with it?

This line of thought figures prominently in popular materialism, and uncritical thought easily falls a prey to it. It is, however, wholly untenable, being based upon a crude and obsolete theory of knowledge. The fact is we do not see causes anywhere. We experience certain effects, but the causes are hidden from us. What the nature of these causes may be, observation does not tell us. We can only infer it from the effects. The problem of cause in the objective world is, therefore, wholly a thought problem. The question is simply one as to how we are to think of the causal ground of the world. Are we to think of it as impersonal and material or as personal and spiritual? One conception is quite as speculative as the other. Matter as cause is in every way as hypothetical as is spirit. Neither is given to us in objective experience. We infer one as much as the other. Materialism in this respect has no advantage over spiritualism. Indeed, if anything, it is at a disadvantage. For while we do not see cause of any kind in the objective world, we do experience it within ourselves. We are conscious of ourselves as agents. This is the only concrete form in which causality presents itself to us. We know from experience what volition or self-determination is. In every other form cause is purely hypothetical. Whether such a thing as impersonal cause is rationally conceivable is, as we have seen, open to serious question. In any case it is not a datum of experience. This is also true of volitional causality so far as the objective order is concerned. We do not observe causality of any kind outside of ourselves. But in our own inner experience we do have a consciousness of volitional causality. We are aware of ourselves as active beings. And since we have direct knowledge of causality in this form, and only in this form, there is a certain presumption in favor of the view that ultimate cosmic causality is of the same type. The actual situation is, therefore, almost the direct reverse of what materialism has assumed. Instead of matter being an empirically real cause and spirit a hypothetical cause, it turns out that spirit is the only cause with which we are directly acquainted and of which we have strict empirical knowledge. From the epistemological point of view the initial presumption, consequently, is in favor of spiritualism rather than materialism.

The positive arguments against materialism may be reduced to four. First, the mental life cannot be deduced or derived from matter. Second, the epistemology of materialism is inconsistent with its metaphysics and its metaphysics makes knowledge logically impossible. Third, as a mechanical system materialism leaves no place for new departures. It explains effects by carrying them back into the cause. All its explanations are thus tautologous.

They mark no progress in insight, and they imply that there is no real cosmic progress. Fourth, materialism, when thought through, leads to agnosticism. Each of these arguments we will briefly expound.

1. Materialism is unable to account for the mental life. This is true both of the lower and the higher forms of materialism, though the difficulties are somewhat different in the one case from what they are in the other. We begin with the lower or atomic form of materialism which conceives of matter wholly in terms of extended substance or force or both together. Where extension and passivity are emphasized as the essential characteristics of matter we have the corpuscular theory. Where stress is laid on its activity we have the dynamic theory. The tendency in modern physics is strongly toward the latter view. But in either case it is simply motion and aggregation with which matter is concerned, and limited in this way it is manifest that it can give no account of mental phenomena. Feeling, volition, and thought cannot be construed in terms of material movements and groupings. The attempt to do so leads to absurdity. The old saying that "the brain secretes thought as the liver secretes bile" rests upon a total misunderstanding of the unique nature of thought. That the mental is wholly unlike the physical is one of the established conclusions to which the progress of thought has brought us. This conclusion has grown out of the more exact definition given to matter and mind, and may be regarded as one of the major insights which we owe to philosophy. It is, however, an insight and not a demonstrated conclusion. If one does not see it for oneself, there is no way of compelling assent to it. The absurdity of saying with Mole-

schott that "thought is a motion of matter"[4] is something
which each one must recognize for himself. "The propo-
sition," says Paulsen, "that thoughts are in reality nothing but movements in the brain, feelings are nothing but
bodily processes in the vaso-motor system, is absolutely
irrefutable; not because it is true, however, but because
it is meaningless. The absurd has this advantage in common with truth, that it cannot be refuted. To say that
thought is at bottom nothing but a movement is almost
the same as to say that iron is at bottom nothing but
wood. No argument avails here. All that can be said is
this: I understand by a thought, a thought and not movement of brain molecules; and similarly, I designate by the
words 'anger' and 'fear,' anger and fear themselves and
not a contraction or dilation of blood vessels. Thought is
not motion, but thought."[5]

When this is recognized and it is seen that physical
and mental facts are completely unlike, the inadequacy
of materialism becomes at once evident. It is still possible to construct phrases that seem to make the mental
commensurable with the physical, but the phrases are
purely verbal. They yield no insight. One may even
go so far as to deny the mental outright. This is the
vogue at present among some psychologists who style
themselves "behaviorists." By identifying the psychical
with the reactions of the organism they seem to think
that they have eliminated not only the soul but consciousness itself. In spite, however, of these denials of its
reality thought remains as much a fact as ever. One
may, it is true, abstract behavior from the rest of life
and make it the subject of separate study. This is quite

---

[4] Quoted by Louis Büchner, *Force and Matter*, p. 135.
[5] Quoted by E. C. Wilm, *The Problem of Religion*, pp. 58f.

legitimate. But as a metaphysics behaviorism is, as Professor Lovejoy has said, simply materialism gone mad. Of it we need take no account.

But while it is manifestly impossible to derive life and consciousness from matter as it is conceived in physics and chemistry, may it not be that these sciences have thought too meanly of matter? Is it not possible that matter has in it the promise and potency of all that is? In addition to its physical properties, such as gravity, affinity, and magnetism, which it manifests in certain relations, may it not in certain other relations manifest vital and mental properties? That this is the case is the assumption of the hylozoistic or "higher" materialism of ancient and modern times. This type of materialism is commonly known as "monism." Even the lower materialism is monistic in the sense that it reduces all reality to atoms that are qualitatively alike. But the monism of the higher materialism is of a different kind. It is "qualitative" like the lower materialistic monism, but it is something more. It is transcendent. It claims to overcome the antithesis between the physical and the mental by a higher synthesis. That it is impossible to deduce the mental from the physical, is admitted. But in the mystic "matter" of hylozoism we have a higher category than the physical. We have in it the common source both of the physical and the mental. Why this common source should be called matter rather than mind, might be a question. Strictly it is neither. But the historic associations of the doctrine are such that there is no good reason for objecting to the use of the term "matter" in this connection, so long as its new meaning is explained. The fact is that this monistic idea of a common source and seat of the physical and the mental is so "loaded" that the materialistic element is controlling in it. Hence the designation of the system as a form of materialism is warranted.

The higher materialism is then monistic in both a qualitative and transcendent sense. But the term "monism" is also used numerically. It affirms one underlying reality as against a plurality of such beings. On this question the higher materialism divides or is in a state of unstable equilibrium. It seeks to retain its connection with the atomic theory of science; but if this is made ultimate, it itself becomes an extreme form of pluralism. Hence some of the profounder materialists stress the idea of one underlying substance or energy. We thus have both a pluralistic and a monistic form of hylozoistic materialism. The difficulties in one are about as great as they are in the other. Both on examination turn out to be merely verbal solutions of the problem created by the essential unlikeness of the physical and the mental.

Against the higher materialism in both its pluralistic and monistic form it may be urged that it departs from the conception of matter that prevails in the physical sciences. Indeed, physics is based on a denial of hylozoism. It was the stricter, devitalized conception of matter that alone made possible the development and progress of the natural sciences. To return to the hylozoistic view would, then, mean a step backward. It would, said Kant, be "the death of all natural philosophy."[6] This point is worthy of note, for modern materialism has always claimed to have the prestige of science on its side. As a matter of fact, it is not science but philosophical materialism that has called for a new definition of matter.

-----
[6] See James Ward, *Naturalism and Agnosticism*, p. 173.

Modern materialistic mysticism finds no support in the physical sciences. This is more clearly recognized to-day than it was a generation or two ago.

The question, however, is not one that science is called upon to settle. It lies beyond its province. We turn, therefore, to an examination of the higher pluralistic materialism. According to this philosophy reality consists of a multitude of material elements which along with their physical properties have a capacity also for thought. It is their main business to run the material universe, but on occasion "they do a little in the mental line." Minds and mental phenomena may, therefore, be referred to them for their explanation. This view at first has a certain plausibility, but the plausibility vanishes as soon as we begin to inquire into the relation of the physical and the mental properties to each other. They are supposed to have their seat in a common substance or agent or element, but aside from this hypothetical bond of unity they represent two totally disparate lines of activity. The question consequently arises as to whether we are to think of them as mutually independent or as standing in a relation of interaction. If we adopt the former view, there is no way of rationally construing the relation of the two to each other. One will inevitably tend to eliminate the other. If the mental activity is wholly self-contained and independent, there is no reason why it should affirm a parallel line of physical activity or any physical activity whatsoever. The ultimate elements would thus be transformed into souls. On the other hand, if the physical activity is recognized as indubitably and as completely independent and unable to transcend itself, there is no logical ground for ascribing true reality to the mental life. Hence it is degraded to the rank of an "epiphenomenon" and treated as a powerless accompaniment of the physical series. In and of itself it *does* nothing and from the causal point of view *is* nothing. It is not even an effect of a material cause, for according to the law of conservation every effect must in turn become a cause; and this the mind cannot become without destroying the independence and self-sufficiency of the physical series. Nor can it be regarded as a passive but real effect, for this would mean the dissipation of the physical energy employed in producing it. The mental must then be looked upon as an inexplicable subjective aspect of the physical. Why it appears at all and what determines the order of its appearance is a complete mystery. The whole thing takes on the character of magic.

The only way to escape this conclusion is to bring the physical and the mental aspects of the elements into interaction with each other. But to do this is to conflict with the law of physical continuity according to which the physical series is a self-contained and closed system, susceptible to no influence from without. To admit that the mental series is in interaction with the physical series would also imply that it is as real a form of energy as the latter, and this would give rise to the question as to which is the ultimate and controlling fact, matter as moving or matter as thinking and willing. Again, if we allow that the elements have an active subjective or inner aspect, it is by no means clear how this aspect or these aspects account for *our* thoughts and feelings. Are they to be regarded as a kind of raw material which can be detached from the elements in which they inhere and then fashioned into souls or into our concrete experiences? Such a crude theory seems to be implied in the idea of a "mind-stuff" which has had some currency in materialistic circles. But only the untutored imagination could find any relief in such a conception. The fact is that these hypothetical inner aspects of the material elements are entirely worthless as an explanation of our own mental life. They complicate and confuse the situation rather than clarify it. If they themselves are psychical in nature, then they are souls; and if so, we not only have our own souls to be explained or explained away but also this multitude of hypothetical souls. Such are some of the difficulties into which the higher pluralistic materialism leads us.

Turning now to the higher monistic materialism we find its attempt to account for life and consciousness equally unsatisfactory. Here instead of innumerable discrete elements, each with an inner and outer aspect, we have two modes of manifestation, one physical, the other mental. The mental mode includes our minds and is supposed to account for them. This view has an apparent advantage over the preceding one since it seems at first easier to pass from a substantial unity to a plurality of manifestations than from a plurality of elements to the unity of our own minds. But on further reflection it becomes evident that virtually the same difficulties beset the monistic type of hylozoistic materialism as inhere in its pluralistic form. For one thing, it is not clear whether the physical and mental "modes" are to be regarded as mere aspects or as real objective attributes. If we take the former view, then they are purely phenomenal, and as such they presuppose a mind or thought of some kind to which they appear as phenomena. Phenomena by their very nature imply a percipient. But a percipient in this case, whether it be found in the human mind or in a *deus ex machina,* would be external to reality and would have no place in the system itself. The system implies such a percipient, and yet with it becomes self-contradictory and absurd.

Adopting the other supposition that the two "modes" are objective attributes and that they are mutually independent, we are first of all at a loss to know how the substance or agent, to which the two attributes belong, can be one. It acts in two incommensurable ways, and how this is possible is completely hidden from us. Neither experience nor reason gives us the slightest insight into its possibility. The unity ascribed to the underlying substance is purely verbal. Furthermore, it is assumed that the thought attribute and the thing attribute run parallel to each other. But no explanation of this parallelism is given us. Sometimes it is said that the two series are identical, but this view from the materialistic standpoint is, as Bowne says, both "thoughtless" and "meaningless." Again, if the two series or attributes are mutually independent and do not in any way interact, there is no reason why thought should not deny the thing attribute altogether. Then, too, the existence of thought as an aspect or attribute of the underlying substance would not account for our own thought and our own minds. The inalienability of personal experience makes it impossible logically to deduce our mental life from the supposed mental life of the Absolute. Monistic materialism thus proves itself quite as helpless over against the facts of consciousness as does pluralistic materialism. For materialism of every kind there is an unbridgeable chasm between the physical and mental. "Matter" as the mysterious ground of both is a mere word. It has no unitary character and no definable nature.

2. The second main objection to materialism has to

do with its epistemology.   Here there are three points deserving of special attention. In the first place, material-'ism, while professing to be empiricistic in its theory of thought and knowledge, is fundamentally out of accord with empiricism—indeed, directly contradicts it.   It assumes a world of things and laws, of substances and causes, which consistent empiricism makes impossible as an object of knowledge or even of faith.   It thus deliberately rejects that positivistic limitation of knowledge which has been characteristic of the empirical school since the time of Hume.   Again, when consistent with itself, materialism is forced to deny the cardinal doctrine of empiricism by teaching that experience is not the determining nor even a real factor in building up the mental life and giving rise to the laws of thought.   From the materialistic standpoint matter is the cause of every mental state and of every form of mental activity.   If, therefore, a perfect physical double of President Coolidge were created, his mental double would also be created. The double would have all the memories of the actual Coolidge though he had had none of his experiences. Experience, according to consistent materialism, is the impotent attendant of nervous change.   In and of itself it does nothing and accounts for nothing.   Materialism, therefore, instead of finding a support in empiricism, overthrows it and is in turn overthrown by it.

In the next place materialism holds that the physical organism not only produces thoughts but produces correct thoughts.   If this were not the case, no knowledge of the material universe would be possible.   But how such a parallelism of thought and thing has been brought about is a question on which materialism does not throw the least glimmer of light.   It simply assumes the parallelism without any serious attempt to explain it. Herbert Spencer, it is true, sought to account for it by the principle of natural selection. His theory was that there is no inherent reason why matter should think rightly. To begin with, some organisms thought wrongly and some correctly. The former came into conflict with their environment and hence tended to be eliminated. The correct thinkers, on the other hand, survived and transmitted to their descendants their correct habits of thought. In this way there has come about a gradual adjustment of the mental to the physical series. The adjustment is not yet complete, but it is steadily moving toward perfection. This interesting theory no doubt contains some elements of truth, but it is wholly inadequate as a solution of the epistemological problem and is, furthermore, fundamentally inconsistent with the materialism upon which it is based. It assumes that our ideas determine at least to some degree the movements of the organism—an assumption which thoroughgoing materialism emphatically rejects. But overlooking this inconsistency we note that the theory, if true, would account for valid thoughts only insofar as they have survival-value, and these form only a small part of the total body of human beliefs and convictions. Again, the theory implies the truth of widespread and long-standing convictions and of all convictions that make for courage and optimism. But these convictions are for the most part antimaterialistic. They are theistic and religious in nature, and thus contradict the fundamental assumptions of Spencer's own system. We must then conclude that his naturalistic account of knowledge is a complete failure, ending in self-destruction. From the materialistic point of view the parallelism of thought and thing remains an opaque fact.

Another epistemological objection to materialism is that as a necessitarian system it makes error as necessary as truth and thus overthrows reason itself. This is a point which we have already elaborated at some length so that it calls for no further exposition.[7] The argument, as it is developed by Bowne, is decisive against necessitarianism in every form.

3. The third general criticism to be passed on materialism is that it is a mechanical system and as such can explain an effect only by carrying it back into the cause. This makes the cause as complex as the effect and reduces all metaphysical explanation to tautology. The cause is constructed so as to fit the effect; matter is said to have in it the promise and potency of all that is to be. There is, therefore, no real cosmic progress and no real progress in intellectual insight. In going backward we potentialize the actual and in going forward we actualize the potential. But the potential is in a sense a duplicate of the actual. If it were not, it would not account for it. All the problems presented by the world as we now know it recur, consequently, in its hypothetical antecedents. The original nebula, if fully understood, would be seen to contain implicitly the world as it exists to-day. Mechanical explanation brings us to nothing simpler. It remains barren and tautologous because of the necessary logical equivalence of cause and effect. On the mechanical plane we cannot pass from the simple to the complex nor from the homogeneous to the heterogeneous. Mechanism contains no principle of differentiation or of progress. It leaves no place for "emergent evolution." From its standpoint nothing absolutely new and unpredictable is

---

[7] See chap. ii, subsection entitled "The Trustworthiness of Reason."

possible. Life and mind must somehow be contained in matter and be resultants of it. Otherwise the mechanical law of cause and effect would be broken.

The theory of "emergent evolution" is interesting as a reaction against the older "resultant" evolution or mechanical type of naturalism. It makes room, as does Bergson's "creative evolution," for the novel and undetermined, and is thus truer to facts than the older theory. But insofar as it regards the new stages of evolution as ultimate and inexplicable it marks no real speculative advance. It substitutes agnosticism for dogmatism and to that extent may be regarded as a forward step. But insofar as it rules out a purposive and creative agent, it becomes itself dogmatic again. And insofar as it refers evolution to an agent which is neither mechanical nor intelligent, it confuses thought rather than clarifies it. The fact is we have only two principles of causal explanation, mechanism which is driven from behind and intelligence which is free and purposive. That which is neither one nor the other is something we cannot construe in thought. We may coin phrases such as "unconscious reason," "pure will," "world-soul" and *élan vital* to represent another principle but there is no clear conception corresponding to any of them. When it comes to causal explanation, we must choose between mechanical necessity and free intelligence. The former, as we have seen, makes real development impossible; only the latter can account for emergent or creative evolution. The theory of emergent evolution stands in about the same relation to the older mechanical naturalism that the current integrating type of sensationalism does to the older atomistic type. Both are confessions of the breakdown of the me-

356 THE PHILOSOPHY OF PERSONALISM

chanical principle, but neither sees as clearly as it might that the only alternative is the principle of intelligence. Only on the assumption of a free and unitary intelligence can the novelties of emergent evolution and the integrating activity of consciousness be explained.

4. The fourth indictment to be brought against materialism is that it leads to agnosticism. The preceding discussion has made this clear. Matter as the source of life and thought is an entirely mysterious entity. We know nothing of its inner nature. The more we seek to penetrate into its true being and the more we seek to understand how the facts of consciousness can be deduced from it, the more hopeless becomes our task. "The really deepest essence of matter," says Büchner, "will probably always remain for us an insoluble problem."[8] "We are incompetent," says Haeckel, "to penetrate into the innermost nature of this real world—the thing in itself."[9] The ultimate principle of explanation, offered us by materialism, thus turns out to be itself unknowable, and instead of casting light upon the world process leaves us in complete darkness. All that we can say of it is that it is a blind and necessary cause. How it acts or why it acts as it does, lies entirely beyond us. To our deepest questions the only answer that can be given is that things are as they are because they must be. Beyond this blind necessity materialism will not permit us to go. From its standpoint there can, therefore, be no rational theory of reality. At bottom everything is pure mystery.

This agnostic tendency in materialism received its most striking and influential expression in the Synthetic Philosophy of Herbert Spencer. During the latter half of

[8] *Natur und Geist*, p. 83.
[9] *The Riddle of the Universe*, p. 292.

the nineteenth century he was the high priest of agnostic materialism or materialistic agnosticism. He himself, it is true, indignantly denied that he was a materialist, and in the cruder sense of the term he was not. What he stressed in his system was its agnostic features. But the main drift of his philosophy was nevertheless materialistic in the monistic and dynamic sense of the term. Though commonly known as agnosticism his system was actually a "monism of force," as R. B. Perry calls it, and is to be placed alongside of Büchner's "monism of matter" and Haeckel's "monism of substance." All three were materialistic systems. In spite of all that Spencer says in a religious vein about the Unknowable, about its being as far superior to mind as mind is to matter, his working conception of it was that of a blind and necessary force. He describes it as "the infinite and eternal energy on which all things depend and from which all things forever proceed." Such an energy, to be sure, might be conceived of as spiritual in nature, and there are not wanting passages in Spencer's writings that suggest a theistic interpretation of it. But the whole bent of his teaching was against any such view. He explicitly rejected theism, attributing it to the "impiety of the pious"; and insofar as he said anything intelligible about the Unknowable he represented it as an impersonal and mechanical force. That there is such a force, one, eternal and absolute, he regarded as "an ultimate truth of which no inductive proof is possible"—a truth "deeper than demonstration, deeper even than definite cognition, deep as the very nature of mind."

Bowne devoted his first book to an examination of *The Philosophy of Herbert Spencer* (1874), and in his last book, *Kant and Spencer,* published posthumously,

358   THE PHILOSOPHY OF PERSONALISM

(1912), he reviewed the first principles of the system again in the light of his own maturer thought. He regarded Spencer as good "cadaver for the dissecting schools," and so used him for many years in his seminar in philosophy. In both his earlier and later work he pointed out the materialistic implications of the Spencerian system and mercilessly exposed its numerous inconsistencies. Spencer, he showed, had an "almost supernatural appetite for self-contradiction." The arguments he employed against his theistic opponents undermined his own position. As Bowne puts it, he mowed down their pseud-ideas but in his enthusiasm mowed off his own legs. "This modern Samson paralleled the ancient by pulling the temple on his own head."[10] There is hardly a fundamental subject on which he does not express himself in contradictory ways. As an object of worship the Unknowable must be absolutely true to its name, but when it comes to its relation to the phenomenal order Spencer, as J. S. Mill said, reveals "a prodigious amount of knowledge" respecting it. It is not only a power, one and eternal, but carries with it the affirmation of absolute and invariable law. So also the self is declared to be only a complex of states of consciousness, but when this view tends toward idealism or nihilism Spencer saves himself by ascribing to the self the power of resistance or, in other words, dynamic reality. Force and matter, he says, are merely "symbols" or "phenomena," and yet he holds firmly and dogmatically to the "persistence of force" and the "indestructibility of matter." His system as a whole is an inconsistent compound of phenomenalism and substantialism, of materialism and agnosticism, and of em-

---

[10] *The Philosophy of Herbert Spencer*, pp. 32, 49.

piricism and rationalism. "Bad science, bad logic and bad metaphysics," as Bowne says, all intermingle in it.

And yet the system had great prestige in its day. Though exposed to the destructive criticisms urged against materialism and, in addition to these, the equally decisive criticisms brought against its agnosticism, it maintained itself for a full generation as the dominant "scientific" or secular philosophy of the time and was regarded by many as the "final" philosophy. Gradually, however, it succumbed to the drastic criticisms to which it was subjected by idealistic and theistic thinkers, and the naturalistic wave which had sustained it receded. Spencer himself, as Bowne said, "had the rather pathetic experience of seeing his system grow obsolete during his own life."

Since the decay of Spencerian naturalism no materialistic system of anything like the same influence has arisen to take its place. But it does not follow from this, as I have already said, that there is no need of studying materialism and subjecting it to a thorough criticism. My motive in here outlining the main arguments against it is not the same as that of the preacher who justified a sermon devoted to a denunciation of Calvinism on the ground that he believed in punishment after death. Materialism is not dead. In one form or another it is a constantly recurring type of human thought. It springs up spontaneously on the sense level, and is implicit in almost all naturalistic systems. To understand its logic or, rather, the lack of logic in it is, therefore, a task incumbent upon everyone who wishes to work his way through to a higher and more consistent world-view. It was for this reason as well as because of the dominance of the current Spencerian naturalism that Bowne devoted so much attention to this type of thought. Nowhere, in my opinion, is there to be found a more penetrating and overwhelming criticism of materialism than in his philosophic works. So decisive did he himself regard the antimaterialistic argument that he said of Romanes, who in his later years recovered the religious faith which in his earlier years he had lost through the influence of atheistic naturalism, that "he must have felt, after coming to himself, like a man who had surrendered his valuables on being menaced with a wooden pistol."[11]

But while theoretical materialism in all its forms is crude, self-contradictory, and altogether incapable of accounting for the phenomena of life and thought, and while both it and practical materialism are directly opposed to the fundamental principles of personalism, there is one point at which materialism as a popular philosophy comes into sympathetic contact with personalism. This is in the field of ethics. Religion and idealism have not infrequently encouraged an unhealthy asceticism. They have also at times cast a halo of sanctity about the *status quo,* no matter how unjust it was and how much of misery it involved. In these ways they have seemed to stand in the way of human enjoyment of the natural goods of life and also have seemed to deny to great numbers of men their economic, social and political rights. Against such injustice and such false asceticism the human spirit has at times risen in revolt, and at such times has found an ally in materialistic philosophy. Materialism, whatever errors and evils may be associated with it, does brush aside many of the conventional sanctities, and in so doing

---

[11] *Kant and Spencer,* p. 311; the *Methodist Review,* 1904, p. 523.

liberates the human mind from bondage to useless and harmful customs and ideas. It emphasizes the present well-being of men as over against a mistaken other-worldliness, and thus seems to be an agent of social progress. It is this fact that has constituted the moral motive of materialism insofar as it has been a popular movement. "Who has nothing more to say about me than that I am an atheist," said the materialist Feuerbach in 1846, "says and knows of me nothing. The question of whether a God exists or does not exist, the opposition between theism and atheism, belongs to the seventeenth and eighteenth centuries, but no longer to the nineteenth. If I am denying God, it means that I am opposing the denial of mankind; it means that instead of a situation full of illusions, instead of a fantastic, heavenly position, which in real life is necessarily accompanied by an actual denial of mankind, I demand man's sensuous real place, which also necessarily means his political and social position. The question of God's being or not being is with me a question of men's being or not being."

With this materialistic insistence on the right of men in general to the natural goods of life personalistic ethics is in complete sympathy. It rejects materialism emphatically insofar as the latter seeks to deduce the moral nature of man from nonmoral elements and insofar as it denies the sacredness of human personality. But it finds the moral ideal in the richness and fullness of life as a whole, and thus makes provision for those economic, social and political goods on which materialism justly lays stress. Insofar, therefore, as materialism is a corrective of a one-sided spiritualism, personalistic ethics is in accord with it. It stands for the rights of all the different aspects of normal life and for the natural rights of all men. This is one of the most characteristic notes in, Bowne's *Principles of Ethics*.[12] He there vigorously contends for the recognition of the claims of the natural life as over against the artificial ecclesiastical ethics, the mistaken asceticism, and other false standards of the past. But this human and democratic note he grounds in a theistic world-view. This gives to it a moral character which it could not have on a materialistic basis. Consistent materialism recognizes no moral imperative, and insofar as it contends for the natural rights of the common man it is voicing a moral sentiment foreign to its own fundamental principles—a sentiment that finds its true basis only in a personalistic view of man and the world.

NATURAL REALISM

By "natural realism" I mean something broader than what is commonly understood by the term. I mean by it substantialistic or metaphysical realism as distinguished both from the epistemological type of realism represented by so-called "critical realism" and the positivistic form of it represented by neo-realism. The latter will come up for consideration in a later section. Here a few paragraphs may be devoted to "critical realism."

As an epistemological theory critical realism is dualistic. It stands directly opposed to the monism both of neo-realism and of absolute idealism, insisting that thing and thought cannot be identified, that thought is other to thing and thing other to thought. But the exact nature of this

---

[12] This aspect of Bowne's ethics has been developed in a significant way by Bishop F. J. McConnell. See especially his *Democratic Christianity, Personal Christianity, Public Opinion and Theology*, and *Living Together*. He says that "Bowne wrote no greater book than his *Principles of Ethics*."

otherness in the case of things it does not define. At least this is the position adopted by such a critical realist as Professor J. B. Pratt. He explicitly states that a critical realist might in his ontology be a dualist, a Platonist, a panpsychist or some other kind of idealist.[13] As he sees it, critical realism is not a metaphysic. It simply asserts the otherness of the object in perception, and in this respect it is in complete accord with personalism. Personalism is quite as emphatic in its epistemological dualism as is critical realism.

But while Professor Pratt regards critical realism as metaphysically neutral, this does not seem to be the view held by most of those who style themselves critical realists. Most of them apparently look upon critical realism as consonant only with a realistic or materialistic metaphysics. Roy W. Sellars, for instance, treats critical realism as the epistemological counterpart of the metaphysical system which he calls "evolutionary naturalism." The two are represented as different sides of the same worldview so that one involves the other. Evolutionary naturalism presupposes critical realism, and critical realism "justifies evolutionary naturalism." "The critical realist," we are told, "knows that physical reality is existent in its own right," and he apparently also knows that nothing really exists except physical reality. At least this is the view of the evolutionary naturalist. He is not simply a metaphysical realist but a materialist; only he wishes to be known as a materialist of the new school. The old materialism he condemns as mechanical, as an absurd "monism of force." It did not have an adequate epistemology, and it lacked appreciation of organization and

---

[13] *Essays in Critical Realism*, p. 109.

novelty.   It did not take evolution nor did it take mind seriously enough.   The new materialism remedies these defects.   It admits that the idealistic critic was right in maintaining that we have no direct perception of material substance or material cause.   We have "knowledge" of the external world but no intuition of it; in other words, the real world is a thought world and not a world of immediate experience.   Again, the new materialism not only admits but stresses the fact of novelty.   Consciousness is something qualitatively new.   Provision is thus made for progress, and the leveling tendency of traditional materialism is avoided.

But on a little further examination it turns out that the new materialism under the name of "evolutionary naturalism" is simply our old hylozoistic friend.   Quite in the style of Tyndall's famous Belfast Address we are told that we have in the past thought too meanly of matter. "Inorganic matter is a far more active, subtle and responsive stuff than the brickbat atomism of the past supposed. It lends itself to mobile integrations which under the hand of time may lead to tremendous novelties."[14]   We must, therefore, enlarge our conception of the physical, and particularly of the brain, so as to make room for such a novelty as consciousness.   We are even told that "consciousness literally assists the brain to meet new situations."[15] But the sting is at once taken out of this heretical utterance by the assurance that consciousness is merely a form of brain activity and that the assistance which the brain receives from consciousness is, therefore, only a case of self-help. The author's materialistic orthodoxy is thus re-

[14] R. W. Sellars, *Evolutionary Naturalism*, p. 263.   Reprinted by permission of The Open Court Publishing Company.
[15] *Ibid.*, p. 313.

established, and matter is again seen to be the sole and all-sufficient causal reality. Mind, it is repeatedly stated, is a physical category.

It takes very little reflection to see that this new materialism is exposed to essentially the same criticisms as the older hylozoism. Its identification of mind and matter or mind and brain is a pure verbalism. It does not carry with it the slightest insight. To say that thinking is a neural process has about as much meaning as to say that red is white. The combination of words is possible, but no real thought is expressed by it. Again the new materialism is necessitarian. It professes to be a synthesis of necessity and freedom, but the synthesis is one in which real freedom, that is, self-determination in the light of an ideal, completely vanishes. Causal necessity reigns supreme, and with it reason, as we have repeatedly pointed out, collapses. Then, too, the new materialism makes possible no real novelty, no real development. It is "evolutionary" only in name. Consciousness, when it first appeared on this planet, was novel in the sense that it had not appeared before, but it was nevertheless "implicit" or "potential" in matter. Inorganic matter was so constituted that under certain conditions consciousness would necessarily appear. But its appearance did not mean the advent of a new entity. "Consciousness is not a new stuff in any metaphysical sense;" it is a function of the physical organism, and owes its origin entirely to material processes of integration. It represents, therefore, nothing metaphysically new any more than the digestive organs do.[16] All that exists to-day was provided for in the inner constitution of matter. There is consequently no

---

[16] *Ibid.*, p. 341.

metaphysical progress. We explain the effect by carrying it into the cause and in juggler fashion we deduce the effect from the cause after we have constructed the cause in such a way as to contain all effects. The barren and unprogressive character of such explanation ought to be evident to everyone.

The agnostic implications and self-contradictory character of the new materialism are also evident. Its conception of ultimate or material reality is extremely elusive. Being is said to be concrete, and its concrete forms are said to have size, impenetrability, structure and capacity for action. But when it comes to the inner nature of being and of particular things, all is mystery. "The physical thing," we read, "unifies itself, much as our minds do through immanent processes;" and again we read that "just as we can change while still feeling ourselves to be the same, so can things which surround us."[17] Now on the conscious and personal plane we understand this combination of unity with plurality and of identity with change. It is given to us in our own self-experience. But how this is possible on the subconscious and impersonal plane is a complete mystery. Indeed, it is not only mysterious, but the very idea of such a combination is self-contradictory. Causal necessity requires us to carry change into being; otherwise the change is not accounted for. But to do so destroys the self-identity of being. Causal necessity also requires us to carry plurality into being; otherwise the plurality is not accounted for. But to do so destroys the unity of being. Nevertheless the materialistic realist has no hesitancy in attributing to physical reality the characteristic qualities of free intelligence.

---

[17] *Evolutionary Naturalism*, pp. 139, 150.

It changes and yet remains the same. It is many and yet one. In its totality it is "a tremendous expanse of heaving, self-organizing, self-differentiating being." But what the selfhood, the unity, and identity of such a being consist in passes understanding. Yet they are blandly asserted. The result is a confused and self-contradictory conception of a mysterious being whose inner activity is absolutely hidden from us and yet whose mills somehow grind out all the multitudinous forms of conscious and unconscious existence in the universe. This conception, we are told, is "the actual *Weltanschauung* of the present." But whether it is or not, it contains nothing that is in principle new. It is really a species of philosophical atavism, a travesty of true philosophy. What true philosophy aims to do is to explain the world, and this it can do only as it finds its ultimate principle in a reality that is intelligible to us. Such a heterogeneous combination of science and nescience as we have in naturalistic realism leaves the world-problem as much of a riddle as ever.

It is not, however, materialistic realism with which we are here concerned, but a natural realism that ascribes metaphysical reality to things as well as selves. This type of realism is inherent in spontaneous thought, and not until modern times was it radically and fundamentally challenged. The grounds on which it is rejected by personalism may be gathered together under four general considerations.

The *first* is negative in character and consists in pointing out that no epistemological proof of realism is possible. The stronghold of realism has always been the immediacy with which material objects seem to be apprehended. We apparently have an intuitive knowledge of them so that to express any doubt as to their extramental existence would seem to call in question the elementary affirmations of consciousness itself.   But this naïve view, growing out of the objectivity of thought, is soon seen to be mistaken.   Physics teaches us that a large part of the object as it exists for the naïve realist is subjective.   The sense-qualities in general are effects in us; they do not belong to the extramental things.   Tastes and colors, odors and sounds, have no intelligible meaning apart from the sensitive subject.   We instinctively ascribe these qualities to the things themselves, but our instinct at this point turns out to be misleading.   And if spontaneous common sense is mistaken with reference to the secondary qualities of things, there is nothing that forbids its also being mistaken with reference to their primary qualities.   Consciousness itself cannot establish the extramental reality of things.   Occasionally an immediate, intuitive, and indubitable apprehension of the primary, as distinct from the secondary, qualities of things is affirmed, but this affirmation is entirely dogmatic without any foundation either in psychology or epistemology.

The more usual method of seeking to prove the realistic position is to say that it is required by the law of causation.   The content of perception may be quite different from the external object, but it is the object nevertheless that is the cause of the perception.   The secondary qualities do not belong to the things themselves but they are stimulated by them so that they have their ground in objective reality.   We do not create our own objects, we find them.   They in a sense coerce us, so that whatever be their real nature we cannot doubt their reality.   The law of causation compels us to admit it.   But while this line of argument has some weight as against solipsism, it

makes no headway against objective idealism. The idealist frankly admits that perception as mental event must
have a cause, but this cause might with Leibnitz be found
in the nature of the soul or with Berkeley in the divine
will and action. There is nothing in the principle of causality and nothing in the physiological and physical antecedents of perception that require us to find its cause in
the external object. Between a perception and the nervous change that precedes it there is no necessary connection, so far as we can see. And there is also no necessary connection between the hypothetical nervous
change and the apparent object. Perceptions often occur,
as in dreams, delirium, and insanity, when there are no
corresponding objects. It is, then, impossible to prove
the truth of realism by means of epistemology.

The same, it should be added, is also true of idealism.
The fact that things exist for us only as we think them
and that thinking is a unique mental process by no
means excludes the view that things have an extramental
existence. This question is one that can be settled only by
metaphysics, by a study of the object itself. So far as
psychology and epistemology are concerned the conflict
between realism and idealism is a drawn battle. By virtually recognizing this fact critical realism marks a distinct
advance beyond the older "natural" realism, which claimed
an immediate and intuitive knowledge of material or
extramental reality. This claim was denied by idealism,
and critical realism admits the correctness of the denial.
Objective reality is something that must be thought; it
cannot be intuited. The question between realism and
idealism is, then, simply as to which has the more satisfactory theory of reality. One is a theory quite as much
as the other. Neither has an intuitive insight into the

nature of the object. To have conceded this, as critical realism does, is to leave the door open to idealism.

Naïve realism is impossible. This is generally admitted. The only form of substantialistic realism that has any hope of maintaining itself is "critical" or "transfigured" realism. By this is meant the realism of the physical sciences, the realism which finds objective reality in the invisible and nonsensible world of atoms and electrons, of force and energy. This type of realism consigns the whole sense-world to subjectivity, and thus loses the powerful support of common sense. All that it has in common with the latter is the belief in existence as extramental and perhaps the assumption that reality is spatial. Apart from these common elements the object is conceived almost entirely differently in the two cases. In the one it is intuited, in the other it is a thought-construct. But more significant than this is the fact that the real world of transfigured realism is one of increasing poverty and worthlessness.

This is the *second* main consideration urged by personalism against the realistic world-view. The richness and worth of the material world lie almost entirely in its secondary or sense qualities, and the range of these qualities is being constantly extended. A world without them, without light and color, without sound, without taste and odor, would be virtually devoid of value. It would be the bare skeleton of being without any sensible content. Yet such is the self-existent world of transfigured realism. In it sense qualities have no place. They may or may not be produced by it, but in any case they represent nothing existentially real. They are not purposed in such a way that they complete nature. They are, rather, a screen thrown over it. Material nature is complete in itself; and as such a self-existent entity it is, as we have seen, increasingly barren of content. This assignment of virtually all the worth of objective experience to more or less masking phenomena and the denial of practically all value to the real world is perhaps not a self-contradictory conception, but it runs so directly counter to a fundamental persuasion of the human mind with reference to the relation of ultimate being and worth to each other that it has little hope of being able to maintain itself against a metaphysical system like that of personalism which "saves" appearances and gives to them an ontological significance by making them expressive of a purpose immanent in nature itself.

The *third* and most important criticism to be passed on natural realism has to do with its conception of reality. For it things are as metaphysically real as persons, and probably more so. Reality as such does not, therefore, imply consciousness. It exists in a subconscious state as substance or energy or both together. There may be different kinds of substance and different kinds of energy. There may be such things as immaterial substances and immaterial forms of energy. But the standard type of reality for the realistic mind is space-filling substance or energy operating in space. The latter is a more refined notion than the former and is somewhat more difficult for the imagination to grasp. But this difficulty is usually overcome by combining the two views. Substance is thought of as the seat of energy, and matter and force are thus united to form the concrete thing. This seems perfectly clear and satisfactory to the mind so long as it remains on the picturing plane. But when we analyze the notion of reality and see that it implies unity in the midst of plurality and identity throughout change, it becomes at once a problem whether these tests of metaphysical reality can be met by an impersonal thing of any kind whatsoever. Space is infinitely divisible, and so also is everything in space. Even if the atom or electron should be indivisible, this would not mean that it is a true unit. For insofar as it occupies space, it has distinguishable parts, and these parts are external to each other so that metaphysically they do not constitute a single, unitary being. All spatial existence by its very nature breaks up into an indefinite plurality, and thus fails to meet the first test of reality, that of unity. Furthermore, no impersonal thing can change or produce change and yet remain the same thing. For change can be accounted for only on the assumption that the being on which it is dependent also changes. Change, in other words, must penetrate into the very core of being, if it is to have a causal explanation; and this means that on the impersonal plane there is nothing in being that endures. All impersonal being or cause dissolves away into the Heraclitic flux. It has no identity, and thus fails to meet the second as well as the first test of reality.

It is, therefore, no mental eccentricity that has led the profoundest minds in the world's history to deny metaphysical reality to material objects. These objects have phenomenal reality. They are no illusions of the individual. As objects of experience they are common to all. They are grounded in objective reality. But when analyzed, it becomes evident to critical thought that they are not self-existent entities. They are simply substantiated or hypostatized phenomena. Viewed as independent things they are inconsistent and self-contradictory. No appeal to the immediacy and finality of experience can blind the human mind to this fact. It is a crude conception of the real, a conception growing out of an incomplete analysis of sense-experience, that has led realists to ascribe metaphysical reality to physical objects. Such objects are real in experience and for the imagination. But when subjected to the scrutiny of thought, their apparent unity and identity dissolve away, and with these attributes goes also their ontological reality. It is only in free intelligence that unity can be harmonized with plurality and identity with change. To it, therefore, reality is to be ascribed in a different sense from that in which it is attributed to impersonal existence.

The *fourth* consideration which leads us to reject natural realism is the unstable position in which it leaves religious thought. By asserting the co-ordinate reality of the physical and the mental it opens the door to naturalism, materialism, and atheism. If nature is a self-running mechanism or a self-existent reality, there is no reason for going beyond it. It is sufficient unto itself and needs no God either as its creator or preserver. Furthermore, if it is the source of all physical phenomena, it is probable that it is also the source of the mental life, for the souls both of men and animals are manifestly dependent forms of existence. They arise in connection with physical organisms and vanish with them. In spite of this they may, it is true, be to a certain extent independent and self-existent. But if their reality is supposed to be merely co-ordinate with that of things and to consist in an immaterial substance or energy, it is very doubtful if their claim to independent existence can be successfully maintained. As compared with the great self-sufficient world of things their being almost inevitably sinks into comparative insignificance. And from this it is but a short step to a denial of their ontological reality altogether. With the progress of science natural law has steadily widened its domain and apparently proved itself more and more adequate to an explanation of the world. Why, then, should we any longer take account of spiritual beings or causes? Their very existence is not only hypothetical but superfluous. So far as science itself is concerned, it has long since escorted both God and souls to the border of the universe and bowed them out with thanks for past services. And there seems no good reason why its example should not be followed by people in general. The ontological reality of things makes unnecessary the ontological reality of spirit, either finite or infinite. This is the natural history of unbelief. Realism leads to materialism.

The only satisfactory way to escape the materialistic or atheistic conclusion is to deny the realistic thesis that matter and material things are metaphysically real. This denial is not new. It has had a long history. In one form or another, though with different degrees of thoroughness and consistency, it has been current among religious thinkers since the time of Plato. It appears in its most extreme and most consistent form in modern idealism. It is also, formally at least, accepted by positivists. But widely current as it is, it is still for most people a hard saying. The average mind and many a trained mind cling tenaciously to the extramental and substantial reality of things. The idealistic and positivistic standpoint seems to them superficial and even frivolous. Francis Bacon likened the moderate forms of idealism represented by Plato and Aristotle to "planks of lighter and less solid wood" that were "preserved amid the waves of time," which submerged the more weighty works of such realis-

tic thinkers as the atomists.[18] A current writer of some
distinction both in the field of philosophy and theology
has compared the entire philosophic movement, insofar as
it has departed from common-sense realism, to the foolish
and disastrous journey of the prodigal son into a far
country, and has said that the epistemological idealist is
like a quack physician who administers a drug that makes
the patient's ailment chronic and thus renders his own
further services permanently necessary.[19] So deep-seated
is the realistic prejudice that to many minds any departure from it seems to suggest intellectual recklessness or
moral irresponsibility or both. But despite this congenital
difficulty, under which the picturing type of mind labors,
the realistic position is not one in which either reason or
faith can rest. Reason is forced to transcend the idea of
spatial or impersonal substance because of its self-contradictory character, and faith is compelled to do the same
because from its standpoint the impersonal can have no
intrinsic worth. Its value is purely instrumental, and
since it is such, no impersonal thing can be self-existent,
for self-existence carries with it the idea of existence for
self, and this implies intrinsic value. The instrumental
position, to which religious faith condemns everything
impersonal, necessarily excludes the possibility of its independent and self-sufficient existence. The moment such
existence is attributed to it the material world bulks so
large in human thought as completely to overwhelm
everything spiritual. The only way to keep the physical
in its place and prevent it from tyrannizing over life as a
whole is to deny to it true ontological reality. It then

---

[18] See C. C. J. Webb, *A History of Philosophy*, p. 63.
[19] D. C. Macintosh, *The Reasonableness of Christianity*, pp. 163–165;
The Problem of Knowledge, p. 334.

becomes simply the spatial and temporal form of the divine energizing, and space and time themselves are seen in their true character as "the two great intimidating phantoms." When thought reaches this conclusion faith has nothing to fear from the world of nature. But let the realistic camel's nose into the tent of faith and there is grave danger that eventually he will destroy it all. Only as we reduce matter to phenomenality can we draw the sting from it and render it religiously harmless.

But while natural realism is both logically and religiously in a state of unstable equilibrium, tending toward naturalism and atheism, it does embody two important truths. As over against solipsism it asserts the independence and universality of the object. Theoretically solipsism is possible. There is no way of logically demonstrating the independent existence of the objects of thought. The psychological distinction betwen subject and object does not necessarily involve their metaphysical otherness. Since nothing exists for me except as I think it, it is abstractly conceivable that the only existence of the world consists in my thinking it. But this abstract possibility involves such a degree of absurdity that no sane person could seriously entertain it. No one could really persuade himself that the Great War and all past history occurred simply in his own mind, and that other people and the starry heavens exist only as his mental states. The existence of an objective order, independent of the individual and open to other minds, is as certain as anything could be. It is the presupposition of all rational intercourse. And insofar as natural realism affirms this fact, it serves as a needed corrective of subjective idealism. It makes the mistake of supposing that independence of finite thought means independence of all thought; this is its radical error. But its emphasis, nevertheless, upon the fact that the objective order is one that we find and not one that we create, is important. The world exists independently of all finite perception.

Natural realism is also right, as over against absolute idealism, in refusing to identify the world with the thought of the Absolute. It is mistaken insofar as it represents the world as self sufficient and independent of the divine thought. The world is dependent on God, but dependence on him is not the same as identification with his thought. Between thought and will we must make a distinction. The world is not simply idea, it is deed. It is the forthgoing of divine energy. It is the translation of divine thought into divine act. This is the differentia of cosmic existence. It is dependent upon the divine will, not identical with the divine thought, and in this sense is objective to God himself. Objectivity, so far as the cosmic order is concerned, does not imply self-sufficiency or independence of any kind whatsoever. Only in finite spirits do we have a measure of independence mingled with dependence. But while entirely dependent on the Absolute, the world as his deed is objective to him, an "other," which he as well as we can contemplate. Insofar as natural realism grows out of and embodies this view, it is in accord with personalism and expresses an important truth.[20]

[20] The realistic element in personalism has been especially emphasized by Ralph T. Flewelling. See his *Bergson and Personal Idealism* and his *Personalism and the Problems of Philosophy*. Professor Flewelling has done much to give currency to the personalistic type of thought, not only by his books but also by his establishment of *The Personalist*, a quarterly journal, and the extraordinary success which has attended his development of the department of philosophy in the University of Southern California.

ABSOLUTE IDEALISM

To absolute idealism we have already devoted considerable attention both in the way of exposition and of criticism. Here we need do little more than sum up what has been said in one connection or another in the preceding chapters.

Absolute idealism is no simple and transparent doctrine. It has assumed a number of different forms. We have distinguished three, the monadistic, Spinozistic, and theistic. But widely divergent as these different forms of Hegelianism are, they are at one in their conception of reality as a rational whole. For each of them logical development is the principle of movement in the universe. Whether this logical principle be embodied in innumerable finite centers, or in a superpersonal Being, or in a personal Deity, it is in each case the constitutive factor in reality. Reality is determined by it, so that apart from it there is nothing real. The real is the rational, and the rational is the real. But rationality may be understood in two different senses: in a broader sense which includes purpose, and in a narrower logical sense, which excludes it. The latter is the sense in which absolute idealism in its nontheistic forms has conceived of the rational, and this also is commonly regarded as the characteristic Hegelian interpretation of the term. From this point of view the changing and developing world is simply the dialectical unfolding of thought. Impersonal Thought or Reason is itself reality.

Against this form of idealism several weighty arguments may be and have been urged. For one thing, it is a necessitarian system, and as such is exposed to essentially the same criticisms as those which we on that ground passed upon materialism. Hegelian necessitarianism, it is true, differs from that of materialism in that it is logical while the latter is causal or dynamic. But the speculative consequences in both cases are virtually the same. Both forms of necessitarianism make real progress impossible. Dynamic necessitarianism carries the effect back into the cause and thus makes the cause as complex as the effect. One may say that the effect is only potentially or implicitly present in the cause, but unless its potential or implicit presence is in some sense actual and in some sense also equivalent to its later state, the effect is not accounted for. The same is also the case with logical necessitarianism. Here the conclusion must be contained in the premises; otherwise there would be no logical connection between them and no way of deducing the conclusion. On this plane, therefore, there can be no real development. Time has nothing to do with rational truths. The logical implications of a thing must coexist with the thing, and this means that the universe as a logically necessitated system, as an implication of pure reason, would be eternal and static. There would be no room for movement or progress. Some extralogical and determining factor would have to be introduced into the system, if the implications of reason were to be prevented from coming to instantaneous realization. Only a supralogical will could transform logical implication into temporal succession.

Logical necessitarianism also overthrows reason in the same way that dynamic determinism does. It makes error as necessary as truth, and thus leaves us with no standard that would enable us to distinguish between them and no means of using the standard if we had it.

Furthermore, absolute idealism has this additional difficulty, that it is forced to refer all human error and evil to the absolute reason and so to introduce into reason itself an element of unreason. The system thus contradicts itself.

A second objection to absolute idealism is that it is as helpless to account for concrete reality as materialism is to account for the mental life. Its conception of reality is, to begin with, abstract. It starts with thought or reason, but thought without a thinker or reason without a reasoner is a pure abstraction. Reality is always concrete. It is an agent. Without an agent there can be no activity, either mental or physical. To make reason or thought the ultimate reality is, therefore, to misconceive the nature of reality. It is also to leave concrete existence unexplained. For there is no way of deducing the thinker from thought. Nor can any form of individual existence be derived from general ideals. Logical abstractions cannot be thickened into real things. In concrete reality there are contingent elements that defy deduction from anything simpler or more general. We may speak of nature as "petrified" or "frozen intelligence" or as "the corpse of the understanding," but these figures of speech in no way relieve the difficulty connected with the transition from universality to individuality. This problem Hegel never solved, and his system at times leaves the impression of being a "spectral woof of impalpable abstractions, or unearthly ballet of bloodless categories."[21]

The fact is that in the world as we know it there are three different stages or degrees of generality, and there is no way of logically binding them together. First, there

[21] F. H. Bradley, *Principles of Logic*, 1883, p. 553.

are the categories of thought, the necessary truths of reason, such as being and causality, space and time. They
outline a possible existence, give us the framework of
reality, but within that framework do not prescribe what
reality must be. The universe might be very different
from what it actually is and yet fit into the categories of
space, time, and causality. No category determines any
specific object or event that falls under it. And the same
holds true of the general laws of the cosmos. These laws
represent a second and more limited stage or range of
generality, and come closer to concrete reality but still
leave it undetermined. They themselves fall under the
categories and are consistent with them, but are not determined by them, and so in turn the detailed facts of
existence fall under the general laws of nature and are
consistent with them but are not determined by them.
The law of gravitation, for instance, is a specification
under the category of causality but not a deduction from
it, and so any concrete object such as a planet or bowlder
fits in with the law of gravitation and other laws of nature but cannot be deduced from them. The world of
facts thus represents a third stage in the cosmic order, and
between it and the realm of law there is no logical bond,
just as there is no logical bond between the realm of cosmic law and that of the categories. Facts, laws, and
categories are three different factors in the objective order, and there is no logical ladder connecting them so that
we can descend from categories to laws and from laws
to facts. The attempt of absolute idealism to bind them
into a logical whole is an impossible task and can only
end by doing violence to the uniqueness and individuality
of the factual order. Between the universal and the par-

ticular and between thought and thing there is a chasm which pure logic can never bridge. Only as we enlarge reason so as to include purpose and will are we able to pass from thought to reality; and even then the transition, though formally intelligible, remains in its inner nature an ineffable mystery.

The failure of absolute idealism to account for concrete reality or to do justice to it, is reflected in its epistemological monism. This doctrine is the third weak spot in its armor. We considered it at some length in Chapter II. We there pointed out that the identification of thought and thing fails to give adequate recognition to the "given" element in experience, that it overlooks the unique character of reality, and that it does not, after all, succeed in overcoming the dualism of human knowing. Things are not simply our thoughts. If they were, we would be condemned to the absurdity of solipsism. And if by "things" we mean divine thoughts, the problem of how we come to know them would still remain unsolved. For us the dualism of thought and thing would continue. But the chief objection to epistemological monism that we pointed out is its inability to account for error. If thought and thing be identical, the thing would in every case be directly apprehended so that there could be no parallax between it and our thought, and hence no error. And if a distinction is made between our thought and the divine thought, it is still maintained by absolute idealism that our thought with all its infusion of error and ignorance is a part of the divine experience, and in that case we are at a total loss to understand how in the unitary experience of the Absolute ignorance and error can coexist with unclouded light and perfect truth. We are,

therefore, justified in saying that epistemological monism
founders on the fact of error.

A fourth argument urged against absolute idealism is
that it is pantheistic and so tends to undermine religious
faith. This, of course, is no argument against it in the
eyes of the unbeliever. But from the standpoint of the
philosophy of religion it is a weighty consideration. Absolute idealism was without doubt originally conceived in
the interest of religion. What Hegel aimed at was a final
synthesis of Christianity and philosophy.[22] And that he
contributed in a profoundly significant way to the revival
of religious faith can hardly be questioned. But the inner
logic of his system, as it wrought itself out, proved eventually to be adverse to religion. It tended to make the
Absolute impersonal and to break down the separateness
and independence of finite personality. Its motive even
here was in a sense religious. It was interested in the
feeling of absolute dependence and of mystical union with
the Deity. But this feeling it exaggerated to such an
extent that it tended to destroy what is most characteristic of religion. What religion is primarily concerned
about is not the metaphysical union of the human with
the divine, but a relation of mutual understanding between them, a relation that expresses itself on our part
in worship and in an attitude of love and obedience. Such
a relation, however, is possible only between persons and
between persons that retain their own distinct individuality. To resolve the divine personality into "a glorified
syllogism," as the more characteristic form of absolute
idealism seems to do, and to dissolve human personality
into a mere phase or mode of the Absolute, is to render

---

[22] See my *Present Tendencies in Religious Thought*, pp. 214ff.

true religious experience impossible and to betray the cause of religion. Pantheism in both the practical and the speculative realm leads to disastrous consequences. And insofar as this viewpoint is the direct or implicit teaching of absolute idealism, it constitutes a fatal objection to that system.

But while the foregoing arguments may be regarded as decisive against the Hegelian philosophy as commonly understood, there are one or two important truths in it which should be noted. Indeed, "immortal merits," as Bowne said, must be conceded to Hegel. It was he who gave to the problem of knowledge perhaps its clearest and sharpest formulation. It was he also who established once for all the doctrine that the real is necessarily rational. Whatever is irrational is unreal and impossible. Only as being is shaped by the categories of thought can it be given an intelligible content. It is therefore, according to Hegel, futile to try to conceive of reality apart from reason. This profound insight constitutes, in spite of all their differences, a permanent bond of union between personalism and Hegelianism. Both are forms of rational idealism, and all rational idealism has its roots in the conviction that only the rational is real. It is this conviction that rules out materialism and natural realism as metaphysical systems. Matter cannot be rationalized without ceasing to be matter. Hence its existence as an ontological entity is rejected, and idealism becomes a corollary of metaphysical rationalism. If the real must be rational, then it must also be nonmaterial or ideal in its nature. On this point both personalism and absolutism are agreed. But when it comes to defining the ideal and the rational, they begin to part company. The tendency in Hegelian absolutism is to restrict the ideal and the rational to thought or to ideas in their logical relation to each other. When taken strictly, this excludes both the will and the self as extralogical factors from the realm of the ideal, the rational and the real, and turns the universe into a logical mechanism. Voluntarism and personalism, from this point of view, are stigmatized as relics of realism.

To this charge personalism replies by pointing out that the purely logical is abstract and has no real existence. The rational is real as opposed to the irrational, but rationality itself is not metaphysically real. Apart from a thinker there is no thought and no rationality. The self is the seat and the source of all that is rational and all that is ideal. To assert the reality of the rational and ideal is, therefore, to assert the reality of the self. To deny the self and assert the reality of its activities is absurd. Without an agent there can be no activities. The reality is always an agent, and since the real is rational, the only reality is a rational agent. The idealism, for which personalism stands, is, therefore, not an abstract, logical idealism but a concrete, spiritual idealism. The reality that lies back of the phenomenal order is the energizing of a free and intelligent spirit. Without this energizing the divine ideas could not be translated into reality. Reason must be linked up with will and embodied in personality before it becomes real. In and of itself it is an empty abstraction. Personality consequently is rational not in the sense that it is logically put together and conforms with certain abstract standards of rationality, but in the sense that it is the source of all rationality and contains within itself the standard by which the categories of thought must be interpreted. In other words, personalistic rationalism is empirical. It finds its ultimate basis and interpretation in self-experience. The self alone meets the Hegelian test of reality. It alone is rational, and that in a double sense. For one thing, it alone has the capacity to reason and to guide itself by rational principles; and, in the second place, it alone combines in its own being unity with plurality and identity with change, and thus meets the fundamental demands which reason makes of reality.

If we are to have a rational metaphysics, it must be personalistic. Our criticism of materialism, natural realism, and absolute idealism has made this reasonably clear. Atheists, as Auguste Comte said, are "the most illogical of theologians, for they occupy themselves with theological problems and yet reject the only appropriate method of handling them."[23] Our choice must be made between theism and positivism, as Bowne clearly saw from the very beginning of his career as an independent thinker.[24] But while this is a significant consideration as over against the impersonal metaphysical systems we have examined, it frankly admits that in positivism theism has a rival that is not so easily dispossessed. Science has given to positivism great prestige, so that this type of thought has to a large extent replaced the older materialism. It is a complex movement, largely epistemological in character, and has had many different centers. In the Anglo-Saxon world it has made itself most distinctly felt in the form of sensationalistic empiricism, pragmatism, and neo-realism, to each of which a brief criticism will be devoted.

[23] *A General View of Positivism*, p. 50.
[24] Compare *The Philosophy of Herbert Spencer*, pp. 244, 258.

Empiricism

Empiricism has not always been positivistic, nor is it wholly such at present. But since the time of Hume this has been its most characteristic form. Berkeley broke its alliance with materialism, and Hume its alliance with spiritualism. These older alliances, it is true, have since persisted to some extent, but the new alliance with positivism has represented the main and most distinctive current in the empiricistic movement. The movement as a whole has had a long and varied history. A brief survey of it was given in Chapter II in connection with our study of the doctrine of the creative activity of thought. We there noted some of the more important changes that empiricism has undergone in the course of its development. Bowne characterized it as "the chameleon of philosophy." Only by continually changing its color to suit the emergency has it been able to maintain itself. This changeability renders it somewhat difficult of exact definition. But insofar as it has a distinctive character it may be defined as the doctrine that the human mind in knowing is purely passive and that experience is the sole source of knowledge. This leaves open the question as to what "experience" and "pure passivity" mean. On these points there has been a great deal of unclearness and confusion of thought among empiricists. The main tendency, however, has been to construe experience as sense-experience and to interpret pure passivity as meaning that the human mind has no power beyond that of reacting in a more or less mechanical way to external stimuli. The self has consequently been virtually eliminated, indeed usually explicitly so, and knowledge has been restricted to what the senses reveal. These conclusions run directly counter to the higher faiths of mankind, and hence one of the chief characteristics of personalism has been its polemic against traditional empiricism. Bowne never wearied of pointing out its errors. Some of them we will here enumerate.

1.   Empiricism has erred in supposing that knowledge can be imported into the mind from without. This is the older and cruder form of empiricism, but it still seems so natural to spontaneous thought that it has not yet been completely overcome. We do not, as did the ancients and scholastics, conceive of objects as throwing off images of themselves which somehow enter the human mind, nor do we employ, as they did, the figure of the seal and the wax to illustrate the process of perception. But we still have people who seem to think that the fact that there is a picture of the object on the retina, removes all the mystery of vision, and we still read of objects as "impressing" or "photographing" themselves upon the mind. We are also told by many realists that the objective world itself somehow builds up perception and reason within us, so that the mind is the direct product of external forces. Again we are assured that our knowledge of the object is so "immediate" that all subjectivity is removed from it and that our thought is completely determined by what it apprehends. But all this rests upon a misunderstanding of the nature of thought. Thought cannot exist apart from thinking; it is not something that can be passed bodily along. No conceivable impression or photograph that the object might produce of itself on the mind would carry with it, or account for, knowledge. In that case we would simply have "an outline *on* the mind, and not a thought *in* the mind." Real subjectivity

would not be reached. Thought is a unique mental reaction, and cannot in the nature of the case be imported into the mind from without. All interaction is mutual reaction. This is true of things, if they are metaphysically real, as well as of minds. When things or minds interact, nothing passes between them except figuratively. Each thing or mind reacts according to its own nature. What particular form the reaction will take will depend upon circumstances. But the essential nature and quality of the reaction will be determined by what the thing itself is. Only as there is a reacting mind can there be such a thing as thought. Chiseling a motto into a stone reveals nothing to the stone, and so it would be with the mind viewed simply as a substance, material or immaterial. No external impression would convey anything to it. Thought cannot be transported into the mind, it can only be evoked from it. It is a radical defect of empiricism that it has tended to look upon the mind as a passive recipient of knowledge rather than its creative source.

2. Empiricism has erred in trying to construct the whole mental life out of sensations. Sensations are subjective. They have external stimuli, but they are not carried over into the mind from without. They are reactions on the part of the mind and hence are purely mental in nature. But they are the most elementary forms of mental reaction, so elementary that they are not supposed to involve self-consciousness or any creative activity of thought. Nevertheless, they are regarded as the source of the higher life of the soul. Reason and all its immanent principles are said to be due to the association of sensations. This doctrine received its classical formulation at the hands of Hume, and for a century after his time

it was the prevailing form of empiricism. Kant and his successors subjected it to a searching criticism, and their criticism finally triumphed over it, at least in its atomistic form.[25] They showed that if we start merely with subjective sensations there is no way of reaching the objective world. Sensations cannot transcend themselves, and so if we only have them, we are necessarily condemned to solipsism. Again, they showed that the association of sensations cannot account for memory or the immanent principles of thought. Succession in experience is not the same as the experience of succession. The latter implies an identical self, gifted with the unique power of recognition. To give to sensations any influence in building up the mental life we must assume memory. But even with this assumption and the assumption of various laws of association they do not enable us to distinguish between what happens together in experience and what causally and logically belongs together. To reduce the latter to the former, as Hume sought to do, is to destroy reason and make all science impossible. Indeed, experience itself would be impossible without the constitutive activity of thought. Apart from thought even sensations would have no unity and identity. A color-sensation cannot become a sensation of color until thought has put its stamp upon it. And so also with the things of experience; they owe their objectivity, and their unity and identity to thought. Without thought there could be no articulate experience. Furthermore, the Kantian critics pointed out that sensations or ideas are mere abstractions apart from the self. The universal fact is not the existence of

[25] It may be of interest to note that it was a personalist, James Ward, who in England did most to destroy the dominant psychological atomism.

thoughts and feelings, but, as Bowne said, the concrete experience that I think and I feel. The unitary and identical self is the presupposition of the entire mental life. The failure to see this has been one of the major shortcomings of empiricism.

3. Empiricism has erred in thinking that the idea of a race-experience removes the difficulties connected with the attempted derivation of reason from sensations. This error was introduced into the empirical philosophy largely through the influence of Herbert Spencer. It had been objected to the earlier individualistic empiricism that the early years of infancy and childhood did not afford sufficient time for the transformation of sensations into such remarkable mental powers as the child of three or four years of age possesses. Hence Spencer proposed that we transfer the genesis of the mental life from the experience of the individual to that of the race. In that way an indefinite extension of time was secured, and thus the earlier objection to empiricism was successfully met. Empiricism, we were now told, is true for the race, while apriorism is true for the individual. But the objection to empiricism, based on lack of time, was unfortunate and misleading. The real objection to it, as we have already pointed out, has nothing to do with time. It is to be found in the complete incommensurability of sensations with their assumed products, and this incommensurability is something which no length of time can overcome. To generate thought out of undifferentiated sensations is as impossible in a million years as in three years. Thought requires a mental subject and laws of its own. It cannot be built up out of sense elements by any mechanical operations of association, no matter how long the operations

may continue.   Furthermore, there is no such thing as
a race experience.   All experience is individual.   There
are a great many individual experiences, and all of these
are connected genealogically with an indefinite number of
other individual experiences in the past.   But each experience is owned by an individual, and it is inalienable.   It
cannot be transferred from one individual to another.   It
cannot be inherited.   Whatever development it undergoes
must take place within the individual.   That there are
many individuals organically related to each other and
that they were all preceded genealogically by an indefinite
number of other individuals, does not in the least degree
altar the fact of the strict individuality of all experience.
The race as such has no mind, no consciousness, and no
experience.   If it did have, its consciousness could no
more be derived from mere sense-elements than that of
the individual.   Racial empiricism from this point of view
would thus have no advantage over individualistic empiricism.   But since there is no such thing as a race consciousness or race-experience, racial empiricism not only
is exposed to the same decisive criticisms as individualistic empiricism, but in addition is forced to face the irrefutable charge of operating with a fiction.

4.   Empiricism has erred in maintaining that a relational conception of the original structure of experience
breaks the point of the Kantian criticism, directed against
the older atomistic sensationalism, and renders unnecessary the assumption of an abiding and unifying self. This
error is of comparatively recent origin, and owes its present currency in no small measure to the influence of William James.   His "radical empiricism" rejected the older
view that discrete sensations are the original raw mate-

rial of experience and that their relations to each other
are added by the mind or some other agency. These relations, according to James, are themselves parts of experience, quite as much so as sensations or things themselves.
Experience is, to begin with, connected. It needs no
extraneous principle to bind it together. It "possesses
in its own right a concatenated or continuous structure."
But how such a conception of experience avoids the Kan-
tion criticism is hard to see. If sensations become anything articulate only as they receive the stamp of thought,
surely a stream of consciousness with its inter-related
parts gives every evidence of being the work of thought.
When confronted with it one cannot escape the question,
How is experience possible? And the only rational answer
is that it is rendered possible only through a unitary and
abiding self endowed with the immanent principles of
reason. Without such a self experience becomes an un-
accountable piece of magic. Indeed, the existence of the
self cannot be denied without being implied. This is evident in the case both of David Hume and William James.
The latter's representation of individual "thoughts" as
"thinkers" is simply a curious way of describing or re-
naming the self. No greater inconsequence is to be
found in the history of thought than the empiricistic denial of the self. "Among all the errors of the human
mind," said Lotze, "it has always seemed to me the
strangest that it could come to doubt its own existence, of
which alone it has direct experience, or to take it at second hand as the product of an external nature which we
know only indirectly, only by means of the knowledge of
the very mind to which we would fain deny existence."[26]

[26] *Microcosmus*, i, 263.

5. Empiricism has erred in limiting knowledge to sense-experience. This has not been true of empiricism as a whole nor does it necessarily inhere in empiricism as such. But it has been true of traditional empiricism. There has, however, been considerable difference of opinion as to the range of sense-experience. Hume limited it to the affections of the passive sensibility, and this, as we have seen, leads logically to nihilism. No knowledge whatsoever is possible on this basis. More commonly sense-experience is supposed to carry with it a knowledge of the world of material things. This empiricistic viewpoint, if strictly adhered to, leads to materialism. It implies that we can know nothing but material objects. The entire realm of spirit lies beyond the range of knowledge, and is to be regarded as an illusion. But this type of empiricism is wholly uncritical. Our knowledge of the external world involves a complex mental activity, and would be impossible to a purely registering intellect. Furthermore, there is not the slightest speculative warrant for assuming that our minds react only to physical stimuli and that our senses, consequently, give us the full measure of reality. It is quite possible that we may have an awareness of reality beyond sense. Such an awareness the mystics have always claimed for themselves, and Royce tells us that they are the only thoroughgoing empiricists in the history of philosophy.[27] Sense empiricism is an unwarranted dogmatism. It falls a prey both to rationalistic criticism and to mystical intuition. William James recognized this, and in his "radical empiricism" made a place for mystical states, ascribing to them a cognitive function. They are, he said, "windows through

[27] *The World and the Individual*, i, p. 81.

which the mind looks upon a more extensive and inclusive world." They vary greatly in vividness with different people and at different times with the same people. But it is in them that vital religious faith has its root. God is primarily not an inference but an object of perception. He himself, as Bowne says, "is the great source of the belief in God."[28]   To restrict valid experience to the physical senses is to be untrue to the empirical principle itself.   For not only have multitudes throughout all the ages been persuaded that they had an experience of a supersensible reality, but what is more patent is that such an experience is given to us in our own self-experience. There is no datum of experience more certain than the unitary and abiding self.   It is the presupposition of all articulate sense-experience, and to deny it in the interest of the latter is not only to violate the fundamental principle of empiricism but to commit intellectual *hara-kiri*.

6.   Empiricism has erred in supposing that it could account for the validity of human knowledge by the theory of natural selection.   This view was introduced into the empirical philosophy by Herbert Spencer.   According to it, false ideas are quite as possible as true ideas, and, to begin with, organisms may have produced the former quite as freely as the latter.   But false ideas brought the organism into collision with its environment. Hence the tendency was for organisms that thought wrongly to be destroyed.   Only right thinking organisms permanently propagated their kind.   The result has been a gradual adjustment of thought to things.   The inadequacy and self-destructive character of this theory, however, become evident on a few moments' re-

---

[28] *Studies in Theism*, p. 81.

flection. For one thing the theory, if true, would account for the validity of ideas only insofar as they relate to survival; and these form only a small part of the total body of our beliefs. Again, the theory requires us to hold that the test of truth is to be found in the age and inspirational value of a belief. Those beliefs that are old and widespread must be true; otherwise they would not have survived. Beliefs, also, that give us hope and courage and that tend to prolong life, must likewise be true. But the beliefs that most completely fulfill these conditions are those of a religious character, and to accept them as valid would be to undermine the theory we are considering. For they imply the existence of God and rational spirits—existences that have no place in the naturalistic empiricism of Spencer. The fact is that on the empiricistic basis there is no solution of the problem of knowledge. Either we must assume an opaque harmony of thought and thing or we must fall into a solipsistic denial of the object, and with that thought itself collapses.

But in spite of the manifest inadequacy, the superficiality, and self-contradictory character of much that has passed and still passes as empiricism, there are two important truths that empiricism has emphasized. First, it has stressed the fact that reality is something given. We do not and cannot deduce it, nor can we construct it out of rational principles. It is imparted to us. We find it, we do not make it. What its exact nature is, is a point on which empiricists, it is true, are divided. Some conceive it realistically and some idealistically. But in either case it is something concrete and factual, an elementary datum, of whose content we can give no further account except to say, if we are theists, that it is due to the divine will. In this respect empiricism is in accord with personalism as against absolute idealism. In the next place, empiricism in its traditional form has rejected the idea of a soul substance. It has interpreted the soul in terms of consciousness. Insofar as it has rejected the reality of the soul or self altogether, it has erred. It has also erred in conceiving the mind as passive. But insofar as it has found the unity and identity of the self in consciousness rather than in an underlying substance, either material or immaterial, it has marked a significant advance and has made a valuable contribution to the personalistic conception of the soul and of reality in general. The personalist finds the essence of the soul in self-consciousness and self-control. This is something empirical, something given. How it is possible we do not know. But it is the only known instance of an actual union of identity and change and of unity and plurality, and as such constitutes the only possible key to ultimate reality. In making this its basal contention personalism is empiricistic, but its empiricism is "transcendental" by way of contrast with the positivistic sense-empiricism of the past.

Pragmatism

Pragmatism is an empiricistic and positivistic reaction against the absolute idealism of the nineteenth century, on the one hand, and its materialism, on the other. Personalism may also be regarded as a reaction against these two types of philosophy, but it differs from pragmatism in that it is not positivistic, nor is it empiricistic in the traditional sense of the term. The polemic of pragmatism is directed chiefly against the intellectualism of traditional

epistemology and the absolutism of traditional metaphysics. This polemic is not novel. James speaks of
pragmatism as simply a new name for some old ways of
thinking. But modest as this statement is, pragmatism
has high notions of its own importance. It aims at a reconstruction of philosophy,[29] is conscious of a universal
mission, and pretends to a conquering destiny.[30] It is not,
however, a systematic whole. It is, rather, a composite
movement, embracing different tendencies which have
been and are capable of being only imperfectly welded
together. It stresses the empirical, the concrete and the
practical. In these respects it is in accord with personalism. Indeed, Woodbridge Riley speaks of pragmatism
as "a doctrine of personalism."[31] But personalism, as he
uses the term, has a much more limited meaning than we
give it. With us it implies both apriorism and a definite
metaphysical theory, and thus runs counter to characteristic tendencies in pragmatism. The objections to the latter movement may be gathered together under four general statements.

1.   The empiricism, upon which pragmatism is based
or with which it is allied, is exposed to most of the criticisms which we have urged against the empiricistic
philosophy in general. It rejects, it is true, atomistic sensationalism, and is not itself a pure sense-empiricism. William James, at least, held that we might have an experience of the supersensible. He saw in mystical states
avenues of approach to a larger and more inclusive world.
This view breaks the earlier alliance between empiricism
and materialism. It leaves the door open to religion. But

---

[29] Compare John Dewey, *Reconstruction in Philosophy* (1920).
[30] Compare William James, *Pragmatism*, p. 50.
[31] *American Thought*, p. 279.

at the same time pragmatistic empiricism denies the reality of the self and looks upon the categories of thought as deposits of racial experience. In so doing it either runs counter to our self-experience or is led astray by an obsolete conception of reality; it reveals lack of insight into the unique nature of thought as something which can arise only within the thinking agent itself; it leaves experience itself entirely unaccounted for; and it leads, when carried to its logical consequences, to hopeless skepticism. The idea, that the conception of experience as relational dispenses with the need of a real self and of the creative activity of thought is, as we have seen, entirely mistaken, and rests upon a singularly superficial interpretation of the Kantian epistemology.[32] If anything, such a view of experience accentuates the need of a unitary and abiding self, endowed with the categories of thought. The only alternative is a complete epistemological agnosticism, according to which experience is to be accepted as an ultimate fact concerning whose presuppositions no questions may be asked. This, of course, is a dogmatic assumption, virtually implying an *a priori* knowledge that there can be no *a priori* knowledge.

2. The pragmatistic conception of truth, in its more radical and distinctive form, misses the essential element, and destroys truth. This is a point of fundamental importance. Unfortunately, pragmatists have not been. so clear and consistent in their utterances on this subject as might have been desired. They are constantly confusing the mark or test of truth with the essence of truth or "trueness." What they especially emphasize in connection with knowledge is its value, its consequences. An

---

[32] See, for instance, John Dewey, *Reconstruction in Philosophy*, p. 91.

idea is said to have meaning only insofar as some particular utility can be ascribed to it. And it is its utility also that is said to determine its truth. But in what sense does utility determine the truth of an idea? Does it simply help us to decide when an idea is true, or does it itself constitute the truth or trueness of an idea? If pragmatists take the former view, their teaching contains nothing novel. It is simply a specification under the Kantian doctrine of the primacy of the practical reason. It does not reject but, rather, assumes the older conception of truth as implying or consisting in some sort of correspondence between the idea and the object. The only difference between it and earlier teaching is its almost exclusive stress upon the practical nature of knowledge. But even here the difference is not so great as might be supposed, for "practical" is interpreted in a broad sense so as to include logical consistency. It might be and is objected to pragmatism that it gives too large a place to sentiment and general utility in its verification of truth. But the same objection is urged against personalism and against voluntarism in general. If, then, pragmatism merely teaches that utility is the test of truth, it cannot be said to have introduced a new conception of truth. All that could be claimed is that it has introduced a new method of verification, and this would be true only to a very limited extent.

But while this interpretation of pragmatism finds some support in the writings of William James and other pragmatists, it by no means expresses their full doctrine of truth nor does it bring out what is most distinctive of the pragmatistic movement as a whole. The unique element in pragmatism is the teaching that utility is not merely the test of truth but its essence. This means that truth does not imply transcendence, that it is synonymous with verification, and that it is identical with the utility or working of an idea. We find this conception of truth repeatedly expressed by James, Schiller, and Dewey. "Theoretical truth," we are told, "is no relation between our mind and the archetypal reality. It falls *within* the mind, being the accord of some of its processes and objects with other processes and objects." "All truths must be verified to be properly true." "Verification and truth are two names for the same thing." "The effective working of the idea and its truth are one and the same thing—this working being neither the cause nor the evidence of truth but its nature."[33] James and apparently Schiller try to combine this conception of truth with the older realistic and transcendental view. But this is manifestly impossible. The two views are contradictory. If an idea owes its utility to its truth, as James occasionally says, it certainly cannot be consistently maintained that its truth consists in its utility. Verification, according to the older view, reveals truth; it does not create it. The identification of truth and utilitarian verification excludes the traditional conception of truth. Dewey, it would seem, sees this more clearly than either James or Schiller and adheres more consistently to the radical and distinctive pragmatistic doctrine.

This doctrine, however, is wholly untenable. To make truth a mere instrument, to degrade it from an end to a means, is to destroy it. Relativity is as alien to the idea of truth as it is to that of duty. The intellect will toler-

[33] Quoted by J. B. Pratt, *What is Pragmatism?* pp. 90–93. This book is an excellent exposition and criticism of pragmatism. See also W. P. Montague, *The Ways of Knowing*, pp. 131–172.

ate the one as little as conscience will the other. Truth is absolute or it is nothing. Again, if truth is simply a concrete process of verification within the individual and if it implies no transcendence, it is difficult to see how we can escape complete skepticism. Truth as mere individual satisfaction does not get us beyond ourselves. Something of the old "spectator, searchlight, notion of consciousness" must be retained if knowledge is to be possible. Furthermore, the radical pragmatist cannot himself escape the older Platonic conception of truth. He tries to prove his own doctrine to nonpragmatists, and in so doing assumes that pragmatism at least is true in a nonpragmatic sense. If the truth of pragmatism were dependent upon its actual utility or verification, it is evident that it would be true only to a very limited extent. Most people find the nonpragmatic conception of truth far more satisfactory. The trouble with radical pragmatism as with philosophical skepticism in general and with theological authoritarianism is that it must use reason, in the Platonic sense, in order to dethrone reason. It must assume the traditional conception of truth in order to establish its own truth. From this fundamental self-contradiction there is no escape.

3. Pragmatism is positivistic in its bent and so leaves us without a rational theory of reality. It does not deny all knowledge of the ontologically real as does pure positivism. It is not dogmatically phenomenalistic. It leaves the metaphysical question open. The older rationalistic metaphysics, to be sure, is untrustworthy. There is no way of logically construing reality. But this does not mean that we are necessarily shut up to complete agnosticism. Pragmatism helps us to a decision or at least shows us

how to decide between competing metaphysical theories. In and of itself it has no metaphysics. It is, as Papini says, like a corridor in a hotel leading into many different chambers. In one you might find an atheist, in a second a devout believer, in a third a pure scientist, in a fourth an idealist, in a fifth a positivist; but in going to and from their respective rooms they all have to use the same corridor.[34] So pragmatism is not confined to any one school of thinkers. It is a method used more or less by all schools. Yet it is not wholly neutral. It favors the metaphysical theory that yields the most satisfactory results. But what particular theory fulfills this condition, is not easily determined. The consequence is that there are not only wide differences of opinion among pragmatists, but also much uncertainty and confusion of thought on the part of many of them. A. O. Lovejoy, for instance, has shown that Dewey in some of his utterances is emphatically realistic, in others quite as distinctly idealistic, and in still others apparently neo-realistic.[35] Bowne used to say of an eminent· pragmatist that in his fundamental thinking he was "afflicted with the blind staggers." This is true of many pragmatists. So unclear, hesitant, inconsistent and often purely negative are they when it comes to the deeper problems of metaphysics that one is almost warranted in saying with Papini that "pragmatism is really less a philosophy than a method of doing without one." In any case, even in its best estate, it gives us no clearly defined and rationally grounded world-view.

4.   Pragmatism is commonly supposed to be favorable to religion, but in its more distinctive form it leads to illusionism. George Tyrrell speaks of it as "an easy and

---

[34] See William James, *Pragmatism*, p. 54.
[35] *Essays in Critical Realism*, pp. 35-81.

illuminative philosophy, particularly pliable to the needs
of the apologist."[36]   And this is no doubt true of it in
the form represented by James[37] and Schiller.   If utility
is the test of truth, much can be said in favor of the truth
of religion.   Its beliefs move in the realm of value-judgments.   They bring with them deep and abiding satisfaction, and if this satisfaction is an evidence of truth, there
is good ground for accepting them as valid.   This is, indeed, the essence of the Ritschlian apologetic.   Popular
pragmatism simply echoes the doctrine of value-judgments as expounded by Ritschl, Herrmann, Kaftan, and
other German theologians.   But in its more radical and
characteristic form pragmatism, as we have seen, identifies truth with utility and denies to it transcendence.   From
this standpoint the good consequences of religion constitute its truth.   God is what he is experienced as, but nothing more.   To affirm his transcendent existence is to go
beyond experience, and this is unwarranted, for truth is an
"experienced relation" and has no meaning apart from it.
The objects of religious faith must, therefore, be referred
to illusion.   Their truth consists in the practical consequences of the belief in them.   The belief has no objective validity.   This is Dewey's position, and it is the conclusion to which radical pragmatism logically leads.[38]

We find pragmatism, then, altogether unsatisfactory
both as an epistemology and a philosophy of religion.
As a reaction against what Schiller has called the "inhu-
man, incompetent, and impracticable intellectualism" of
such an absolute idealist as F. H. Bradley, it is intelligible

[36] *Through Scylla and Charybdis*, p. 192.
[37] Compare J. S. Bixler, *Religion in the Philosophy of William James*
(1926).
[38] For a more detailed criticism of Dewey's view of religion, see
E. S. Brightman's *Religious Values*, pp. 140-152.

and to a large degree commendable. But as an independent philosophical movement it is too superficial and too self-contradictory for even the American get-rich-quick type of mind to be long content with it. A. E. Taylor looks upon it as already a "spent force." The trouble with pragmatists, as he points out, is "that they all show a great impatience with the business of thinking things quietly and steadily out," and that "none of them seems to appreciate the importance of the 'critical' problem." Pragmatism thus seems "less a definite way of thinking than a collective name for a series of guesses at truth."

But while this rather severe stricture upon pragmatism as a philosophy pretending to "a conquering destiny" is in my opinion justified, it should not blind us to the large element of truth in the pragmatistic movement. In its emphasis on the importance of both the concrete and the practical it is in full accord with personalism. This was cordially acknowledged by William James. He regarded Bowne and himself as fighting "in exactly the same cause." "Our emphatic footsteps," he said, "fall on the same spot."[39] It may be that he exaggerated his points of

---

[39] These words are taken from a letter written by James to Bowne. The letter is so interesting and instructive that I quote it here in full. It is the clearest and completest statement we have of James' relation to personalism.

HAARLEM, Aug. 17, '08.

MY DEAR BOWNE:

Owing to various distractions, duties, and impossibilities I have only just "got 'round" to the reading of your "Personalism," and I must immediately send you a word of "reaction" on its contents. It seems to me a very weighty pronouncement, and, form and matter taken together, a *splendid* addition to American philosophy. Your youthful tendency to a certain snappishness of statement has toned itself down into patience, but you have clung to your old directness and simplicity and to your avoidance of overtechnicality in language. The book represents very obviously a process of mature evolution, with the phases gone through remaining in the result, some of them (in my own opinion) rather in the form of cicatricial than in that of living tissue. The shortness of the book is wonderful, considering the great amount of vigorous thought-operation embodied in it—that is what makes it so weighty. After one reading one gets only the generalized impression, and I shall not pretend to go into any detail. It seems to me that you and I are now aiming at exactly the same end, though, owing to our different past, from which each retains special verbal habits, we often express ourselves so differently. It seemed to me over and over again that you were planting your feet identically in footprints which my feet were accustomed to—quite independently, of course, of my example, which was what made the coincidences so gratifying. The common foe of both of us is the dogmatist-rationalist-abstractionist. Our common desire is to redeem the concrete personal life which wells up in us from moment to moment from his fastidious (and really preposterous) dialectic contradictions, impossibilities, and vetoes. But whereas your "transcendental empiricism" assumes that the essential discontinuity of the sensible flux has to be overcome by higher intellectual operations on it, quite à la Kant, Green, Caird, etc.; my "radical" empiricism denies the flux's discontinuity, making conjunctive relations essential members of it as given, and charging the conceptual function with being the creator of factitious incoherencies. You don't stop with the abstract syntheses of the intellect, however, you restore concreteness by the "will," etc., whereas I *keep* the full personal concreteness which I find in time and the immediate particulars that fill it. I have been tremendously confirmed in my radical empiricism, and emancipated, by Bergson's writings. He treats (as you probably know) the whole intellectual function as being primarily practical. By it we jump or fly over the surface of experience and perch on distant spots conceptually, for our advantage here and now, instead of wading through the intervening concrete particulars, as animals without intellects have to do. New values, indeed, arise by the use of the intellectual function, but it gives no insight into forces or activities, which must be lived directly or represented sympathetically, not *conceived*. All this is entirely congruent with your scheme; so I think we fight in exactly the same cause, the reinstatement of the fullness of practical life, after the treatment of it by so much past philosophy as spectral. I personally prefer my own directer method; but so far has the *thinking* (at any rate the "academic") mind been warped away from directness by school traditions that I have no doubt your more complex treatment will prove by far the more effective in the philosophy market. By the school traditions I, of course, mean the contempt of sensation, the insistence on an intellectual synthesis, the spewing out of "time," the appeal to infinite regress as fatal, and the like. I prefer simply to short-circuit all this as so much artificiality. But the essential thing is not these differences, it is that our *emphatic* footsteps fall on the *same spot*. You, starting near the rationalist pole, and boxing the compass, and I, traversing, the diameter from the empiricist pole, reach practically very similar positions and attitudes. It seems to me that this is full of promise for the future of philosophy.

My wife awaits me to go to the church to hear the organ. We sail for home on Sept. 22nd, in good health, as I hope the whole Bowne family is. Don't think of answering this—at any rate not by writing!

Yours fraternally and sincerely,

WM. JAMES.

agreement with him. But in any case it is a matter of interest that the chief pragmatist found so much to approve in the philosophy of personalism as expounded by its American founder.

Neo-Realism

The new realism is another empiricistic and positivistic reaction against both the materialism and the absolute idealism of the past century. It differs from pragmatism in that it is more naturalistic and more intellectualistic. It is also more rigid in its positivism. Pragmatism by its stress on utility as the test of truth leaves the door open to the older substantialistic belief in God and the soul. At least this is true of it in its modified form. Neo-realism, on the other hand, repudiates every form of moral or spiritual ontology.[40] Indeed, in the older substantialistic and dynamic sense of the term it repudiates all ontology. Substance and cause it relegates to the limbo of discarded ideas. In their stead it puts the interconnected elements of our actual experience—elements, however, that are supposed to exist independently of their being experienced. The result is a kind of phenomenalized metaphysics, a system which, as Doctor Brightman says, "is peculiarly subtle, abstract, elusive, and revolutionary."[41] Several older types of thought reappear in it, particularly materialism, Platonism, and Spinozism. But under the influence of positivistic science all are lifted to a more or less ethereal plane and thus take on a different character. The fundamental sympathies of neo-realism are, I think it may fairly be said, materialistic. But the

[40] See R. B. Perry, *Present Philosophical Tendencies*, p. 344.
[41] Essay on "Neo-Realistic Theories of Value" in *Studies in Philosophy and Theology*, edited by E. C. Wilm, p. 27.

materialism which it favors is not "the rocky-mountain-tough" type current a generation or two ago, but, rather, a materialism sicklied o'er with the pale cast of thought. With lumpish matter and metaphysical forces the new realism will have nothing to do. It even transcends the physical realm and attributes reality to the logical universals of Plato. A new and strange combination of hitherto discordant doctrines is thus effected. The materialistic lion is so tamed that it lies down peaceably with the Platonic lamb.

But while neo-realism is more "tender-minded" and intellectually more respectable than the older materialism, it is none the less pronounced in its antipathy to idealism. As an empiricistic philosophy it rejects the absolutism of idealism, but its polemic is more particularly directed against its subjectivism. It is itself sometimes called the "great objectivism." But to combine a thoroughgoing objectivism with a positivistic antisubstantialism is no easy task. The result is much unclearness of thought and diversity of opinion among neo-realists. The movement, however, both in its English and American form, has certain well-marked characteristics so that it may be treated as a whole.

1. The first criticism to be passed on neo-realism has to do with its doctrine of mind. This doctrine is essentially Humian, though it transcends Hume in two respects. It adopts the current relational conception of consciousness as against the earlier atomistic view, and it assimilates mind to things in a way that Hume did not. But fundamentally neo-realism and Hume are in accord in their theory of mind. Both reject the reality of the self and thus expose themselves to a double criticism.

For one thing, they do violence to the facts of experience and fall into the fallacy of abstraction. The actual empirical fact is not that sensations, percepts, and concepts exist but that I feel, I perceive, I conceive. In thought we may distinguish between the various forms of mental activity and the mental agent; but in reality the distinction is invalid. There is no such thing as "a definite act of perceptivity" apart from a perceiver.[42] The assumption that there is, is the basal error of neo-realism and of positivism in general. The analyzing and classifying processes of thought do not necessarily have their counterpart in reality. Failure to grasp this elementary truth vitiates a large part of neo-realistic speculation. The neo-realist, it is true, counters with the charge of "pseudo-simplicity." But this is only a negative way of asserting or assuming that the method of analysis and abstraction is the key to the structure of reality—a view which has no support in a sound theory of knowledge and which, as applied to the self, contradicts the facts of experience. The denial of the self is unempirical and rests on a logical fallacy.

In the next place, it renders impossible any explanation of the unity and identity of consciousness. The notion that the relational as distinguished from the atomistic theory of consciousness renders unnecessary a unitary and abiding self is, as we have already pointed out, wholly baseless. Rather does it make this need all the more manifest. The only way to escape it is to have recourse to a dogmatic agnosticism. Bertrand Russell tells us that the real man has no numerical identity, that he is really a series of momentary men, each different one

---

[42] Compare A. N. Whitehead, *Religion in the Making*, p. 108.

from the other.[43]   But if this be so, how account for his apparent unity and self-identity?   Russell's theory leaves these basic facts of consciousness as mysterious as ever. The only rational explanation of them is the one they themselves give.

The attempt of American neo-realists to assimilate mind to matter by making both different groupings of the same "neutral entities" is akin to the Spinozistic reduction of thought and extension to modes of one underlying substance.[44] We have in the one case many entities and in the other a single substance, but the entities are every whit as abstract and hypothetical as the Spinozistic substance. Furthermore, they fail to make even the formal provision for connection and unity that Spinoza's theory did.   But what I wish here especially to emphasize is that the relationship which Spinoza and the neo-realists have sought to establish between mind and matter is purely verbal. Not the slightest glimmer of insight into the kind of unity that binds together thought and things is furnished us by either theory.   If we should adopt the extreme behavioristic view of consciousness, to which neo-realism seems at times inclined, we would, it is true, have an assimilation of mind to things, but then we would have no mind or consciousness left. Organic reaction is not thought. The reaction of the brain to external stimuli does not imply consciousness any more than the process of digestion does.   If any one thing has been made clear by the patient labor of the centuries, it is the unique character of the mental life.   Dogmatically to deny this uniqueness, as some neo-realists do, is to revert to the precritical stage of thought.

[43] *Mysticism and Logic*, p. 129.
[44] Compare R. B. Perry, *Present Philosophical Tendencies*, pp. 315f.

2. The epistemology of neo-realism is equally unsatisfactory. We discussed it briefly in Chapter II. It seeks to overcome the dualism of thought and thing by denying the otherness of thought. Ideas, we are told, are identical with things. There is no separate class of ideas, but only the one class of things, "ideas being the sub-class of those things that happen to be known." Things enter the mind, and when they do so they become ideas. Ideas, therefore, are simply things in a certain relation, the relation, namely, of being known. The apparent absurdity of this doctrine is in part removed when we remember that by "things" are not meant the substantial things of common sense but aggregates of qualities. To ascribe objectivity to some of these qualities seems rather strange in view of the historic distinction between secondary and primary qualities. And still more strange is the ascription of objectivity to concepts and relations. Here we have an idealistic element foreign to naïve as well as to scientific realism. But however strange this transfigured conception of reality may be, it does render the neo-realistic identification of ideas with things less absurd than it may at first have seemed.

When, however, we reflect that the diaphanous things or objects of neo-realistic theory are declared to be wholly independent of mind and to be completely constitutive of knowledge, serious difficulties at once arise. First, we recall the creative activity of thought. This is not a doctrine that can be set aside by vague metaphorical statements about things entering the mind or by dogmatic assertions about the identity of ideas and things. Analysis of the thought process makes it as clear as the day that a thing can exist for us only as we think it. Objectivity

is not something imported into the mind.   It is something which the mind by virtue of its own activity recognizes and thus creates for itself.   In the next place, the
ascription of independent objectivity to the secondary
qualities of things not only conflicts with scientific theory
but on being analyzed seems to have no intelligible meaning.   We can understand what the idealist means when
he says that the primary qualities are as subjective as the
secondary qualities, but when it is said that the secondary
qualities are as objective as the primary qualities are commonly supposed to be, thought begins to grope.   For what
a taste is when it is not tasted, what a smell is when it is
not smelled, what a sight is when it is not seen, what a
sound is when it is not heard, would seem to be meaningless questions.   These sense qualities are constituted
by experience and apart from it have no assignable content.   In and of themselves they are even more unknowable and self-contradictory than Kant's things-in-themselves.   Furthermore, the neo-realistic identification of
ideas with things would seem either to exclude the possibility of error or to require us to think of error itself as
objective.   The latter paradoxical and self-contradictory
conclusion has been drawn by some neo-realists.   Others,
such as R. B. Perry,[45] ascribe the possibility of error to
"subjectivity."   This reminds one of Hume's statement
about the "mind's propensity to feign."   In a left-handed
way it acknowledges the creative activity of thought, and
also seems to reinstate the old epistemological dualism.
The latter conclusion is unavoidable unless Professor
Perry means by "subjectivity" simply organic reaction
and by "truth" simply successful organic reaction, in

---

[45] *Present Philosophical Tendencies*, pp. 324ff.

which case not only truth but consciousness itself would vanish. Into such difficulties as these we are led by neo-realism, and from them there is no escape so long as we adhere to its epistemological monism.

3. The neo-realistic theory of reality is based upon two false assumptions, and as a result is incomplete, inconsistent, and hopelessly abstract. The first assumption is that substance and cause are obsolete and misleading categories. A Roman Catholic writer has said that the new realists seem to be afflicted with substance-phobia.[46] For this fear there may be some ground. The idea of substance has often been wrongly conceived and has led to much gratuitous mystification. But it is not an idea that can be dispensed with. It involves the notion of cause and expresses the idea of ground and connection. Without it being would dissolve away into a groundless flux. There would be no abiding reality and no connection between its broken and dissolving fragments. Science would have no rational basis. Not even solipsism would be possible. Nihilism would be the outcome. Such conclusions are, of course, not drawn by those who deny the validity of the categories of substance and cause, but this is due to the fact that their denial of these categories is always half-hearted and hardly more than an excuse for rejecting the metaphysics and theology of the past. For they at once proceed to reinstate the discredited categories under other names. They deny them insofar as they seem to imply a coherent world-view, thus justifying the incomplete, fragmentary, and agnostic character of their own philosophy. But at the same time they inconsistently apply them to phenomena. This inconsistency

---

[46] Sister Mary Verda, *New Realism in the Light of Scholasticism*, p. 110.

is inherent in every positivistic system.   Such a system,
to save itself from the Heraclitic flux, must become a kind
of hypostatized phenomenalism.   Phenomena or abstractions from them are declared to be independently real.
The resulting philosophy may be crudely naturalistic, or
it may be a highly sophisticated construction like neo-
realism with its neutral entities and its objective universals.   But in either case it is a confused and inconsistent
compound of phenomenalism and substantialism.   No
philosophy, no science, and no coherent thought can get
along without at least the surreptitious presence of the
categories of substance and cause.   Only verbal denials
of these categories are possible.   "The most confirmed
metaphysicians, and the most harmful," as Bishop Mc-
Connell has well said, "are those who disavow metaphysics."[47]

The second false assumption that underlies neo-realism
is the belief that the ultimate structure of reality can be
revealed only by logical analysis.   This assumption, when
consistently carried out, leads to the "logical atomism" of
Bertrand Russell.   According to it there is no abiding
existence of any kind.   Nothing exists except for a mathematical instant.   Every concrete thing or mind is an
infinite succession of different things or minds. How this
succession is possible and what the source of these in-
stantaneously fleeting things and minds is, we do not
know.   They and their order of succession are ultimates
without ground or rational bond.   The question as to
their source and causal relation is, therefore, either meaningless or illegitimate.   The same is true of the "neutral
entities" of R. B. Perry.   They are the last terms of logi-

[47] *Is God Limited?* p. 11.

cal analysis, "the alphabet of being." They have no "home." They simply are what they are and find a place only when they enter into relationships. But how they enter into these relationships and what they are apart from them we do not know. We are simply told that they are and that they have an independent character of their own. To this hopelessly abstract conception of reality we are led by the analytic method when applied in positivistic fashion to the world of experience. This method assumes not only that the laws of thought in general are valid for reality but that the analyzing and classifying processes of the human mind correctly reproduce the objective order —an assumption without foundation either in experience or in reason. The method of analysis taken by itself can give us no coherent world-view. It is in this respect as helpless as the anti-intellectualism of pragmatism. Of both pragmatists and the new realists W. H. Sheldon has justly said that "no systematic metaphysic has issued from their minds, nor have they essayed any great plan of reality—and consequently they have little or nothing to teach."[48]

4. In the field of religious thought neo-realism is sterile. The system is not necessarily antireligious or atheistic. This is evident from the fact that not a few neo-realists take a sympathetic attitude toward religion, and some of them seem at times to be almost on the threshold of personalism.[49] R. B. Perry, for instance, says that neo-realism is "theistic and melioristic in its re-

---

[48] *Philosophical Review*, 1920, pp. 35ff. For an excellent detailed exposition and criticism of neo-realism, see Professor Sheldon's *Strife of Systems and Productive Duality*, pp. 172ff.

[49] See the searching criticism of Professors Perry and Spaulding by E. S. Brightman in *Studies in Philosophy and Theology*, edited by E. C. Wilm, and also in his *Religious Values*, pp. 152–161.

ligion." Others, however, like Bertrand Russell, are radically atheistic. The complete purposelessness of human life and the absolute hopelessness of man as regards the future seem to him "so nearly certain, that no philosophy which rejects them can hope to stand." The most elaborate study of religion from the neo-realistic standpoint is found in S. Alexander's great work on *Space, Time, and Deity*. Here a distinction is made between God as an ideal and God as an actual existent. As an ideal God is nonexistent. What he stands for is the quality next higher to that which has been attained, that is, the quality beyond spirit or mind. What this quality is we do not and cannot know. All that we know is that it is different in kind from spirit and that the universe is at present engaged in bringing it forth. If it ever should actually be brought forth as an empirical quality, it would, I suppose, cease to be deity. Deity would then be transferred to the next higher empirical quality as yet unrealized. But for the present deity is the unrealized and perhaps unrealizable quality next to mind or spirit. What it may turn out to be we do not know, but the infinite world is struggling toward it and, insofar as it does so, is to be identified with God as actually existent. God, thus understood, may be said to be the "mind," and the world the body. But as such he does not know nor is he either good or evil. He is a nisus, not an accomplishment, the power that makes for deity, not deity itself. Why such a nisus, such a hypothetical striving of the cosmos, should be called God is not quite clear. He or it is explicitly said to be a creature. The real creator is Space-Time, not God. But if God be merely an unconscious and nonmoral nisus or impulse toward deity, of what religious value is he? Manifestly, such a conception furnishes no ground for religious faith. If religion had no better philosophical basis than this, it would be condemned to complete intellectual bankruptcy.

Other neo-realists, it is true, seem to have a more positive conception of God; but he is to them, after all, only a finite God, not a God structurally related to the universe, but, rather, an appendix to it. In neo-realism itself there is nothing that points clearly and unmistakably to a religious view of the world. Rather does its logic point in the opposite direction. It has been somewhat playfully said of S. Alexander that he introduced "God" into his system in order to qualify as a Gifford lecturer. Certainly, there is nothing in his philosophy as such that requires God and nothing that even fits the name of Deity, as this term has commonly been understood. The chief religious significance of neo-realism lies in the fact that it imposes no such veto upon faith as did the so-called scientific philosophy of half a century ago. Its positivism as applied to nature represents a distinct advance beyond materialism, and so also does its recognition of concepts and relations as having a coequal reality with sense qualities. By thus breaking down the exclusiveness and arrogance of "matter" it has opened the door, though a narrow one, to belief. But that it is in and of itself entirely inadequate as a philosophy of religion, is evident from the ventures which its representatives have already made in this field.

Objections to Personalism

We have thus far passed in review the leading systems of philosophy which may be regarded as rivals of personalism, and have found them all radically defective in one or more respects. But how about personalism? Is it not equally vulnerable? Many think so, and hence it becomes necessary to consider briefly the objections that are raised to it. Five of these may be mentioned.

1. It is said that the personalistic view of nature is out of harmony with common sense and with science. In response to this criticism it may be pointed out that every one of the philosophies we have considered, and natural science also, is in some important respect out of accord with common sense. Common sense does not recognize the subjectivity of the secondary qualities, but this is recognized by natural science and by all the different types of philosophy except neo-realism; and neo-realism in turn denies what is still dearer to common sense than the objectivity of the sense-qualities, namely, the substantiality and dynamic efficiency of the material object. Whether natural science favors any one type of philosophy above another is an open question. The answer will depend on what is understood by natural science. Most scientists no doubt believe in the extramental and substantial reality of the primary qualities. But this is only a relic of their earlier common-sense realism. It is not inherent in science itself. Science has nothing to do with substantial or causal reality. It is concerned simply with phenomena. Whether there is such a thing as substantial or dynamic reality is a moot question. But it is not a question that can be decided by science itself. It lies beyond the scientific domain. Science in the strict sense of the term is philosophically neutral. To suppose that science favors realism as over against idealism or positivism as over against substantialism is to misunderstand the nature of science. The arrogance of science may lead to

positivism, and its inherited sense prejudice may seem to involve realism. But neither of these types of philosophy is an implication of true science. Personalism is in every respect as consistent with empirical science as is any form of realism or positivism. Indeed, personalism and idealism in general accept essentially the same view of natural science as does positivism. They regard it as limited to phenomena, to their relation and correlation, and as having in that respect a perfectly free field untrammeled by philosophy of any kind. They differ from positivism only in this, that they consider science to be as independent of antimetaphysics as it is of metaphysics. The assumption that personalism is in any sense in conflict with science rests on a complete misunderstanding both of science and of personalism.

2. It is sometimes asserted that personalism is an eclectic system, lacking in logical thoroughness. This charge is brought against it by William James[50] and R. B. Perry.[51] James sees in it a thing of compromises, a system that seeks above all things a *modus vivendi*. He misses in it the radical and aggressive note and so declares that it lacks *prestige*. Perry in a similar vein assigns personal idealism to an unstable intermediate position. From the practical point of view he concedes that it has a certain advantage over absolute idealism, but logically he holds that it is at a disadvantage both as compared with Hegelian absolutism and with panpsychistic and pragmatistic pluralism. The latter is the conclusion to which it would logically come if it rejected the Kantian epistemology, while, if it accepts this theory of knowledge, it is on "a slippery inclined plane with the Absolute waiting at

---

[50] *Pragmatism*, p. 18.
[51] *The Present Conflict of Ideals*, pp. 202, 218.

the bottom." Personalism, it is consequently claimed, lacks inner coherence and consistency. It is insecurely poised on a narrow divide between opposing systems, and destined eventually to fall to one side or the other and thus lose its present identity.

In reply to this criticism the personalist admits that his philosophy is, in a sense, of the mediating type. It is a philosophy of conciliation.[52] It acknowledges that there are elements of truth in the other systems of thought. We have shown how personalism finds itself in accord with the realistic conception of a dynamic otherness in nature, with the Hegelian conception of the rationality of the real, with the empiricistic recognition of a given element in experience, with the voluntarism of pragmatism, with the positivistic element in the neo-realistic conception of nature, and even with a certain aspect of materialistic ethics. We have also in earlier chapters shown how personalism steers a middle course between metaphysical monism and pluralism, between a dynamic realism and a purely logical idealism, between a crude substantialism and an antimetaphysical positivism, between agnostic dualism and epistemological monism, between empiricism and apriorism, and between pragmatic relativism and intellectualistic absolutism. A certain element of truth is recognized in each of these competing views, and personalism seeks to do justice to them all. But this is by no means its animating and constructive principle; it is simply incidental to the system, an evidence of its comprehensive, not its composite, character. Personalism is distinctly not an eclectic or compromise philosophy. It is a philosophy born of one great generating insight—the in-

[52] Compare R. T. Flewelling's *Creative Personality: A Study in Philosophical Conciliation.*

sight into the unique epistemological and metaphysical significance of personality. Around this one insight the whole system revolves, and that it is able to take up into itself without contradiction so many factors that have previously been regarded as mutually discordant is proof of the fruitfulness of the fundamental principle by which it is animated. There is, as a matter of fact, no conflict between it and the Kantian theory of knowledge. Rather is its basic doctrine, its transcendental empiricism, the direct outgrowth of the Kantian epistemology. It was Kant who furnished the logical justification of the principle that the categories of thought do not explain intelligence but are explained by it. It is, then, a mistake to suppose that the logic of Kantianism is opposed to personal idealism. Rather is it to be viewed as structural within the personalistic system, a vital factor in its organic unity.

3. It is objected to personalism that it is too systematic, too sharply defined, and too thoroughly rationalized. This objection comes from the metaphysical skeptic. He is not a complete agnostic. He does not reject metaphysics altogether, but he has become distrustful of the finished systems of the past. He is very much impressed with empirical science, and seems to think that it has somehow discredited the theistic arguments. Occasionally he becomes a quite thoroughgoing empiricist, and tells us that "we have no experience of universes that would warrant us in denying that a very marvelous universe can grow up blindly."[53] This, of course, means that reality or the universe may as well be irrational as rational, and if so there is no reason why any sort of ab-

----
[53] Durant Drake, *Journal of Religion*, 1925, p. 138.

surdity should not be possible in it. But the man who objects to the systematic completeness of personalism does not usually go so far as this. He thinks that theism is nearer the truth than antitheism. But it is nevertheless too much of a closed system for him. It implies too finished and static a conception of reality. He wants something vaguer and less clearly defined, and so argues for a modified theism—a theism which recognizes a certain kinship and a certain fellowship between man and the cosmos but does not seek to determine more precisely what it is that makes possible and justifies this feeling of *rapport* with the universe. He seems to think that this sort of intellectual twilight is more congenial to the modern scientist when he comes to religious questions than the noonday brightness of personalistic theism.[54]

In response to such an æsthetic and half-hearted objection to personalism one can hardly do more than insist on the rights of the intellect. One may point out, as we have already done, the self-contradictory character of the empiricism upon which it is based. One may also show that in all fundamental thinking concerning the world we must choose between a view that is essentially mechanistic and one that is essentially personalistic. There is no really tenable or even intelligible middle ground. Nor will the human mind be long content with merely a vague mystical feeling. For a while the baffled intellect may find refuge in it. But eventually it will assert its right to know, and then it will be satisfied with nothing short of "an unusually obstinate attempt to think clearly and consistently." If metaphysics be understood

[54] A good illustration of this standpoint is found in an article by G. B. Smith, entitled "Is Theism Essential to Religion?" in the *Journal of Religion*, 1925, pp. 356–377.

as such an attempt, as William James says it should be, it is not difficult to understand why so much of current philosophy and theology is *anti*metaphysical. The tendency at present is to discredit the intellect and to adopt the cheap and easy method of appealing exclusively to emotional and mystical values. That this appeal has some justification, personalism is only too willing to acknowledge. But it is equally insistent that the intellect too has its claims and must not be put off. Skepticism in this realm is certain to result in the recrudescence of a crude naturalism and the stifling of that elevation of spirit which, as Hegel says, is the essence of religion. Only in such systematic completeness as we have in the personalistic philosophy can both mind and heart find ultimate satisfaction.

4. It is insisted that the self or personality is composite and that it cannot, therefore, be regarded as metaphysically real. This is the most formidable attack upon personalism. The attack has come from two quarters. It has emanated both from empiricism and from abstract logic. The empiricist analyzes the self into a plurality and succession of mental states or into a series of pulse-beats of consciousness, and insists that there is nothing more to it than the discrete or related elements revealed by this analysis. There is no metaphysical glue in the form of a soul that binds together the coexistent and successive states of consciousness. These states are themselves ultimate. They presuppose no unitary and self-identical spiritual substance; rather do they themselves give rise to the appearance of unity and identity in our conscious experience. This appearance is, therefore, illusory. There is no abiding and unitary self.

To this line of argument the response is threefold. First, the facts of the mental life, perception, memory, and thought, are wholly incapable of explanation apart from the assumption of a real self. Without such an assumption consciousness is reduced to a dissolving flux devoid of all ground and connection. Second, it is a radical error to assume that the self, if real, must manifest itself as a distinct and separable object in the stream of consciousness. As the subject of the mental life it is, of course, distinguishable from its states, but for that very reason it cannot be identified with any one of them or with what is objectively or subjectively revealed by any one of them. The eye does not see itself and yet without the eye there would be no vision. So it is with the self. To suppose that the self as mental substance or agent ought to have an entirely separable existence of its own, which might somehow be apprehended apart from or alongside of its own psychical filling, is to revert to an obsolete conception of both substance and cause. But, in the third place, it does not follow from this that the self, if real, is merely an inference. While it is not an object of knowledge in the same way that the things of sense are, it is nevertheless given immediately in experience. This experience is something unique. Perhaps it might be well to use a distinct term for it, and to say with C. A. Richardson[55] that we "realize" what a self is. We have a "concrete realization" of its existence. But whatever term we use, we have a direct and valid experience of the self, and this experience is of "infinitely greater importance" than any mere inference. As an inference we might with some show of reason declare the belief in a

---

[55] *Spiritual Pluralism and Recent Philosophy*, pp. 13f., 19, 139.

self to be unwarranted, but as an experience we cannot escape it. In the very act of trying to analyze it away we assume its existence. The denial of a self, as H. A. Youtz says, would be impossible were it not for the presence of a self to make the denial.[56]

The objection to the reality of the self from the standpoint of abstract logic grows out of the fact that we do not see how unity and plurality, and identity and change can be combined in the self. These attributes are logical opposites and exclude each other. The soul is, therefore, a self-contradictory conception and hence cannot be real. The reply to this objection is found in the fact that reality is deeper and richer than our formal logic. It is given to us in our experience, and as such is first, not second. It also has a way of harmonizing conceptions that seem logically contradictory. Unity and plurality, for instance, and identity and change, when abstractly viewed, contradict each other. But when interpreted in the light of the soul's own experience, they are seen to be entirely harmonious with each other. One, indeed, implies the other. The soul is not constituted by a combination of abstract categories, nor can it be dissolved away by an analysis into them. Rather do the categories derive their whole content and meaning from their realization in self-consciousness. The self meets the test of reality as does no other form of concrete existence.

5. It is urged that personality implies limitation, and, consequently, cannot be attributed to the world-ground or Absolute. This objection rests upon a misunderstanding of what is implied both by personality and by the idea

---

[56] *The Supremacy of the Spiritual*, p. 47. This book is a finished and stirring exposition of the bearing of personalism on the psychological and social problems of the day.

of the Absolute.[57] The absolute is sometimes interpreted as meaning the unrelated, and in this sense the term is inapplicable even to the world-ground, to say nothing of a personal Creator. But this interpretation of the term has no justification either in etymology or in philosophy. The word "absolute" comes from the verbal adjective, *absolutus,* which means, not the unrelated, but the perfect, the complete, the unconditioned, that which is not dependent on anything else.[58] Thus understood there is nothing in the term that is necessarily inconsistent with the idea of personality. For personality in and of itself does not imply dependence upon anything else. It is not infrequently said that consciousness requires an object and that the Absolute cannot, therefore, be a conscious Being. But this argument mistakes a mental form for an ontological distinction. The Absolute Person creates his own objects or makes himself his object. Indeed, it is only in this form that personality attains to completeness. Our personalities are limited and imperfect. If we were less limited, we would be more truly personal. Full personality exists only in the Absolute. Only in him do we have complete self-knowledge and complete self-possession.[59] Instead, then, of the idea of personality being inconsistent with that of the Absolute, the two are, rather, mutually congenial. It may even be convincingly argued

---

[57] Doctor Brightman has justly characterized this objection as "logomachy which vanishes with a clear definition of terms" (*Religious Values*, p. 24).

[58] Compare L. Stählin, *Kant, Lotze, Ritschl*, p. 201.

[59] A. C. Beckwith attributes the widespread assent given to this conclusion to its "bold and startling paradox" rather than to its inherent consistency. See his well-known book, *The Idea of God*, p. 293. This book, while written in excellent style and containing much valuable information, reveals, it seems to me, a seriously confused and unsettled state of mind on the author's part when it comes to the problems of metaphysical theology.

that the idea of the Absolute can be consistently thought through only on the personal plane, so that we are warranted in saying not only that the Absolute *may* be personal but that he *must* be personal. A personalized Absolute can alone meet the demands of reason.

This completes our survey of the objections to personalism. There is not one of them that cannot be met with a fair measure of success. But this does not mean that there are not depths of mystery before which personalism as well as every other philosophy must be silent. All that personalism claims is that it represents the line of least resistance to thought; and that this claim is justified has, I trust, been substantiated by the foregoing study of the chief rival philosophies and the objections which they have raised to personalism. Nothing does so much to strengthen one in his personalistic faith as a careful, critical examination of other and competing systems of thought. Such a study makes it clear that, while theism has its manifest limitations and difficulties, still more serious difficulties inhere in all the other systems. Every philosophy is necessarily imperfect. For human knowledge at the best is extremely limited; it is but a candle-light in the immense darkness of the universe. But in addition to its own greater self-consistency and rational probability personalism has this advantage over most of its rivals, that it assures us that, where knowledge fails, we may believe. It is, indeed, itself a faith quite as much as a philosophy, and as such it stands structurally related to that higher type of idealistic and religious thought which since the time of Plato has commanded the assent of many of the world's profoundest minds. In its essential nature it is not a novelty, it is, rather, a reaffirmation of "what theistic thinkers have been saying from the beginning."[60]   Its uniqueness consists in the greater logical thoroughness with which it. has carried out the theistic idea.   In it the philosophy of religion has received its completest, most self-consistent, and in this sense most radical expression.

THE DEVELOPMENT OF PERSONALISM

It now remains for us, in conclusion, to outline the main stages in the development of the personalistic worldview, and in doing so the best method will be to summarize the contributions which leading thinkers have successively made to it.   In the selection of a list of thinkers for this purpose, there will be no attempt at completeness.   Many distinguished names might be added to the list that I shall give.   For personalistic theism is the accumulated product of the life and thought of the centuries, and a great many minds have made important contributions to the completed structure.   But those whom I shall mention may perhaps be accepted as fairly representative of the different lines of thought that have prepared the way for present-day personalism, though many others would be entitled to a place in the personalistic Hall of Fame.

1.   To Plato the debt of personalism is manifold. The superiority of thought to sense, the conception of immaterial existence, the objectivity of the ideal, the speculative significance of self-activity, the shadowy and unsubstantial character of matter, various arguments for the existence of God and the immortality of the soul—all these characteristic elements in personalism appear in his

---

[60] B. P. Bowne, *Studies in Theism*, p. vi.

teaching. What is philosophically most significant in them is their ascription of true being only to the logical, the ideal, and the self-active. This meant, at least by way of implication, the virtual limitation of metaphysical reality to the realm of spirit, to what we would call the personal.

2. Aristotle in the general drift of his teaching was less personalistic than Plato, but in at least two respects he marked an advance beyond him. For one thing, he emphasized the view that reality is concrete and individual, and thus corrected a rather strong tendency in Plato toward, an abstract metaphysical universalism. In the next place, he gave to his world-view a more distinctly spiritual and monotheistic cast by substituting for the Ideas, the Demiurge, and the World-Soul of Plato a single self-conscious Being, a "prime" or "unmoved mover."

3. Plotinus also made two important contributions to the development of personalism. He affirmed more emphatically and defined more precisely than had heretofore been done the immateriality of the human as well as the divine spirit, bringing out more clearly the unique and active nature of self-consciousness. Then, too, he reduced nature more completely than Plato had to pure phenomenality. He saw in it absolute nonbeing, a mere outer husk behind which the truly active reality existed in the form of souls and spirits. In this respect he anticipated the modern panpsychistic form of personalism.

4. Augustine might in a sense be called the first personalist. To him we owe (1) a more highly developed conception of the unity of the mental life, (2) a new insight into the significance of the will in the life both of God and man, (3) the earliest clear formulation of the

great truth that self-certainty is more immediate than our knowledge of the external world and hence should be used as the starting-point of philosophy, and (4) the first clear grasp of the fact that a valid metaphysics must be based on the self-knowledge of the finite personality. The last two of these insights were nothing short of revolutionary, and though their full import was not recognized until centuries after the time of Augustine, they eventually lifted from off its hinges the earlier uncritical objectivity of thought and literally turned the world upside down. They not only put thought above thing but the thinker above thought.

5. The philosophical significance of Thomas Aquinas from our standpoint consists chiefly in the fact that he gave a more personalistic cast to the teaching of Aristotle at two important points. He ascribed efficient as well as final causality to God and thus made the world directly dependent upon the divine will both for its origin and its preservation. This gave a more distinctly personal character to God than Aristotle had done, who conceived of him as the "unmoved mover," whom the world loved but who did not himself love the world. Then, too, Thomas interpreted the somewhat vague and apparently universal "active reason" of Aristotle in an individualistic sense. In this way a basis was established for the belief in personal immortality, since, according to Aristotle, the active reason, and it alone, is immortal.

6. Descartes revived the Augustinian doctrine of the primacy of *self*-certainty, and made it basal in his system. At the same time he broke the spell which the Aristotelian distinction between matter and form had exercised over the human mind for almost two thousand years, and

put in its place a radical distinction between thought and extension or mind and body, thus making the mind independent of the body and by virtue of its own unique self-identity capable of an immortal destiny. In these two ways he contributed powerfully to the development of the personalistic type of thought.

7. Leibnitz corrected the universalistic tendency latent in the Cartesian system and carried by Spinoza to its logical pantheistic conclusion, by defining more precisely the nature of individuality and by ascribing to the individual a large degree of metaphysical independence. Substance as realized both in the Infinite and in finite monads he conceived of as psychical and active. Thus he laid the foundation for the immaterialism and the activism of modern personalism.

8. Berkeley was more thoroughgoing in his immaterialism than Leibnitz. He denied completely the substantial reality of the material world, reducing it to a series of presentations produced in finite minds by the Infinite. To souls alone and to God did he ascribe metaphysical reality. His system was thus, in the strict sense of the term, a personal idealism, the first of its kind in the history of speculation.[61]

9. Kant was not himself a metaphysical personalist,

[61] In an unpublished dissertation on *The Relation of Bowne to Berkeley* Dr. Gail Cleland has maintained the thesis that the framework and much of the content of Bowne's philosophy came from Berkeley. He puts the Berkeleian influence above that of Kant and Lotze. In support of this conclusion he shows with painstaking thoroughness that there is throughout a close kinship between the philosophy of Bowne and that of Berkeley. But this kinship, as Doctor Cleland admits, does not necessarily indicate a direct dependence of Bowne on Berkeley. It is quite as probable that both men drew to a considerable extent from a common theistic tradition. The same is also to be said of the resemblances pointed out by Dr. G. H. Jones between Bowne and Lotze.

but indirectly he probably did more to promote the spread of personalism than any other thinker.   By his doctrine of the creative activity of thought he gave to the spiritual individualism of Leibnitz and Berkeley a definiteness of content that it had previously lacked and also supplied it with a firm epistemological basis.   By his conception of personality as an end in itself he laid the foundation of ethical personalism, and by his doctrine of the primacy of the practical reason he justified the belief in God, freedom, and immortality.   In his synthesis of apriorism with empiricism is also to be found the justification of the profound metaphysical significance attributed by personalism to self-experience.   Almost a full personalistic creed might thus be deduced from certain phases of the Kantian philosophy.

10.   Whether Hegel may with propriety be classed as a personalist or not, is a question.   But in any case he made one very significant contribution to the personalistic philosophy.   He established the rationality of the real. In this truth is to be found the ultimate basis of the immaterialism of Leibnitz and Berkeley, and of idealists in general.   The material or space-time world cannot meet the test of rationality.   It is shot through and through with inconsistencies and contradictions, and hence must be condemned to phenomenality.

11.   Lotze corrected the Hegelian tendency toward an abstract and universalistic type of metaphysics by successfully maintaining that reality is concrete and individual, that it is infinitely richer than thought, and that in the form of personality it offers an adamantine resistance to every dissolvent that thought is able to apply, for without a thinker there can be no thought.   The self is a pre-

supposition of thought. True existence must, therefore, be something more than thought; it must be existence for self. Lotze thus transformed the logical rationalism of Hegel into a personal rationalism, and the absolute idealism of Hegel into a personal idealism.

12. Bowne transcended Lotze in two main respects. First, he took the idea that personality is the key to reality and made it the central and organizing principle of his entire philosophy. This Lotze did not do. He saw that self-experience is the solvent of such fundamental antinomies as those between unity and plurality and between identity and change, and occasionally gave clear and effective expression to this thought. But it can hardly be said that he did anything enthusiastic with it. At least he did not elaborate and systematize it. Bowne, on the other hand, seized upon this facet of the soul's life and turned it into a steady glow. He made it the one great illuminating principle of his entire system. Through all the ramifications of metaphysics he carried it as a torch and found that it revealed the way to a unified view of reality and to a solution of the basic difficulties that confront human thought so far as such a solution is possible. He thus became the systematizer of personalism. To him we owe what I have called systematic methodological personalism. In the next place, he supplemented Lotze's conception of reality as self-existence by introducing into it as an essential and controlling factor the thought of *free* self-activity. Lotze, of course, also recognized the fact of freedom, but he did not, like Bowne, give to it a place of coequal importance with self-consciousness. Bowne made freedom a touchstone of reality. Only that which is free did he regard as truly real. He also made free-

dom, as Lotze did not, a fundamental presupposition of epistemology. He showed that without it there could be no distinction between truth and error, no standard of truth, and no way of using such a standard if there were one. For him freedom was thus constitutive both of knowledge and of reality. No other writer, so far as I know, has done so much as he to bring out the epistemological and metaphysical significance of freedom.

This brief survey of the historical development of personalism reveals in a general way what the whole book has sought to show, namely, that personalism is no mere novelty, no vagary of an individual, no philosophical "sport." It represents one of the oldest and broadest currents in the history of human thought; it stands organically and structurally related to the spiritual philosophy of all the ages. It is the ripe fruit of more than two millenniums of intellectual toil, the apex of a pyramid whose base was laid by Plato and Aristotle.

INDEX

Absolute, the, 34f., 39f., 46f., 50f., 197ff., 425f.
Academicians, 141
Activism, 202ff.
Agnosticism, 140ff., 356ff.
Albertus Magnus, 256
Alexander, S., 298, 416f.
Anaxagoras, 90, 296
Anaximander, 90
Anaximenes, 89
Animal automatism, 323
Anselm, 144, 256, 259ff.
Apriorism, religious, 251f.
Aristotle, 27, 64, 93, 127ff., 140, 182f., 192, 215, 226, 240, 265, 277ff., 296, 298, 309, 319ff., 429
Arnal, A., 38, 43, 48
Arnold, Matthew, 187
Atomism, materialistic, 191, 340
Atomism, psychological, 121, 134, 389f., 392f., 398, 408
Augustine, 21, 126, 141, 152, 237, 242, 265, 271, 429
Authority, 95, 143, 247, 255f.

Bacon, Francis, 374
Balfour, A. J., 62
Beckwith, A. C., 426
Behaviourism, 345
Berkeley, George, 62, 77, 95, 117, 121, 131, 193, 229, 387, 431
Bigg, C., 330
Bixler, J. S., 404
Boethius, 81
Bois, H., 48
Bosanquet, B., 31, 57, 190
Bowne, B. P., 19, 32, 63, 77, 82, 85, 136, 148ff., 188f., 194, 198, 220f., 224f., 226, 232f., 246, 253, 272, 293, 303, 311f., 314, 326, 329, 334, 357ff., 362, 386, 405f., 433f.
Bradley, F. H., 31, 196, 244, 252, 380, 404
Brightman, E. S., 18, 20, 32, 51, 86, 90, 404, 415, 426

Browning, Robert, 34
Büchner, L., 204, 356
Buckham, J. W., 82
Burnet, John, 277

Caird, Edw., 32, 315
Calkins, Mary W., 32, 76
Carr, H. Wildon, 57, 76
Causal argument, 274ff., 285
Causality, principle of, 60, 206, 212, 215, 263
Causality, volitional, 210, 305, 343
Cell, G. C., 17
Christianity and idea of personality, 21, 78ff.
Christianity and personalism, 80, 254ff., 327ff.
Cleland, Gail, 431
Clement of Alexandria, 262
Comte, Auguste, 40, 386
Conceptual argument, 259ff.
Contingency, argument from, 286
Contradiction, law of, 42, 216
Copernican astronomy, 329
Cornford, F. M., 264, 279
Cosmological proof, 276ff., 291ff.
Cratylus, 140
Creation, 35, 45, 50, 54ff., 64, 79, 282ff., 328
Creative activity of thought, 54, 96, 114ff., 181, 411f.

Darwinism, 301f., 329
Democritus, 70, 90, 117f., 138f., 191
Descartes, 71, 112, 119, 126, 141, 152, 260, 266, 323, 430
Dewey, John, 88, 109, 398f., 401, 403.
Drake, Durant, 421
Dualism, epistemological, 100ff.
Dualism, metaphysical, 112ff., 119
Duncan, George M., 151

Ego-centric predicament, 246

435